THE
ARCHAEOLOGY
OF
COLORADO

E. STEVE CASSELLS

Johnson Books: Boulder

D1502136

© 1983 E. STEVE CASSELLS
Cover Design: Joe Daniel
Cover Illustration: Clovis point (Point B) from the Dent site
ISBN 0-933472-76-5

LC Catalog Card No.: 83-082868

Printed in the United States of America by
Johnson Publishing Company
1880 South 57th Court
Boulder, Colorado 80301

Contents

Acknowledgements

This book would not have been possible without the kind help of many individuals.

Many photographs were loaned by people who were sympathetic to the cause. Too numerous to be mentioned here, they have been credited in the captions.

A number of professional and avocational archaeologists generously took the time to review the drafts of various chapters. I am grateful for their comments, and I of course accept responsibility for any errors that appear in the text. Reviewers included Dennis Stanford, Marie Wormington, Frank Adkins, Jeff Eighmy, Bruce Jones, Jim Benedict, Jack Smith, Emerson Pearson, Linda Gregonis, Bill Buckles, Frank Frazier, Ann Johnson, Bruce Rippeteau, and OD Hand.

Helen Pustmueller (University of Denver), Liz Morris (Colorado State University), Ann Hedlund, Joe Ben Wheat, and Priscilla Ellwood (University of Colorado Museum), and Bob Ackerly (Denver Museum of Natural History) were very gracious in allowing me access to their museum collections.

Obscure manuscripts were provided to me by Cal Jennings, Carl Conner, John Gooding, Bruce Jones, Marie Wormington, Ed Simonich, and Sarah Nelson.

My treatment of the topics in the book benefited greatly from extended conversations with Marie Wormington, Cal Jennings, Bill Buckles, Joe Ben Wheat, Ann Johnson, Emerson Pearson, Jeff Eighmy, Caryl Wood Ravanelli, Dennis Stanford, Frank Eddy, Jim Benedict, Jack Smith, John Gooding, and Willard Louden.

The excellent pen and ink cultural reconstructions in Chapters 5-9 were rendered by the accomplished artist-historian Robin Farrington.

The present readable condition of the text is in great measure the result of assistance by Johnson Books Editorial Director Michael McNierney.

I have been fortunate to have had the help of these many individuals. They corrected me when I strayed too far from the legitimate data, helped remove ambiguities in the text, and encouraged me to persevere. They all deserve more than my meager accolades.

Lastly, I want to pay homage to my wife and children, Jill, Mara, and Josh, and to my parents and in-laws, Ed, Virginia, Bud, and Margaret, for being so supportive and understanding throughout the research and writing. Without them I would have despaired long ago. It is to these seven that I dedicate this book.

Preface

This book deals with the early inhabitants of what is now Colorado. It has been my intent to portray prehistory here in a way that would prove both interesting and informative for a wide audience. Trying to strike a balance between the needs of the professional, the serious avocational archaeologist, and the more casually interested lay person is not an easy task, and only time will tell if I have succeeded.

Rather than document every site known or recorded in the state (26,000 prehistoric ones alone), I have attempted to provide a representative sampling of them and their associated materials, and in some cases, a history of the investigations. These are synthesized into a broad view of prehistoric lifeways.

Instead of citing all pertinent literature in the text, as is common in professional papers, I have listed the references at the end of each chapter in the order of their appearance. These in turn lead the reader to the complete bibliography at the back of the book. Although I wish that all of these items cited were readily available to anyone who wished to read further, I was occasionally forced to mention obscure or unpublished manuscripts. For this I apologize.

My interest in archaeology stems from early grade school forays through Honolulu's Bishop Museum, at which time I supposedly announced my future profession. This fascination was further enhanced as I grew up in western Nebraska, walking across numerous sandy blowouts with my mother, searching for tiny flakes and arrowheads dropped by some unknown hunter. High school was a time for playing in rock and roll bands and roping calves. Any trace of the early glow of prehistory was masked for many years. But then, in 1967, my path crossed that of Dr. Larry

Agenbroad, both of us having arrived at Chadron State College (Nebraska) at the same time. He came to teach, and I to learn. His enthusiasm for prehistoric elephant hunting was contagious, and it rekindled my desire to track the Ancients. Subsequent exposure to Idaho buffalo jumps and the massive bone bed at Colorado's Jurgens site were the final nails in my career decision.

My work in the archaeological profession has been varied and rewarding, leading me through a college teaching appointment, federal and state positions, and into private consulting. Throughout it, I have observed the unflagging interest in archaeology shown by many individuals. They may have paused to marvel at intricate rock art on a massive sandstone slab or perhaps walked through a narrow and low T-shaped doorway in a Mesa Verde cliff dwelling. And they want to know more.

I hope that this book will serve, in however small a way, to perpetuate and enhance the attraction in those people who have already had a glimpse into the past. Perhaps some will use this book as an entrance into the field. Hopefully, professionals and serious avocationals will be able to use the data and observations in their research as well.

It is my deep desire to see Colorado's heritage fully appreciated and cherished by people today and protected for the benefit of future genera- tions. The hunter of the Columbian mammoth is gone forever. No more Ice Age bison are felled with stone-tipped spears or driven over cliffs. When all of our archaeological sites have been destroyed, this non-renewable resource will be exhausted. For this reason, I want to encourage you, the reader, to take a conservationist's position. You are the ultimate steward of our prehistory and can contribute either to its preservation or to its accelerating destruction. I pray that you will choose the first of these two paths.

1 Introduction to an Exciting Science

The word "archaeologist" may conjure up a vision of Indiana Jones, a skull in one hand, a bull whip in the other, dodging boulders and a hail of spears and arrows. Or perhaps one might see a pith-helmeted, khaki-clad fellow bent over a minute fragment of pottery, meticulously cleaning it with a camel hair brush, measuring it in millimeters, mapping and photographing it in its ancient bed. With his computer-like mind, he recognizes the significance of the small bit of fired clay, and hoisting it into the air, declares to all around that he has the link between two cultures that had heretofore eluded all scientific inquiry.

Although they may contain some truth, these stereotypes, like most, are oversimplified and overworked.

It is true that archaeologists find small vestiges of previous human inhabitants to be of great interest. This is because of the nature of most prehistoric sites. Seldom will fieldwork expose a pristine, intact "living floor" or "activity area" such as was revealed to Howard Carter when he first looked into the tomb of King Tutankhamen by flickering torchlight and glimpsed "wonderful things," or as when Italian workmen began to uncover the rooms, streets, and human bodies of Pompeii, frozen fast into their forms of 24 August, A.D. 79 by ash of the suddenly violent Mt. Vesuvius. Instead, most archaeological excavations recover only a minimal amount of broken and discarded debris of earlier human occupations, some of which is randomly scattered about. The bulk of the original artifacts have probably decomposed, leaving behind only those items which are of stone or which have been artificially hardened into a stone-like form (e.g. pottery). Some plant and animal remains might survive, depending on the circumstances of their deposition and the acidity of the soil. Architectural elements may be sufficiently intact for interpretive purposes but are often so subtle in form as to be easily overlooked, such as a dark circular soil deposit, a post mold, which reveals where a pole once stood as part of a small hut.

These data are but scraps of the once vital cultures they represent, but they are usually the only evidence available. At least as far back as the Italian Renaissance, prehistorians have taken what clues were available and tried to see more clearly the lives of their predecessors.

Archaeologists today are not antiquarians in the classic sense, collecting "things" for their intrinsic value (as an Indiana Jones might do). Instead, archaeology seeks to "look through" the artifacts to those who used them in an attempt to understand the culture of the times. Archaeologists are essentially cultural anthropologists who work with past cultures. The paradigms and goals of cultural anthropology are fundamentally the same as those of archaeology.

A cultural anthropologist is interested in the nature of human beings, how they collectively think and act. Research is directed toward document-ing patterns in political, religious, and economic systems, kinship organi-zations, and other related aspects of culture. In addition, the an-thropologist compares various cultures to determine the reasons for differ-ences between them. Whether cultural diversity and change were brought about by environmental or other factors, the processes would certainly be focal points of the investigation. In order to reach reasonable conclusions about cultures, the anthropologist enters the field and observes people firsthand. Data are collected through a variety of techniques, including interviews, observations, and participation in the various community ac-tivities. Given a sufficient period of involvement, the anthropologist can be expected to produce a reasonably accurate ethnography detailing the par-ticular group studied, perhaps including a comparative analysis with surrounding villages or language groups.

The archaeologist likewise endeavors to recover such data from the particular culture under study, but the methods differ. Participant-observation and interviews are impossible. Discovery, documentation, analysis, and comparisons of site and regional data are, by necessity, the means of reaching back into time beyond written records. The basic aims of archaeology are to reconstruct the lifeways and culture histories of prehis-toric peoples, to delineate culture changes in societies, and to generate possible explanations for these changes.

This task is not easy. To illustrate, imagine yourself totally ignorant of modern Western society. Being the investigator, you have been provided with one of every item in the Montgomery Ward catalog (a reasonable source of the spectrum of American artifacts). Of course, since you must be under the same constraints as other prehistorians, those items that will decompose readily have been deleted from the assemblage. That will take care of all items of wood, cloth, paper, and the like. What will remain is composed of metal, glass, ceramics, and plastic. To be sure, you would have more artifacts to examine than the average archaeologist, as modern technology has developed a great number of non-perishable items. However, you may perceive that an analysis of American culture based on the partial inventory of a mail-order catalog would at best be described as incomplete.

One advantage that the archaeologist does have, however, is context. A pile of artifacts from Montgomery Ward might be hard to sort into functional categories. But if each item were placed in its proper location in the various rooms of a house, according to its use, then analysis of its function would be aided immeasurably. Pots and pans have more meaning when arranged by the stove, rather than in a pile alongside a road. An arrowhead, recorded in place after having passed through a bison rib cage, says much more to a prehistorian than it can if it is thoughtlessly ripped out of the ground and glued into a colorful mosaic on a coffee table. Excavation is a destructive process, even when undertaken by a professional archaeologist. Thus it behooves the investigator to document as fully as possible the find *in situ* (in place) for the benefit of future analysis of the entire site and for providing comparative data for other studies.

Archaeologists are committed to the scientific method. Detailed descriptions are essential if cultural patterns are to be discovered, tested, and compared. Interdisciplinary cooperation with physical anthropologists, geologists, paleontologists, geochronologists, zoologists, botanists, ethnographers, and historians, as well as with a variety of technicians, has led to a number of significant breakthroughs in archaeological method and theory. Archaeology is not a static discipline but is continually developing.

The term "culture" is one that is often misused in modern conversation and literature. A survey of existing definitions of the term in modern anthropology has turned up over one hundred and sixty different versions. It would be pretentious to attempt one here that would prove satisfactory to all. What can be said with certainty is that culture is not people and is not things. ("Things," or the actual artifacts produced by an individual or group, are often termed "material culture.") For the purposes of this book, culture will be considered as patterned behaviors, values, and beliefs generally accepted and held in common by the members of a society.

Keeping this in mind, and understanding that prehistoric archaeology seeks to delineate *prehistoric cultures*, one must appreciate the immensity of the task. Using the articles discarded or otherwise deposited in the soil, along with any other associated empirical data that can be generated, the archaeologist moves cautiously toward the elusive goal of determining the patterned behaviors, values, and beliefs that were generally accepted and held in common by the members of the prehistoric society.

Archaeology is an exciting science. It provides an avenue along which one can reach into yesterday and possibly attain a greater understanding of the variety of life experiences. It provides us with a time-line upon which we may test hypotheses about environmental change and cultural adaptation. Perhaps we can yet learn from history (and prehistory) and avoid unnecessary complications and catastrophes that might spell an end to humankind as we now know it.

References

On culture and cultural anthropology:
Kluckhohn and Kelley 1945; Kroeber and Kluckhohn 1952.

On archaeological methods:
Hester, Heizer, and Graham 1975; Joukowsky 1980.

On the development of American archaeology:
Willey and Sabloff 1974; Fitting 1973.

2 The New World in Global Perspective

Colorado is in no way a microcosm of global or even North American cultural evolution. What has taken place here, though, is largely the result of outside influences bringing about a cumulative heritage over many thousands of years. However, the results in Colorado may not clearly reflect the main cultural contributions from New World contemporaries and Old World predecessors. For that reason, it seems important to briefly consider the broad scope of human evidence in order to better understand Colorado's place in world prehistory.

Humankind and Culture in the Old World

The earliest cultures of the world arose in Africa, Asia, and Europe, and the time of their origins is still in question. It seems that with each new field season in Africa the age of humankind is pushed back additional millenia. At present, fossils belonging to the genus *Homo* are thought to date to around three million years before present (B.P.). From that point forward there is a reasonably clear picture of physical and cultural development that culminates in civilization as we know it.

The early development of humankind, including the emergence of a fully modern *Homo sapiens sapiens*, falls within a major geological period known as the Pleistocene (Ice Age). During this time, a dramatic series of climatic fluctuations caused the periodic formation and melting of massive continental ice sheets and mountain glaciers. The process involved at least four major periods of advance, known in Europe as the Günz (the oldest),

Mindel, Riss, and Würm glacials. In North America, the same periods are known as the Kansan, Nebraskan, Illinoisan, and Wisconsin (named for the southernmost states penetrated during each glacial). These four advances were separated on both continents by major warm intervals termed interglacials.

The Pleistocene climatic shifts affected the entire globe. During glacials, with sea water locked up in continental ice, ocean levels dropped as much as 110 meters, exposing large expanses of continental shelf and sea floor. Temperate zones crept closer to the equator, pushed by the expanding arctic biomes. The warmer interglacials caused ice sheets to melt and recede and sea levels to rise.

From the earliest hints of the human line, perhaps three million years ago, until the end of the Pleistocene at about twelve thousand years ago, the way of life can be described as foraging or hunting and gathering. Social organization consisted of small band-level groupings, probably much like extended families. From this time, no domesticated plants or animals are known. Survival depended upon a knowledge of wild game habits and migration patterns and upon the ability to find edible wild plants. Bands perhaps moved from one ecological niche to another as various species ripened.

Southern and eastern Africa hold a wealth of fossil bipedal hominids dating back to the earliest known cultural period—the Lower Paleolithic. The principal artifacts known from the earliest part of this period are crude pebble tools (or core tools). It is quite likely that other items (e.g. branches, unmodified rocks, bones) were also used, but they either have not survived or are not recognizable as definite implements. There is also some question about just who made and used the pebble tools. Small proto-humans, the Australopithicines, do not seem to many observers to be likely candidates; it is still unclear whether or not these creatures are even actually hominids (in the human lineage). Another early (two million years B.P.) hominid now seems most likely to be the first stone tool maker in Africa, but only continued fieldwork and analysis will finally unravel these and other puzzles. Right now, the physical evolutionary scheme is being debated furiously, with fossil specimens lumped or split into one genus and then into another, and we will have to be content with viewing the earliest chapters of humanity "through a glass darkly."

At some point around one million years B.P., *Homo erectus* appears in Africa. This physical type was first classified by Dr. Davidson Black on the basis of a single molar. The oldest *Homo erectus* remains are from Africa, with younger finds from Asia and Europe. These progressively later exam-

OLD WORLD			NEW WORLD		
Date (B.P)	Stage	Species	Date (B.P.)	Stage	Culture
4,500-present	Civilization	Homo sapiens sapiens	1,000-contact	Postclassic	Aztec, Inca
			1,700-1,000	Classic	Maya, Nazca
9,000-4,500	Neolithic	Homo sapiens sapiens	4,000-contact	Formative	Anasazi, Mississippian, Olmec
12,000-4,000	Mesolithic	Homo sapiens sapiens	8,000-2,000	Archaic	Late Archaic Middle Archaic Early Archaic
40,000-12,000	Upper Paleolithic	Homo sapiens sapiens	pre-12,000-6,000	Lithic	Plano Folsom Llano (Clovis)
100,000-40,000	Middle Paleolithic	Homo sapiens neanderthalensis			
pre-3 m.y ?-100,000	Lower Paleolithic	Homo erectus early Homo Australopithecus			

Figure 2-1   Summary of Old World stages and New World equivalents.

ples of *Homo erectus* outside of Africa coupled with the early Australopithicines and early *Homo* finds in Africa, have given the Dark Continent the title of "Cradle of Humankind."

Homo erectus appears to have evolved culturally as well as physically. The crude pebble tools from the beginning of the Lower Paleolithic have become more complex by the end of the period. At that point, especially in China, a flake technology can be observed, complementing the core tool tradition. *Homo erectus* learned to control fire and began to engage in a less creative activity—cannabalism.

Following the extremely long Lower Paleolithic is the Middle Paleolithic. Beginning perhaps 100,000 years ago, the period is characterized by a new human species—*Homo sapiens neanderthalensis*, "Neanderthal Man." Though often characterized as the stereotypic "cave man," the

Neanderthals possessed complex tools, were successful hunters and gatherers, buried their dead (often with funerary goods that suggests a thought of afterlife), and adjusted well to an often stressful climate in the northern latitudes. They were anything but "slow."

The Upper Paleolithic, growing out of the Middle Paleolithic around 35,000 years ago, was a period of continued cultural and physical development. But this time, the modern *Homo sapiens sapiens* (once termed Cro-Magnon) is present. With the new physical form came a complex blade technology that was a refinement of the pebble and flake traditions. Art became abundant in the form of transportable items and rock paintings, peckings, and incisings. Bones were modified into a variety of implements, including needles, awls, hammers, and shaft straighteners.

The northern continental ice sheets retreated at the end of the Paleolithic, about 12,000 years ago. The human population was increasing, but many of the larger Pleistocene animals (e.g. mammoth, bison) became extinct or their territories coalesced near the Arctic. Human survival in the face of the environmental shift depended upon significant cultural adjustments.

During the new era, known as the Mesolithic (Middle Stone Age), hunter-gatherers were forced to abandon a lifeway dependent upon large game and concentrate instead on a wide assortment of wild plants, marine and freshwater resources, and small game. The substitutions in the food base compelled concomitant technological innovations and the honing of human abilities. The Mesolithic was a time of regional cultural diversification, brought on by the need to exploit foodstuffs that varied considerably according to the specific local ecosystems. Some cultures conquered the water while others laid claim to the expanding woodlands.

Although the Mesolithic was a time of rapid cultural change, the hunter-gatherer mode of life from the Paleolithic remained basically intact. The resource base was still composed entirely of wild plants and animals. As a result, sedentary life was impractical for all but those in the richest environs (e.g. some coastal situations). However, humanity had demonstrated considerable resiliency and adaptability and was on the threshold of a major step that would forever change life as it had been known.

Sometime around 10,000 years ago, domestication of plants and animals began, giving rise to a new cultural period, the Neolithic (New Stone Age). Best evidence today places the initial innovation in the Middle East. Cultivated crops and farmyard animals are so much a part of our life today that it is easy to take them for granted. However, from a cultural perspective, domestication is probably a greater achievement than recent beginnings of the conquest of space. The whole process of deliberately selecting particular genetic traits (long before the research of Mendel) and rearing generations of various crops and herds required a tremendous mental leap.

No longer would hunters be forced to relocate because of game migrations. Never again would women be required to travel to distant climes to retrieve the only available seeds and fruits of that season. Permanent villages rose in locales conducive to the cultivation of wheat and other crops. Pigs and sheep were bred and raised with the intent of slaughtering them for their meat and hides. The development of irrigation eventually allowed the extension of farming into marginal regions. Populations increased, land became valuable, and walled cities proliferated.

Some (including this author) think that the Neolithic Revolution was the prime mover in the advent of war. Prior to the invention of farming, surplus foodstuffs were unknown. A vast accumulation of material possessions would be a liability to the family unit when camp was broken and the next long trek commenced. Defending a plot of land was not practical or necessary. War as "sustained, major conflict between opposing forces," is clearly impossible among foragers. It requires logistical support that would have been unimaginable in those simpler days. Territoriality was probably of only minor import in the Paleolithic, but in the Neolithic and after it became central to the maintenance of life and culture. With land and its fruits and the goods made possible by the leisure and specialization that a stable agricultural economy allows, a peaceful people had much to defend and a warlike people much to take.

The Middle East, though probably the earliest place in which farming took place, cannot claim to be the only center of agricultural innovation. Domestication occurred as independent invention in several other nuclear areas of the world. Various rices are known early in Southeast Asia, India, China, and Africa. Peoples in the New World domesticated and developed corn, beans, squash, potatoes, tomatoes, and tobacco.

The Neolithic—with the introduction of the means of maintaining a dependable food supply and the beginnings of settled village life— provided the prerequisites for the development and spread of civilization.

The term "civilization" is regularly misused by the general public and mass media in dealing with prehistoric cultures. From an archaeological standpoint, civilization denotes a very particular level of cultural achievement in which the society is characterized by high specialization within the division of labor, a stratified social structure, monumental architecture, and the use of writing. Technically, humankind leaves prehistory at this point, as the invention of writing advances its possessors into recorded history. In the Middle East, this level was achieved over 6,000 years ago. Other parts of the world were not far behind.

On To The New World

During the millions of years of the Lower and Middle Paleolithic of Africa, Asia, and Europe, the Western Hemisphere appears to have been unoccupied by human groups. The spacious tracts of water known as the Atlantic and Pacific proved to be adequate barriers against potential world travel. However, some limited opportunities for access arose as time passed.

The climatic oscillations during the Pleistocene and the corresponding fluctuation of sea level in response to the forming and melting of land ice provided humans with periods of time in which pedestrian travel into North America was possible. The Bering Strait, a narrow gap between Siberia and Alaska, was at various times dry land up to 1,500 kilometers wide. The sea floor there is quite shallow, less than 40 meters in places and would have been exposed each time substantial quantities of sea water became locked in the continental ice sheets. This process took place several times over the past 40,000 years and undoubtedly many times before that, although evidence for the latter is lacking due to subsequent reworking of the surface geology.

Although prehistoric peoples may have had other motives for entering the New World, one of the more popular archaeological speculations is that hunters followed herds of mammoths and other large game across the strait and into the unglaciated and tundra-covered portions of Alaska. It has been suggested that once the early peoples reached the interior of Alaska, they would have found the route south blocked by the same massive ice sheets that had been directly responsible for lowering the sea level and allowing access to the continent in the first place. This ice barrier would have caused an interlude in their travels until the next warming trend developed, opening up a corridor and permitting passage to the unglaciated regions of the south. Questions have arisen about the validity of the corridor concept; some archaeologists doubt that southward movement of peoples from the Alaskan inlands was ever significantly impeded.

Given the above model, one would expect that the oldest New World sites would be found in the northwestern Arctic and youngest in Patagonia. Actually, the greatest number of early dates that have been accepted

THE NEW WORLD   13

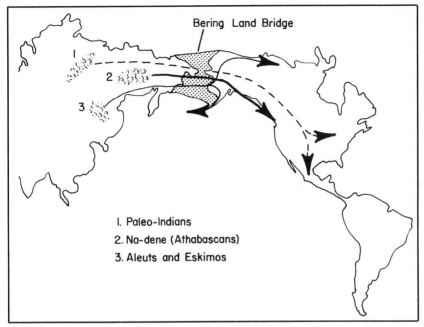

Figure 2-2   Turner's speculative population sources in Asia and proposed migration routes to the New World, based on dental evidence. (Modified from Folsom and Folsom 1982.)

without question have come from the American Southwest, the Plains, and the Eastern Woodlands. This is not to say that early sites are not known in the vicinity of the Bering Strait. Old Crow Flats in the Yukon yielded a date of ca. 27,000 B.P., and other very early sites have been reported throughout the New World. But most, if not all, lack some of the criteria demanded by the archaeological community as a whole, including a definite and clear association of undisputed artifacts in a well-stratified site that can be reliably dated by conventional methods. It is anticipated that sites in the 25,000 year range will be found and accepted by all, but at present, those sites enjoying nearly universal endorsement are considerably younger (ca. 12,000 B.P.). Recent excavations at the Meadowcroft Rockshelter in Pennsylvania have yielded stratified human remains that have been dated to over 19,000 B.P. Although the date is still somewhat controversial, it does appear that a groundswell for its support is building.

The presence of the Bering Strait land bridge is not the only evidence used by prehistorians to demonstrate a New World cultural continuum with Asian roots. Physical anthropologists have verified that only fully modern *Homo sapiens sapiens* have been found in the Americas, suggesting an entrance no older than the Late Paleolithic. These scientists have documented a variety of genetic traits held in common by modern Asians and Native Americans, including similarity in teeth (shovel shaped incisors) and blood types (both have A and O and lack B). However, the modern American Indian is not identical to the modern Asian, a probable result of continuing evolutionary processes, affected by new genetic material from several waves of immigrants. Christy Turner has examined the dental remains of over 6,000 skeletons from the New World, Russia, and Siberia. These collections represent a wide variety of populations separated geographically and chronologically. His findings bear out previous cultural studies of Native Americans. Tooth patterns distinguish between the main body of Indians with origins in an initial immigration perhaps over 20,000 years ago, the Athabascans (Na-dene) who arrived later (Turner speculates 14,000 - 12,000 years ago), and the most recent colonists, the Aleuts and Eskimos. Based on Old World comparative samples, the early Paleo-Indians of pre-20,000 years B.P. originated in the Lena Basin of Siberia. The Athabascans, including the Navajo, Apache, and several of the Northwest Coast groups, have dental affinities to peoples from the forests of northeast Siberia. The Aleut-Eskimos show a genetic connection with the Amur Basin on the Chinese-Soviet border, south of the other two points of origin.

Jesse Jennings has aptly described these hardy nomads who were willing to brave the harsh life of the north: "There was an endless land filled with natural riches to be conquered by a tiny, arctic-hardened, cold-screened population of more than average toughness and viability."

In addition to their genetic baggage, the newcomers to the Western Hemisphere brought cultural attributes that had been honed in the midst of the European Ice Age and which would serve as buffers between the foragers and the environment of a new land. Clothing, tools, hunting/gathering skills, and shelters likely crossed the Strait *in toto*, though much of the actual evidence has failed to survive.

With the cumulative knowledge of the myriad generations arisen from the African continent during the Lower Pleistocene, humankind stepped into a new land just before the sea door closed for the last time. As time passed, isolation in conjunction with a functional stone age culture brought about lifeways that were both unique and yet held some developmental parallels with Old World counterparts right up to the time Europe "discovered" America.

References

On the Pleistocene and sea level fluctuations:
Müller-Beck 1967.

On fossil hominids of the Old World:
Day 1965; Howell 1968; Howells 1959; Johanson and Edey 1981;
Almquist and Cronin 1978; Phenice 1972; Poirier 1977.

On Old World cultural developments:
Braidwood 1967; Hester and Grady 1982; Clark 1977.

On Old World and New World domestications:
Struever 1971.

On the Bering Land Bridge:
Laughlin 1967; Müller-Beck 1967; Jennings 1968; Wormington in prep.

On the corridor through the North American ice sheets:
Jennings 1968; Hester and Grady 1982.

On the Old Crow Flats site:
Irving and Harington 1973; Bonnichsen 1978.

On other very early sites in the New World:
Bryan 1978; Wormington in prep.

On the dating of the Meadowcroft Rockshelter:
Haynes 1980; Mead 1980; Adovasio, et al. 1980.

On Turner's analysis of Siberian and New World teeth and early New World migrations:
Turner 1981, 1983; Folsom and Folsom 1982.

3 Colorado's Environment

Colorado is as complex geologically, ecologically, and topographically as any state or province in North America. It contains a multitude of life zones, a dramatic range in elevation, and a reasonably full representation of geologic formations. The Continental Divide courses north and south, forcing drainage patterns into basins dominated by the Mississippi, Missouri, Rio Grande, and Colorado Rivers. Colorado has been divided into three provinces: plains, mountains, and plateaus, each encompassing roughly one-third of the state.

Geology

The oldest rocks in the state are the Red Creek Quartzites from the Uintas in the northwest (2.3 billion years old). The youngest are still forming today from material washed or blown down from the mountains and plateaus and deposited in the basins and valleys and on the prairies.

Between 2.3 billion years ago and the present, a great deal of geological activity has taken place. According to plate tectonics theory, Colorado is part of the North American Plate, a large land mass once attached to Europe, in turn part of the supercontinent Gondwanaland. North America has since slid 1,500 miles to the west, riding up over part of the Pacific Plate. From about 600 to 300 million years ago, seas covered much of Colorado. Then a period of intense plate movement appears to have caused some cracking and breaking of the earth's crust along a north-south zone that intersects Colorado. This resulted in the formation of the original Rocky Mountains, a process known as the Colorado Orogeny.

These mountains eroded over the next 200 million years until a second major uplift began around 60 million years ago. This event is termed the Laramide Orogeny. The formation of these second Rocky Mountains is thought to have coincided with the actual separation of North America from Europe and the creation of the Atlantic Ocean.

The movement of the plates seems to have slowed since then, but a more recent bowing up of the American Southwest that formed the Colorado Plateau about five million years ago (the Miocene-Pliocene Uplift) is believed to have had its origins in plate motion as well. The uplift of the Colorado Plateau brought about a significant increase in stream gradient, regenerating slow drainages into young rivers that could downcut quickly. As a result, the plateau country was broken up into what were to become major basins. The most spectacular feature of the increased downcutting was the carving of the Grand Canyon.

Between the Laramide Orogeny (second Rockies) and the Miocene-Pliocene Uplift, massive volcanic activity brought about the San Juan Mountains and adjacent areas. Then, following the Miocene-Pliocene Uplift, more volcanic action took place in the San Luis Valley area, along with localized flows in the Golden vicinity and Mesa de Maya, and eruptions in the Rabbit Ears Range and the Spanish Peaks.

For about three million years, the Pleistocene enveloped Colorado, bringing massive glacier building to the mountains. Ice carved broad U-shaped valleys there and pushed rock into linear moraines along the glacial borders. The climate in the adjoining plains and plateaus would have been correspondingly harsher. Near the end of this time, the terminal Pleistocene, the first evidence of humankind in Colorado appears.

Topography

The Great Plains cover much of the central continent, stretching east from the Rockies to the Eastern Woodlands and north from Mexico into Canada. The Plains of Colorado are contained within the portion known topographically as the Central Plains.

Westward from Kansas, the elevation of the flat land increases, a result of the uplifting of the Rocky Mountains. Over a distance of 150 miles, the land rises about 2,000 feet, from 3,386 to 5,200 feet above sea level. Extreme deformation of the horizontal bedrock sediments that underlie the plains can be seen at the contact with the mountains, where the sandstones and shales protrude out of the ground at an acute angle in response to the

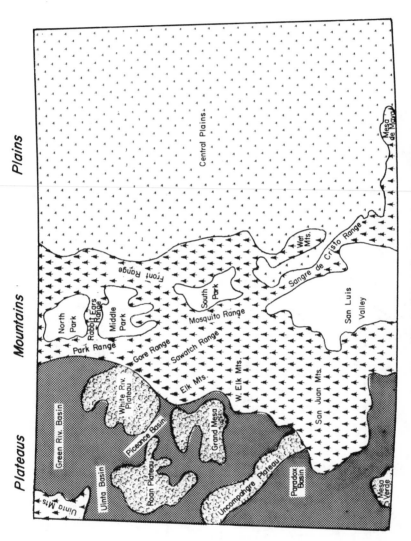

Figure 3-1   Topographic areas of Colorado. (After Chronic and Chronic 1972.)

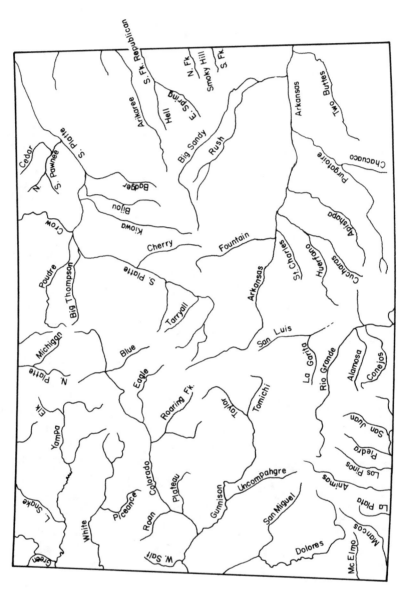

Figure 3-2   Major drainages in Colorado.

intrusive igneous and metamorphic rocks that compose the mountains. Red Rocks near Morrison and the Garden of the Gods near Colorado Springs are notable examples of this.

Colorado's High Plains are the conduit for eastward flowing streams that have captured snow melt in the mountains. There are two major drainages: the South Platte River and the Arkansas River.

The South Platte begins in South Park and courses to the northeast, gathering momentum from tributaries such as the Big Thompson and the Cache la Poudre. After crossing the plains of Colorado, the river enters Nebraska, joins the North Platte, and feeds into the Missouri at Omaha.

The Republican and Smoky Hill Rivers have small headwaters in northeast Colorado. They join in eastern Kansas and terminate in the Missouri at Kansas City.

The Arkansas River, with headwaters in the Mosquito Range near South Park, flows east across southern Colorado, then to the southeast across Kansas, Oklahoma, and Arkansas, emptying into the Mississippi River.

These eastern river systems conduct water from the mountains through what is otherwise a dry region. For the most part, the western plains sit in the rain shadow of the Rockies. Were it not for the dependable flow of the rivers, the plains could scarcely be occupied today. Prehistoric and modern migration and settlement patterns are intimately linked to these drainage systems.

Colorado's mountains are perhaps the most spectacular component of the state. Summits with elevations in excess of 14,000 feet can be found in various ranges. Most of the peaks are part of a north-south alignment. The main exception is Colorado's portion of the east-west Uintas, jutting in from Utah.

The extreme elevation of the mountains forces water-laden air from the West Coast to rise, cool, and contract, causing precipitation to fall in the high country. When the air mass reaches the east side of the Front Range, it drops, warms, and expands; precipitation generally stops, causing the "rain shadow" effect.

Snow melt from the mountains serves to sustain life in all the surrounding states, as well as many non-contiguous ones. In addition to the eastern streams already mentioned, the southern mountains feed water into the Rio Grande, San Juan, and Dolores River systems. The Rio Grande becomes a major New Mexico and Texas drainage, eventually flowing into the Gulf of Mexico. The San Juan runs west through the Four Corners region and meets the Colorado River at Glen Canyon. The Dolores courses northwest and joins the Colorado near Moab. Four major drainages originate in the

Western Slope mountains of Colorado. The Gunnison River flows out of the Elk Ranges and merges at Grand Junction with the Colorado River. The Colorado River begins near Middle Park and flows across Utah and Arizona and into the Gulf of California. North of the Colorado are the White and Yampa. Each flows west into Utah and joins the Green, which then turns south into the Colorado River. The North Platte has its headwaters in North Park, drains north into Wyoming, turns east, and links with the South Platte in Nebraska.

All of these rivers have served to downcut the mountain ranges, significantly modifying the terrain. This, in turn, has opened up a variety of routes for human travel into what otherwise would be nearly inaccessible ground.

Within the mountain province are four large open valleys (parks), each locked in by surrounding mountain ranges. North Park, Middle Park, and South Park were formed as basins to the west of the Front Range. Their geological composition is much like the foothills area of the plains, with basin floors composed of sediments laid down from mountain erosion. All of these parks are well-watered, serving as temporary holding areas for new snow melt. The fourth park, the San Luis Valley, is on the southern state border and is thought to have formed as part of the Rio Grande Rift (a large north-south split in the earth). It is the largest of the intermontaine basins and at present contains between 10,000 to 13,000 feet of gravel, sand, clay, and volcanic deposits on top of the original valley floor. The northern half of the valley does not open into the Rio Grande drainage system. Instead, runoff in the San Luis and La Garita Rivers is trapped subsurface in the deep sands. Although this ground water was of little use to aboriginals, it has been a source for artesian systems in the valley over the past 50 years or more.

The last of the three topographic provinces in Colorado is the plateau country of the west. Formed primarily during the Miocene-Pliocene Uplift, the region is characterized by large mesas separated by equally massive basins. For the most part, the caprock is sedimentary, having been lifted up in one piece. One notable exception is the younger Grand Mesa that has a basalt flow surface.

The uplift of the sediments caused fracturing in places, leading to rapid weathering. As a result, basins expanded outward because of the erosion of regenerated streams, isolating the plateaus and creating diverse ecosystems.

Plant and Animal Life

Most of the variation in plant and animal life in Colorado can be attributed to one primary factor: elevation, which ranges from 3,386 feet in the southeast to a maximum of 14,431 at the summit of Mt. Elbert. Other factors involved in the patterns of life include water (atmospheric, surface, and ground), soils, and aspect of exposure. However, these are all tied directly to ground elevations in one degree or another.

From a standpoint of floral distribution, Costello has divided the state into three geographic areas that closely resemble the physiographic divisions of Chronic and Chronic. Costello sees these regions as the plains, mountains and plateaus, and the semi-desert.

The eastern plains are primarily a mixed-grass or short-grass prairie, with wheat grasses, blue stem, blue grama, and buffalo grass as major components. Costello suspects that the land was once a tall-grass prairie but that grazing (including by bison) brought it into a "disclimax" state. Major drainages support deciduous trees (e.g. cottonwood, willow) and a variety of shrubs in their immediate vicinity. Forbs (any herbaceous plant other than grass), such as prickly pear and yucca, can be found throughout.

The mountain and plateau area has been divided by Costello into five subcategories: piñon-juniper, mountain shrub, ponderosa pine-Douglas fir, spruce-fir, and alpine.

The piñon-juniper zone exists between 5,500 and 7,000 feet in south-central Colorado, and from 5,500 to 8,500 in the west-central and southwest part of the state. It is found along the lower reaches of the Dolores, San Juan, Uncompahgre, Gunnison, Colorado, and Piceance rivers, to name a few. Mesa Verde and the Uncompahgre Plateau have large populations of piñon-juniper. This community also exists at the contact of the Rocky Mountains with the prairie in the southeastern counties of El Paso and Pueblo. An isolated grove (1,000 acres) on the hogback west of Fort Collins in northern Colorado may indicate a much wider distribution of this forest type in earlier times.

The mountain shrub is a transitional zone intermediate between the upper coniferous forests and either plains, semi-desert, or piñon-juniper communities below. North of Denver, along the Front Range, the dominant shrub is mountain mahogany mixed with a variety of smaller plants such as skunkbrush, serviceberry, and rose. South of Denver and on the Western Slope, the main component is oakbrush with an understory of serviceberry, bitterbrush, and rabbitbrush.

Between 8,500 and 9,500 feet, the ponderosa pine-Douglas fir zone occurs. Grasses and forbs can proliferate beneath ponderosa due to the open nature of the tree growth patterns.

The spruce-fir zone predominates above the ponderosa pine-Douglas fir zone. Englemann spruce and alpine fir are the most common species, with lesser numbers of blue spruce and white fir. The unforested North, Middle, and South Parks exist in the midst of this zone. Vegetation in the parks is principally sagebrush and mixed grasses, intersected by localized riparian (stream bank) communities.

The last of the mountain-plateau zones is the alpine. Found above 11,500 feet in the northern part of the state and above 12,000 feet in the south, it is characterized by a lack of trees. A transitional community of stunted conifers may exist as a buffer between the spruce-fir and alpine areas, but the zone itself is a tundra. On shallow soils between the rocks, grasses, sedges, forbs, and a few small shrubs will grow during the short summers.

The western basins of Colorado are occupied by semi-desert species. Generally located below 7,000 feet, the communities are usually of greasewood (in high alkaline soils), saltbush (in drier, well-drained, less alkaline soils), or sagebrush. The sagebrush often grows at elevations just above either greasewood or saltbush.

Animal populations across the state are not as fixed or as easily demarcated as vegetation. Some species, such as the mule deer, coyote, and raptors (hawks, eagles, owls) range throughout the three regions.

Others—including the pica, marmot, elk, bighorn sheep, and blue grouse—are restricted to the higher elevations of the mountain province.

The mountain lion has an extensive territory that includes both plateau and mountain regions.

The pronghorn (antelope) is a short-grass prairie animal and maintains healthy numbers on the eastern plains where the human population is sparse. The bison was abundant on the plains (and present in the mountains as well) until the second half of the nineteenth century when wholesale slaughter by Anglo hunters practically eliminated them. Elk were once a plains species too, but they have retreated into the isolation of the mountains.

Migratory waterfowl (geese, ducks) are basically funneled along the east side of the Front Range, flying south in the fall and north in the spring. The prairie chicken appears to be restricted to the plains, while the sage hen is more of a plateau-basin species.

Prehistoric hunters and gatherers in Colorado were generalized feeders and would probably take whatever game was available. The most important species probably included bison, mule deer, elk, mountain sheep, rabbit, pronghorn, and available birds. There is some Western Slope evidence for fish as well (chub, squawfish).

Overall, Colorado has provided a rich and varied environment for its inhabitants. Early hunters could escape the hot, dry periods on the plains by climbing a few thousand feet into the mountains. Seasonal rounds would yield such nutritional foodstuffs as piñon nuts and other seeds. Large high country game could be taken in the summer, while other large game would be abundant in the lowlands during the cooler times of the year. Geological deposits were ample for those seeking raw material from which to fashion stone tools.

Although the available resources did not approach the quantities available in the Eastern Woodlands at the same time, the populations of Colorado were lower and the demand less. Living in Colorado with primitive technology would have been rigorous, but it was not without its rewards. Adaptation to the environmental constraints allowed for what appears to have been a reasonably good life.

References

On Colorado's provinces:
Chronic and Chronic 1972.

On Colorado geology:
Chronic and Chronic 1972; Chronic 1979.

On continental drift:
Heirtzler 1968; Runcorn 1962; Tarling and Tarling 1971.

On the Great Plains:
Webb 1931; Wedel 1961.

On Colorado plant communities:
Costello 1954.

4 Dating

Relative Dating

Before moving into the chapters dealing directly with the actual data recovered in Colorado, some mention should be made of dating techniques most commonly applied to the finds.

Many sites are not dated by what would strictly be termed absolute or chronometric dating. Perhaps the least sophisticated (in terms of technological involvement) means of determining the antiquity of a site is by *relative dating*, the judgement that one find is older or younger than another, without the application of a specific calendrical date.

Relative dating originated with Nicholas Steno, a Dane and one of the "Fathers of Geology." In 1669 he published the *Prodromus*, which contains his observation that stratified sedimentary rock had its origins as horizontal layers, with the lowest levels older than the highest. This has been termed the law of superposition and is a major principle in modern geology.

Assuming that soil formation follows the law of superposition, when cultural remains are found at different levels, it can usually be stated that the lowest cultural stratum is the oldest and the highest is the youngest. This is the simplest of the relative dating methods.

There are some factors that may complicate such an interpretation, such as rodent activity that can move items from one level to another. If someone had dug through cultural deposits and thrown the debris and soil into backdirt piles, the result would be inverse stratigraphy, with younger remains beneath older ones. However, these sorts of complications can usually be spotted if the field archaeologist is vigilant.

Once a relative sequence is established based on the order of occurrence in the soil, it can be applied to similar finds elsewhere. Though no absolute age can be assigned to a new site by this method, it can often be placed within the relative culture sequence by matching artifact types and styles to those in the established column.

Dendrochronology

One of the most useful absolute dating methods in southwest Colorado is *dendrochronology* or tree-ring dating. It works by determining cutting dates for log beams (usually within structures). If one assumes that a beam was cut shortly before the construction of the room in which it was found, then a good age for the use of the room may be obtained.

Dendrochronology was refined by the astronomer, A. E. Douglass, in the early 1900s, but it had been an area of speculation and research since Theophrastus in the third century B.C.

In 1901 Douglass began studying tree rings in order to discover relationships between sun-spots and vegetation growth patterns. He suspected that annual growth rings would indicate fluctuations in climate: wide rings would be evidence of better growth conditions and narrow rings worse ones. He collected many samples of living trees, gaining several hundred years of growth information in some single logs. When he reached the maximum age possible with living trees, he began to overlap their rings with old logs incorporated in historic buildings. In this way the chronology began to expand back into antiquity.

Earl Morris, one of Colorado's pioneer archaeologists, provided Douglass with his first prehistoric samples in 1918—specimens from two Anasazi ruins in New Mexico, Aztec and Pueblo Bonito. The following year Douglass and Morris designed an increment borer that could extract tree-ring samples from a ruin beam without undermining the beam's strength and damaging the integrity of the site. That accomplished, a widespread program of tree-ring sampling was undertaken. What resulted was thrilling for Southwestern archaeologists. Though Douglass did not have the actual link between his living tree series and the earlier series that was beginning to accumulate, he was able to judge from the earlier "floating chronology" that, for example, Pueblo Bonito was constructed 40-45 years before Aztec.

Collection of specimens continued over the years, and the prehistoric record grew. In 1923 the National Geographic Society, at the suggestion of

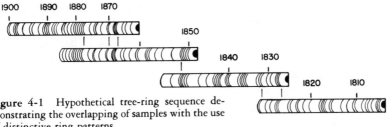

Figure 4-1 Hypothetical tree-ring sequence demonstrating the overlapping of samples with the use of distinctive ring patterns.

Neil Judd, underwrote a program to further enlarge the known sequence. This work, when connected with the previously accumulated data, led to an unbroken, though still floating chronology spanning 585 years. Though this method was extremely valuable in recognizing climatic fluctuations endured by the prehistoric populations and in helping to establish the relative dating of sites, it still did not provide absolute dates.

In 1929 the breakthrough occurred—a dramatic event that must have rivaled the greatest "eurekas" in the history of archaeological science. That year, Lyndon Hargrave and Emil Haury were part of the "Third National Geographic Society Beam Expedition" which was attempting to find the missing link between the two chronologies.

On 22 June 1929 at the Whipple Ruin (near Show Low, Arizona, in a Mormon farmer's barnyard), they collected a buried beam that was numbered HH-39. Douglass took the fragile sample to a nearby shed and counted the rings, determining that they went back to A.D. 1237 (20 years older than the modern series previously extended). They still did not know how big the "gap" was, however. That night, in a Show Low hotel room, with Haury, Hargrave, and Neil Judd looking on by the light of a hissing gasoline lantern, Douglass began comparing the HH-39 rings to the modern and floating chronologies. According to Haury, when final recognition took place, Douglass said:

> I think we have it. Ring patterns between 1240 and 1300 of the historic sequence correspond in all important respects to the patterns in the youngest part of the prehistoric sequence. This means that there was no gap at all. The overlap of the two chronologies was only 26 years and there was no possible way to join the two on the evidence we had. Beam HH-39 has established the bridge.

The way dendrochronology works is fairly easy to explain, though its implementation is quite complicated and fraught with pitfalls. To begin with, not all trees produce suitable rings for dating. It is true that they all have annual growth rings, but different species respond differently to environmental influences. Soft woods of the *Populus* genus (e.g. cotton-wood), for example, grow quite rapidly and with generally uniform ring widths. They do not have the necessary idiosyncrasies that can mark a unique climatic pattern and allow for overlapping of samples from prehistoric sites of unknown ages.

Many prehistoric houses were constructed with beams of coniferous trees. Ponderosa pine and piñon are usually good species for dating, though juniper can provide analytical difficulties. These types of tree rings have extremely variable widths, with narrow rings coming during poor growing seasons (low moisture or colder climate) and wider bands during more favorable times. Taken over a long period of time, the ring patterns can be seen as distinctive, much like fingerprints. When one starts from a known date (modern cut tree), it should be fairly obvious how a chronology could be constructed by overlapping samples from progressively older sources.

However, problems in dendrochronology are numerous, limiting its application. The Southwest is an area of variable rainfall and temperature, an ideal environment for producing regional idiosyncrasies in ring patterns. Other parts of the country, with more constant climates, have trees with more uniform rings (complacent rings) that are practically useless for dating purposes. One problem directly related to Southwestern dating is that even though a sample may tell the archaeologist in what year it was cut, it may not necessarily accurately date the construction of the room from which the sample was taken. A tree may have been dead for many years before it was cut down and used. In addition, since trees were difficult to fell with stone tools, if beams could be salvaged from abandoned buildings, they would logically be incorporated in the new structure right along with the more freshly-cut specimens. Only when patterns within rooms can be discerned (e.g. 90% of a room's beams cut within a few years of each other) can some confidence be placed in the assigning of a construction date.

The difficulty in the actual correlations of an archaeological specimen with the known chronology should not be understated. The center for such work is the Laboratory of Tree-Ring Research at the University of Arizona (established in 1938 by A. E. Douglass). Regional chronologies from all over the country are housed there, and collection from various areas is continuing, since no one chronological series can be applied to every site (even within the Southwest). Microscopic details are often the only clues that can tie a site of unknown age into a master time-table. At this point, Southwestern sites that fall within the past 2,000 years in age can potentially be dated by dendrochronology.

Radiocarbon Dating

Age determination of archaeological sites through *radiocarbon* dating is the most practical and widest-used method in the United States at present. Reasonable accuracy can be expected for samples up to 50,000 years old. Since it appears that human presence in the New World is younger than this maximum range, radiocarbon is an ideal approach.

Radiocarbon dating was originated by Willard Libby in the 1940s while he was at the Institute of Nuclear Studies in Chicago. In 1960 he was awarded the Nobel Prize in Chemistry for his discovery.

The process leading to an organism's datability is somewhat complex. Libby's idea was that cosmic radiation produces neutrons which react with nitrogen 14 to bring about the formation of carbon 14 isotopes. It was assumed that the cosmic ray-produced C 14 oxidizes into carbon dioxide and blends into the atmosphere. With air movement around the world, it was calculated that a rapid dispersion of C 14 takes place globally. Plants take in the C 14 with the CO_2 and retain it at a predictable level that remains in equilibrium throughout the organism's life. Since C 14 is a radioactive isotope, it decays at a given rate (a half-life of 5,730 ± 40 years), and when absorption ceases at the organism's death, the level of C 14 begins to diminish, since there is no commensurate C 14 intake to maintain the balance. According to the half-life principle, radioactive isotopes are never fully exhausted from a sample. Each half-life reduces what remains by one-half. Thus two half-lives result in a remainder of one-fourth of the original quantity, rather than approaching zero. By the end of nine half-lives, radiocarbon still remains, but it is such a small amount that it cannot be accurately measured.

When a sample is taken to a laboratory, the carbon is converted into gas (CO_2, methane, or acetylene) and then counted in a device similar in function to a Geiger counter.

Though charcoal is probably the best and most common form of organic material used for radiocarbon dating, theoretically any once-living organism, plant or animal, can be dated.

Problems with C 14 dating come from a variety of factors. For one thing, it appears that the concentration of radiocarbon in the atmosphere has not been constant through time and plants have absorbed varying amounts according to when they lived. These fluctuations have been plotted, and a closer fit between radiocarbon years and calendar years can now be made.

Contamination of organic samples by a variety of materials can drastically affect the reliability of the date. Coal, perhaps from local seams,

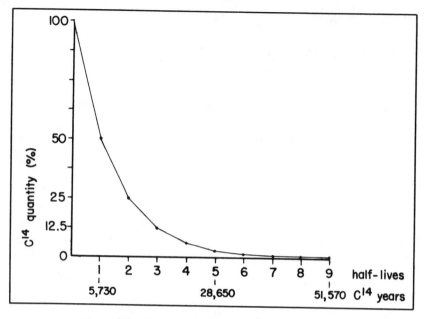

Figure 4-2   Decay rate of carbon 14 for nine half-lives.

mixed inconspicuously with charcoal in a hearth, can make the resultant date far older than it should be. Modern rootlets in a sample can cause the date to be too young. Other contaminations by careless excavators can also take place. However, today radiocarbon laboratories are quite conscious of these types of problems and take great care to assure that the resultant dates reflect the actual age of the sample.

Radiocarbon dates are expressed with an error factor, as in 9600 ± 130 B.P. (Frazier site). This indicates that the actual age of the site probably lies within 130 years on either side of 9600 years before present (B.P.). If one were to increase the number of standard deviations, making a wider range of variation, the probability of accuracy would also increase. Radiocarbon dates are not as specific in age determination as dendrochronology, for example. However, given the greater time depth possible, being able to know within a few per cent is quite satisfactory. Without C14 dating, the vast majority of sites in the Americas would, at best, be tied together in a "floating" chronology of only limited value.

Obsidian Hydration

Obsidian hydration is a dating method that measures the amount of water absorbed on the surface of obsidian (volcanic glass). Since obsidian builds a hydration layer at a fixed rate, flaking of the material during tool manufacturing leaves fresh unhydrated surfaces. Years later, when the tool is recovered by an archaeologist, it can be examined microscopically and the water layer measured. With knowledge of the rate of hydration per year, the thickness of the water layer should indicate the year of the tool's manufacture.

Obsidian hydration techniques are of limited value in Colorado, primarily because the raw material is not very common. There are portions of the southern state where it does occur naturally, and of course, it could be carried in from the outside (e.g. Yellowstone or New Mexico).

Environmental variation appears to affect hydration rates, and the recognition of this problem has brought about the development of regional chronologies, rather than a single master rate. The technique is still being refined, but it can be valuable, especially in conjunction with other dating methods.

Archaeomagnetism

Archaeomagnetism is a dating method based on the identification of past movements of the earth's magnetic poles. These migrations are quite well known and have been tracked and plotted from various vantage points on the earth's surface. Dating of the ancient virtual geomagnetic poles (VGP) has been accomplished in Europe by historical documentation. In the United States dendrochronology has provided the absolute chronology for pole movements.

In addition to the polar shifts, the other component of this dating method is the presence of magnetically-sensitive minerals in clay, such as in a clay-lined hearth or a clay-plastered floor. The mineral-laden clay would have been applied to the feature surface during its construction in prehistoric times. At a later date, when the hearth was filled with burning fuel, or perhaps when the house burned down, the clay would be heated to a point where the minerals became somewhat fluid, allowing them to align with the current magnetic field. This would be much like releasing the damper on a compass and allowing the needle to point north. Upon cooling, the

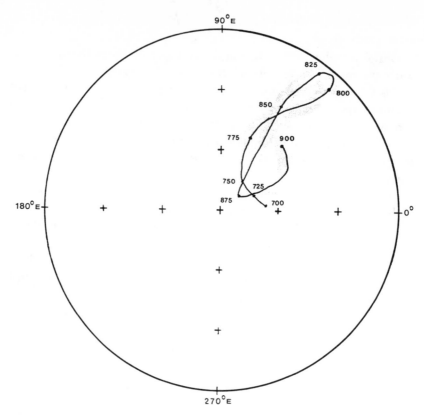

Figure 4-3   Virtual geomagnetic pole paths as determined by the Dolores Archaeological Program during the 1978 through 1980 field seasons. The center of the polar projection represents true north. Dates along the curve are in years A.D. (Based on data in Hathaway, Eighmy, and Kane 1983; courtesy Jeff Eighmy.)

particles would be frozen in place in the baked clay, oriented to north as it existed at that time.

Upon discovery by the modern archaeologist, the sample is capped with plaster of Paris and marked with the modern direction to magnetic north. This piece of clay is then removed to an archaeomagnetic laboratory. Through the use of a magnetometer, the earlier alignment can be determined in relation to the modern alignment. With knowledge of the chronology of polar migrations, a date for the firing of the clay can be ascertained.

The Dolores Archaeological Program in southwestern Colorado has recently produced some interesting data. The investigators dated sites in the project area by means of ceramics and architectural styles, stratigraphy, and radiocarbon and tree-ring dating. They then compared the results with archaeomagnetic data from clay features in the same sites and have been able to plot 36 virtual geomagnetic pole positions and modify the initial master curve for the Southwest between A.D. 700 and 900. This is indeed a significant contribution.

Archaeomagnetism is an excellent tool, especially when used in conjunction with other conventional approaches. The prerequisite of having prepared clay features usually means that plenty of wood will also be available for radiocarbon and tree-ring dating to serve as cross-checks. Since the method is fairly new, experimentation to increase its reliability is still in progress.

Summary

Dating sites and establishing cultural chronologies are integral and very difficult aspects of archaeology. The unique characteristics of each excavation require the investigators to call upon all of their training and mental skills to deduce chronology and cultural affiliations from discarded artifacts and abandoned dwellings. The interpretations of future archaeologists will hinge on the fieldwork and analyses of today.

References

On relative dating:
Hester and Grady 1982; Hester, Heizer, and Graham 1975.

On dendrochronology:
Hester and Grady 1982; Hester, Heizer, and Graham 1975.

On A. E. Douglass:
Anonymous 1962.

On Earl Morris and tree-ring dating:
Lister and Lister 1968.

On closing the gap between the modern and floating tree-ring series:
Haury 1962.

On radiocarbon dating:
Hester and Grady 1982; Hester, Heizer, and Graham 1975; Suess 1965.

On obsidian hydration:
Hester and Grady 1982; Hester, Heizer, and Graham 1975.

On archaeomagnetism:
Eighmy 1980; Hathaway, Eighmy, and Kane 1983.

5 The Paleo-Indians

As archaeology attempts to expand the field of knowledge deeper into the past, it inevitably becomes involved with the problems of origins. In the New World, as we have seen, a search for the origin of our species is not relevant. The problem here centers on prehistoric immigration: when did it occur and where did it come from? The first humans to enter the Americas appear to have come from Asia, a likely time being at or near the end of the Pleistocene, perhaps 18,000 to 20,000 years ago, just before the great ice sheets retreated for the last time.

In order to demonstrate a link between the traditions of the possible Old World parent culture and the recent arrivals to North America, a search for similarities in the tool kits of both groups has been launched. But early North American Paleo-Indian projectile points do not look like any found outside this hemisphere. They are extremely well-made, are often long and symmetrical in outline, and have had large flakes removed from the basal portion of the blade, leaving wide grooves called "flutes." This unique fluting appears to be a New World invention. Marie Wormington has suggested that the earliest newcomers from Asia brought a tool kit consisting of choppers (large handaxe-like cutting tools), flake tools (made from flakes struck from a core or parent chunk rather than from the core itself), discoidal scrapers, crude blades, and possibly some refined bifacial (flaked on both sides) leaf-shaped blades. Although this tool assemblage has been at least partially documented in some New World sites, chronological problems remain to be solved.

Early in this century, the antiquity of human beings in the New World was very much in doubt. There was little evidence to support a great age for the presence of native peoples, and the few claims that had been made were quickly and devastatingly criticized by the noted physical anthropologist, Aleš Hrdlička. The result was that most archaeologists so feared the inevitable and scathing critiques of their interpretations and field methods (often justified) that they concluded that discretion was the better part of valor and abandoned the study of early man in favor of safer fields.

But in the 1920s, something happened to change this unfortunate situation forever. George McJunkin, a cowboy, found bones eroding out of an arroyo wall in a box canyon near Folsom, New Mexico. He eventually mentioned the place to Carl Schwachheim, an avocational paleontologist from Raton. Schwachheim tested the site and notified the Colorado Museum of Natural History about the discovery.

In 1926 J. D. Figgins, director of the museum, began excavations there with the intention of recovering paleontological specimens. During the course of the season, the excavators found several fragments of projectile points in direct association with the bones of fossil bison. Realizing the astonishing importance of this, Figgins left one of the points *in situ* and removed the surrounding block of earth and undisturbed bones, taking it back to the Denver museum. That winter of 1926-27, Figgins announced

Figure 5-1   Carl Schwachhiem points to an artifact *in situ* at the Folsom site, while Barnum Brown (American Museum of Natural History) looks on, 1927. (Western History Department, Denver Public Library.)

the discovery to his colleagues around the nation but received few positive responses. Many scholars assumed that there had been a mixing of a younger cultural stratum with the older bison bones. After all, the bison were an extinct species, too old, in all probability, to be contemporaneous with New World humans.

Determined to adequately demonstrate the relationship between early man and the bison bones, Figgins resumed work at Folsom in 1927. After finding four projectile points but having disturbed them in the process, he discovered a fifth in place. Figgins immediately sent out telegrams to various archaeological experts, inviting them to the site. Of those who came to examine the discoveries were Barnum Brown of the American Museum of Natural History, Frank H. H. Roberts, Jr. of the Smithsonian Institution, and Ted Kidder of Phillips Academy, Andover. These three respected scholars accepted Figgins's evidence for the association of man and extinct bison. However, it wasn't until the third season of work, with its additional discoveries of projectile points and bison bones, that there was general concurrence throughout the American archaeological community.

Although the actual count is not known, the Folsom site contained between 25 and 50 individual bison identified as *Bison antiquus figginsi*, an extinct species larger than our modern form. The animal carcasses had been butchered and the bones disarticulated (cut apart at the joints). Barnum Brown noted that most of the caudal vertebrae (tail bones) were missing. He surmised that since the tail would be removed with the rest of the hide, this was an indication that the Folsom bison had been skinned.

The projectile points found there were termed Folsom points, named after the nearby town, and the site became known as the type station for the Folsom culture. These thin projectile points have concave bases, fine flaking along the edges, and distinctive wide flake scars (flutes) on both faces, extending nearly the length of the blade.

It was the discovery at Folsom and its eventual acceptance by scholars as a legitimate archaeological site that initiated Paleo-Indian studies. Without the aid of radiocarbon dating, no one knew exactly how long prehistoric hunters had lived in the New World, but the association of artifacts with extinct Pleistocene fauna indicated a far greater time depth than previously thought.

In 1932 mammoth elephant bones were discovered near Dent, Colorado. With them were several fluted projectile points larger than those from Folsom but with some similar characteristics. This was the first good association in America of man with mammoth, and it indicated a human presence older than that revealed at the Folsom site. The projectile points found at Dent were later named Clovis points and have been found over much of the United States, often with mammoth bones.

Then in 1934 near Fort Collins, the Smithsonian Institution opened excavations at what was to become one of the most famous archaeological sites in America. The site, named Lindenmeier, contained an abundance of previously undocumented types of Folsom artifacts. The discoveries there contributed to a more complete picture of life in the terminal Pleistocene and added momentum to Paleo-Indian research.

While it is true that later investigations in Colorado have provided more detailed information about early man than did those excavations of the 1930s, the Dent and Lindenmeier projects stand out as significant mile markers in our journey toward understanding New World prehistory.

Pre-Clovis

Dutton and Selby

With some of the historical background for New World Paleo-Indian studies in mind, it is now appropriate to examine what may be the earliest remnants of human activity in the state.

During the mid-1970s, a Smithsonian Institution archaeologist, Dennis Stanford, was alerted to two locations in eastern Colorado where large mammalian bones had been exposed during construction activities. Upon realizing that the skeletal remains were those of mammoths, Stanford began excavating the Dutton and Selby sites, as they are now known, with hopes of finding evidence of human hunting and butchering activities. With the mammoth bones were also those of horse, camel, bison, antelope, deer, and smaller species. Dates on camel bone from Selby of 16,630±320 B.P. (years before present) and from Dutton of 13,600±485 B.P. have placed the deposit in the pre-Clovis range.

The mammoth bones were disarticulated and broken, many with spiral fractures, bone flaking, and polish. Considerable experimentation on modern elephant bones has since led Stanford to conclude that breakage of fresh mammoth bones can be accomplished by percussion from large rocks. As further evidence of human agency, some of the bone flakes from the two sites had striking platforms (remnants of the point of percussion where the flakes were originally detached). Based on these findings, Stanford originally suggested that the sites may have been pre-Clovis kills and processing areas, but through further analysis, he now thinks this interpretation is equivocal.

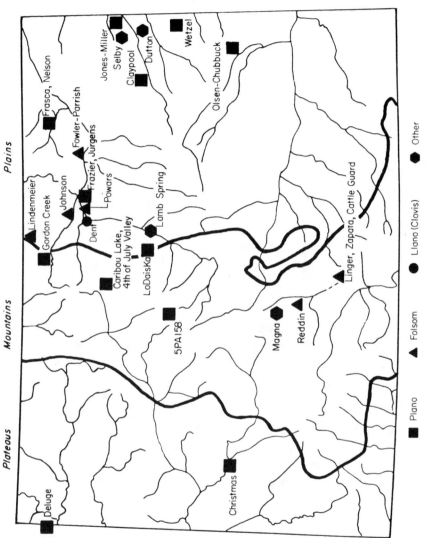

Figure 5-2 Principal Paleo-Indian sites in Colorado.

Lamb Spring

Further to the west, near the Denver suburb of Littleton, is the Lamb Spring site. Like Dutton and Selby, it contained faunal materials perhaps related to pre-Clovis occupations in North America. It was first excavated in 1961-62 by Waldo Wedel and C. L. Gazin of the Smithsonian and has since been re-investigated by Dennis Stanford from 1979 to 1981.

Lamb Spring, from prehistoric times until about 1970, was apparently a dependable water source, attracting both animals and humans. Archaeological excavations there exposed a deep level with camel, horse, and mammoth bones overlain by bison remains of Paleo-Indian age. Higher up were younger Archaic, Woodland, and historic artifacts.

The mammoth bones are from at least 23 individuals, 14 or more of which were within a single linear pile. Some of these bones show edge rounding and fractured surfaces, perhaps due to water movement, but many do not, indicating that for the most part the Lamb Spring mammoth bone bed is a primary deposit (that is, undisturbed by subsequent geological or other processes). The mammoth bone was dated 11,735 ± 95 B.P. and 13,140 ± 1000 B.P., both older than usual Clovis sites that have been dated to around 11,200 years ago.

Who or what was responsible for the death of the mammoths has not yet been determined. A large boulder with battering damage on one end was found in the mammoth level, and it was originally suspected of having been been used to break the mammoth bones. However, its stratigraphic relationship to the bones is now in question; it may have intruded into the mammoth zone from the overlying Paleo-Indian bison level via an intersecting stream channel. Some crudely flaked stones found with the mammoth bones have been dismissed as "geofacts" (rocks appearing to have tool-like qualities but actually produced through natural geological processes). Numerous flaked bones and bone flakes were also found, and it is of interest that the more fragile bones in the deposit were complete, while the structurally stronger long bones (legs) were usually highly fragmented.

Among the Dutton, Selby, and Lamb Spring sites, the evidence for humans in pre-Clovis times is greatest at Lamb Spring. But until confirming data can be found, including *undisputed* man-made artifacts with the bones, human presence before 11,500 years ago will have to remain an open question.

Figure 5-3   The Lamb Spring site with mammoth bones exposed at the bottom of the excavation unit. (Jim Grady).

Figure 5-4   1973 oblique aerial photo of the Dent site (arrow), located above an old channel of the South Platte River. Note Union Pacific railroad tracks. View is to the west (Frank Frazier.)

Clovis

Dent: The Original Find

There is no argument about the validity of the Clovis Complex, a lifeway that began over 11,000 years ago and lasted throughout much of North America for hundreds of years. At present, the Clovis evidence is the earliest universally accepted for people in the New World. Clovis is considered to be the oldest of three Paleo-Indian divisions and is also known as the Llano Complex, named for its appearance on the Llano Estacado (Staked Plains of Texas). Clovis remains are rare, but limited numbers have been found in many parts of North America.

Based on evidence from these sites, some generalizations about the Clovis lifeway can be made. The majority of the sites are kills. Animals actively sought by the hunters include mammoth, bison, horse, camel, and some lesser species. Kills are usually found along tributaries of major streams in areas of ponded or slow-moving water. It is assumed that the large animals were dispatched with spears while bogged down in mud. In the case of mammoths and bison, analysis of skeletal remains indicates that females and young were most often killed. The tool kit of Clovis hunters included large fluted Clovis points, scrapers, blades, hammerstones, flake knives, choppers, and bone tools, including bone points.

Early in 1932, none of this was known. But that spring, flooding along the South Platte River eroded soils and gravels out of a bank near the Dent railroad depot, revealing several large animal bones. These were observed by a Union Pacific Railroad Section Foreman, Frank Garner, who reported the discovery to the Dent Depot Master, Michael Ryan, Sr.; Ryan's son, Michael, Jr., told his professor at Regis College in Denver, Father Conrad Bilgery. That fall Bilgery and his students undertook the initial excavations of the site. The bones turned out to be mammoth.

On 5 November the excavations exposed a long fluted point among the mammoth remains, putting Colorado on the map for the first site in the New World with firm evidence for the association of man and mammoth. Because of the site's importance, Bilgery was joined by J. D. Figgins, now regarded as an early man expert because of his highly acclaimed discoveries at Folsom, New Mexico. A second fluted projectile point was found on 7 July. Apparently a third projectile point had been picked up in 1932 by Mr. Garner near a mammoth tooth but was unreported until 1955. Bilgery's projectile point was not stored at the museum and has since been lost, although the cast remains.

Figure 5-5   1933 photo of Dent excavation at the time point B was discovered. Father Bilgery is at lower left (white shirt and vest). Fredrick Howarter, the field director, is lower right. Figgins is not pictured. (Denver Museum of Natural History.)

Deeply mired in a small waterhole on Colorado's plains and pierced by numerous spears tipped with fluted points, a Columbian mammoth is about to succumb to a band of tenacious Clovis hunters.

Figgins was impressed by the site and soon published the results of his investigations. He noted that there was a minimum of 12 individual mammoths present, mostly females and young (Bilgery said 14). Figgins also stated that in addition to the projectile points, there was a high percentage of "bowlders . . . occasionally as large as 20 inches in circumference." He observed that the "bowlders" did not commonly occur in the vicinity, implying that they were carried in by the hunters to assist in the kill.

Bilgery was apparently not as convinced of the man-mammoth association, having suspected that the entire deposit of bones and artifacts had been washed in, perhaps even at different times. In correspondence with Figgins a few years later, he stated:

> Once more I wish to draw your attention to my conviction that the flint-blades of Dent were simply washed in with the bones of the mammoth and, hence, they need not be of the same type. They may be artifacts of different tribes. The fourteen mammoths surely were not killed by man.

ROBERT NOEL
FARRINGTON

A subsequent re-investigation of the Dent site by Frank Frazier and Linda Spikard confirmed Bilgery's observation that the bones and projectile points were actually redeposited. Frazier does not think that the bones moved very far in the washing or slumping action, since they do not show the kind of polishing, rounding, or sorting that would be expected in long distance stream transport. However, any bone or artifact assemblage that has been geologically redeposited *at all* is difficult, if not impossible, to interpret culturally. Its original context has been lost.

I was able to interview Frank Frazier in 1982. He provided the following details on the redeposited nature of the Dent site and explained the presence of the "bowlders" Figgins saw as potential weapons used by the hunters.

There are several old terraces along the South Platte River, now standing well above the present river bed. One of the more significant terraces, from the standpoint of early man studies, is the Kersey Terrace. Several good Paleo-Indian sites have been found in this river deposit along the South Platte. Much of the Kersey Terrace is of a sandy composition, and it is in this stratum that the Dent bones were found. Above the Kersey terrace and farther back from the river is the Louviers Terrace, an older alluvial deposit. In it are coarse gravels that are distinguishable from the Kersey material. One good indicator of Louviers gravels is that, at least in the Dent area, ground water has built up calcium carbonates on the *bottoms* of the cobbles. Such deposits are not found in the Kersey level. Yet the gravels found with the Dent mammoth bones had the carbonate coating—but not on the "bottom" of the stones. The coated surfaces were oriented randomly in all directions. This supports Frazier's conclusions, suggesting that some sort of slumping or washing had moved the upslope Louviers gravels (as well as any mammoth bones lying on or near the surface of the Louviers Terrace) down onto the Kersey level. From a practical standpoint, this could have been a distance of 50 feet or less.

Frazier indicated that the Louviers gravels are commonly up to 20 inches in circumference, the size indicated by Figgins for his "bowlders." This is only about six inches in diameter. Figgins had been correct in stating that these large cobbles were not a normal part of the Kersey deposit, but they do occur in abundance in the adjacent Louviers Terrace, and their presence does not have to be explained by human transport.

A sample from some of the Dent bone was radiocarbon dated by George Agogino at 11,200 ± 500 B.P., an excellent Clovis date anywhere in the United States. Based on the date, these mammoths were contemporaries of man. However, it is doubtful that man was directly responsible for their demise, although there is some evidence for the mammoths having come into contact with one or more hunting parties during their lifetime. The lack of butchering scars on the bones would suggest that the animals were not cut up following their deaths.

Another indication that Dent is not a kill site is that it lacks the sort of typical features found elsewhere that explain mass bone accumulations through hunting. Normally one would not expect many mammoths to be killed at any given time, as the difficulties in bringing down such a large animal with spears would probably allow all but a few to escape the hunters. Those mammoth kills where *many* animals have been found are usually at isolated springs or ponds that would have attracted game over many seasons, allowing a slow accumulation of bones. Dent, on the other hand, is directly on the South Platte River, a major and permanent drainage in northern Colorado. Unless the Dent area was a favored crossing of the river, a plausible idea but one for which we have no evidence, there is no apparent reason why the immediate Dent locale would attract animals for successive kills. Yet 12 to 14 mammoths were found together here.

The three fluted projectile points still remain to be explained. The presence of this type of spear point with numerous bones elsewhere is testimony to its lethal capabilities. An alternate explanation for the Dent artifacts is that one or more of the Dent mammoths had been speared by hunters and then escaped, the stone projectile points still lodged inside. At a later date, the herd died of some unknown catastrophic cause while still carrying the Clovis points. Such a senario is not without precedent. A fully articulated (and thus unbutchered) mammoth was found at the Escapule site in southern Arizona. With it were two Clovis points. The animal was near three major mammoth kills (Naco, Lehner, Murray Springs) and has been interpreted as "one that got away."

What really transpired at Dent over 11,000 years ago will probably never be known with certainty. There is no doubt that mammoth hunters were on the Central Plains at that time, but their connection to the Dent site is at best inconclusive.

Perhaps because Figgins regarded the fluted points from Dent as Folsom variants, no new name was applied to the point style in 1933. The term Clovis point was later given to the type specimens found by John Cotter during the 1936 and 1937 field seasons at Blackwater Draw near Clovis, New Mexico. Had Figgins taken the opportunity to name the type, we might today be talking about Dent culture rather than Clovis.

Dutton

Other mammoths have been found in Colorado, and at least two of them are probably legitimate Clovis-age finds. A level at the Dutton site overlying the pre-Clovis bone bed contained a complete Clovis point, several scrapers, flakes, and the skeletal fragments of mammoth and horse. Stanford has interpreted this level as a Clovis camp. A date of 11,710 ± 150 B.P. from *below* the Clovis zone would allow for the camp's placement at a slightly younger age, comfortably within the documented Clovis range of variation in the U. S.

Claypool

There is a good possibility that a Clovis site was found in the sand dunes of the eastern Colorado plains, although as at Dent, there are interpretive problems. Known as the Claypool site, it is most familiar as a Plano (late Paleo-Indian) camp, but it also contained mammoth bones and two Clovis points. Because the site had been deflated (removal by wind of sand and dust, allowing artifacts from different levels to mix), the actual relationship of the Clovis points and the mammoth bone could not be determined. The initial geological interpretation of the site's geology by Hal Malde was that the mammoth bones were in a 200,000 year-old formation, far too old to have a human association. A re-investigation by Dennis Stanford and John Albanese has since cast some doubt on the original findings. They have concluded that the stratum containing the bone was part of a localized inter-dunal pond deposit of Late Pleistocene age and that the man-mammoth relationship is probable. Unfortunately, no *in situ* Clovis-age materials remain, and verification is not possible.

The San Luis Valley Mammoths

In the 1940s, C. T. Hurst (founder of the Colorado Archaeological Society) mentioned that mammoth bones were present at at least nine locations in the San Luis Valley, as well as at one locality in the Gunnison Valley to the northwest. He did not have substantial evidence to support a human association with any of the remains.

Since that time tantalizing data (unpublished) has emerged from the valley, but it lacks qualities that would unequivocally prove that humans hunted mammoths there. In 1972 Joe Ben Wheat of the University of Colorado Museum excavated a fossil waterhole named the Magna site along the northern edge of the San Luis Valley. Out of the buried depression came numerous mammoth bones, teeth, and ivory, some of which had cut marks perhaps due to butchering. No stone tools were found with the bones. Upper levels contained ground stone artifacts and flakes that were probably Archaic-age or younger. About 100 feet away, on an old erosional surface, Wheat collected two artifacts of interest. One was a highly patinated biface with a single shoulder, somewhat resembling a Sandia point. (In New Mexico this point type was reported to be underlying a Folsom level in Sandia Cave, although some questions about the validity of this type have since arisen.) Wheat also found a thick biface made on a side-struck flake, a manufacturing technique closely comparable to Upper Paleolithic traditions in Japan, the Asian continent, and the Solutrean of western Europe. The weak association between these surface artifacts and the mammoth bone provides little support for an interpretation of Magna as a Paleo-Indian site.

Summary

Taken as a whole, the evidence for early mammoth hunters in Colorado is scarce. Dent, probably not a kill, may reveal that hunters had come into contact with mammoths, although they presumably did not successfully down any of them. Dutton and Claypool provide only hints of Clovis hunting and camping. What relation man had to the mammoths at the lower level at Dutton, Selby, Lamb Spring, and Magna is not known at this time.

Folsom

Overlapping and following the Clovis Complex, during a time when the populations of mammoths, horses, camels and other Pleistocene megafauna (big game) were declining, is the Folsom Complex. The first discovery at Folsom, New Mexico, previously discussed, was responsible for stimulating the quest for early man in the New World. But New Mexico does not have a monopoly on the scattered remnants of Folsom culture. Colorado has eight documented Folsom sites and perhaps hundreds of isolated surface finds.

Lindenmeier

The Lindenmeier site in the foothills northeast of Fort Collins is one of the most famous in the country. It was discovered in 1924 (two years *before* the Folsom, N.M., finds) by three artifact collectors: Judge Claude C. Coffin, his son Lynn, and C. K. Collins. Major Roy G. Coffin, the judge's brother and a geology professor at Colorado State College, was later involved in collecting and digging at the site. After the initial discovery in New Mexico had demonstrated the significance of the distinctive Folsom points, and Denver University professor Etienne B. Renaud had published descriptions of Lindenmeier surface collections, Major Coffin was concientious enough to contact the U. S. Geological Survey and the Smithsonian Institution. Regardless of the damage done by collecting and excavation by the relic hunters—the Coffins continued to dig adjacent to the Roberts units until 1938—the fact that they did encourage professional investigations is to be commended. The site was opened by Frank H. H. Roberts of the Smithsonian in 1934 and was backfilled for the last time following the 1940 field season.

One aspect of Lindenmeier's significance is that it was a camp, rather than a single kill site. Data related to a wide range of domestic activities, tool production, and social organization were recovered.

Artifacts found included a variety of scrapers, knives, engraved bone (including possible gaming pieces), bone needles, and the fluted Folsom

Figure 5-6   Looking north down Trench A at the Lindenmeier site in 1935. (University of Colorado Museum.)

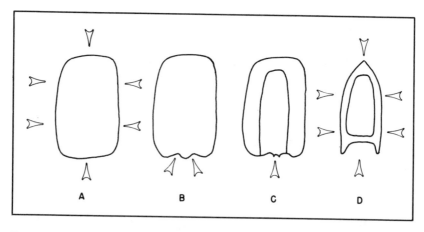

Figure 5-7   Folsom manufacturing stages, with small arrows denoting the areas flaked. A—flaking of preform; B—isolating the nipple; C—indirect percussion on nipple removes flute; D—final edge shaping.

points. Remains of wild game brought back to the camp by hunters included pronghorn, rabbit, fox, wolf, coyote, turtle, and bison.

Since the fluting of projectile points is a difficult and delicate process, one would expect a number of specimens broken during the knapping to have been left in the manufacturing area. Partly finished and ruined points were indeed found at Lindenmeier. Based on inferences from point fragments broken during production at Lindenmeier, the following sequence of manufacturing stages has been postulated.

In Stage A the preform is made with blunted ends by both percussion and pressure flaking. At the end of this stage, the biface has been thinned considerably.

Stage B entails the isolating of a "nipple" on the basal edge through the removal of flakes around it on both faces with pressure flaking. This action also begins to produce a concave edge.

In Stage C a channel flake is removed from one face, probably with indirect percussion. To accomplish this, the tip of an antler tine could be placed on one side of the nipple and then struck on its other end with a hammerstone or antler baton, sending a shock through the tine and onto the nipple. Properly positioned, this blow would result in the removal of a thin channel flake up one blade face to create the flute.

Stages B and C would then be repeated, setting up a new nipple and driving off a channel flake from the reverse face.

The projectile point's shape is refined in Stage D. A tip is formed, the blade is narrowed, and the base is indented more deeply. Stage D is probably accomplished entirely with pressure flaking. In order to reduce chances of the sinew binding being cut when the point is seated in the shaft, the lateral edges near the base would then be ground smooth with a piece of sandstone, known as an abrader. Most Paleo-Indian points have this basal grinding.

Edwin Wilmsen, in studying the lithics of Lindenmeier, used some of the data to infer the shadowy outlines of social organization at the camp. Typically, evidence of this nature is beyond the reach of normal archaeological approaches. Through an examination of flaking attributes on the Folsom points, he was able to distinguish several non-functional traits that clustered in two separate locations in the site. These characteristics were all produced as finishing steps in point manufacture. They include point shape (outline), parallel or expanding flakes, perpendicular or oblique flaking, and degree of fluting or only basal thinning. On the basis of statistically significant differences in the two areas, and with support from the ethnographic record of hunter-gatherer groups, Wilmsen saw Lindenmeier as the scene of periodic gatherings of:

> geographically-distinct but interacting groups, each identified with one of the stylistic sets of projectile points, (where they) participated in common social and procurement systems but were sufficiently indepen-dent to maintain some degree of stylistic distinction.

In 1959 Vance Haynes and George Agogino collected a C14 sample that yielded a date of 10,780 ± 375 B.P., well within the range of Folsom dates from elsewhere on the plains. Wilmsen submitted some charcoal collected from a lens in 1939 and sealed in glass at the Smithsonian ever since. It provided an earlier date of 11,200 ± 400 B.P., overlapping the older Clovis culture.

Fowler-Parrish, Powars, and Johnson

Northeastern Colorado contains several other Folsom localities including the Fowler-Parrish site in the South Platte drainage near Orchard. Seven-teen whole or fragmentary Folsom points were recovered from the site, and at least two separate bison bone beds were identified in place. However, extensive deflation of the sand and previous heavy surface collection ham-pered the interpretation of the probable kill site.

Upstream near Greeley is the Powars site, dug in the 1930s by an amateur (Powars) and reported by Frank H. H. Roberts, Jr. Like Fowler-Parrish, it was located in a sand dune but differed in that it was a camp rather than a kill. Over 2,000 artifacts were taken out of the site.

The Johnson site, located on the Cache la Poudre River near La Porte, yielded a small assemblage of Folsom artifacts similar to those at Linden-meier.

Linger

The San Luis Valley, geologically unique in the state, also has the distinction of containing an unusually high number of Folsom sites.

In 1941 C. T. Hurst excavated at the Linger site, exposing the remains of five *Bison antiquus* and 22 Folsom artifacts in a sand dune. Both the *Denver Post* and the *Rocky Mountain News* carried stories on the discovery, and numerous arrowhead hunters descended on the Valley with hopes of adding to their collections. As a result, considerable damage was done to the archaeological resources over much of the area.

In 1974 Dennis Stanford re-investigated Linger and identified what he thinks are three functionally different areas within the site. Tight concen-

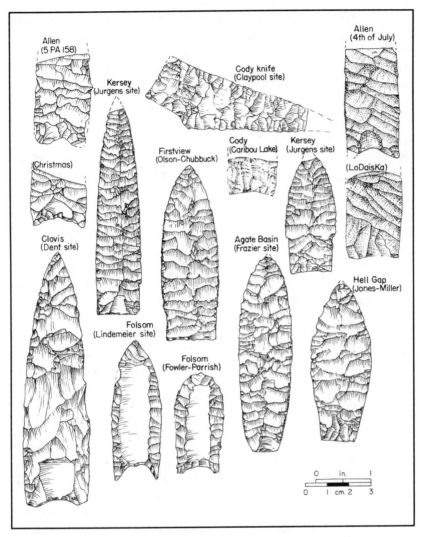

Figure 5-8   A sample of Paleo-Indian artifacts from Colorado.

trations of bison bone were found scattered across the large blowout, and Stanford has postulated that these are the remains of animals killed either while handicapped by the dune sand or while watering at an inter-dunal pond. Lighter and wider areas with bone fragments were interpreted as butchering areas. A third type of activity area had numerous flakes and some burned bones. Meat may have been guarded at these localities while awaiting transport to camp, or the areas may have been camps. Two bone dates from Linger are 9,885 ± 140 B.P. and 8,480 ± 85 B.P., slightly younger than anticipated, but since bone dates usually are younger than comparably-aged wood samples, they are certainly not much out of line.

Zapata

The Zapata site near Linger was probed by non-professionals in early years but has recently been excavated by Stanford. The results were not as great as at other sites in the area, but Folsom points were recovered.

During the 1960s Jerry Dawson found a partial human skullcap on the surface of a deflated sand dune at Zapata, and it is quite possible that this bone is of Folsom age. Until something like a flourine test can be run (to determine if the human bone is contemporaneous with the fossil bison at the site), its actual significance will have to remain unknown. The site was incorrectly identified by Dawson at the time, leading to the name "Linger Skull" in the literature.

Cattle Guard

A third dune field locality in the San Luis Valley is the Cattle Guard site, excavated in 1981 by Sloan Emery and Dennis Stanford. It has been interpreted as a short-term hunting camp. A variety of artifacts were found, including Folsom points, channel flakes, gravers, flake knives, and abraders. Raw stone materials for the tools came from as far away as New Mexico and Texas. Partial bison remains in the camp appear to have been carried in from distant kills.

Reddin

To the north of this concentration of Folsom sites is the Reddin site, discovered by Gordon and Paul Reddin and subsequently examined by Dennis Stanford. It has yet to be excavated, but the surface materials suggest an interesting combination of activity areas. Point tips and broken points near some ponds are probably evidence for kills, while flakes found on a nearby ridge may indicate camping activity. Future work by the Smithsonian is planned for the site.

Summary

Colorado contains far more evidence of the Folsom culture than of those peoples preceeding it. This may be indicative of an increasing population. The technique of fluting projectile points, apparently invented in Clovis times, was perpetuated by Folsom peoples. Some of the big game previously hunted (e.g. mammoths) was now gone, but these foragers adjusted and managed to sustain themselves on the available resources. And then, after surviving for perhaps 1,000 years, Folsom lithic technology seems to have been replaced by innovations in projectile point hafting that did not require fluting.

Plano

As evidence of Folsom peoples fades out about 10,000 years ago, new stone attributes begin to appear. Fluting is discontinued, and long, finely flaked lanceolate blades compose the bulk of the projectile points. Many of these sites on the plains are either bison kills or are associated with them. The Plano continued until about 7,000 years ago when it gave way to the Archaic Stage. Colorado is rich in extremely well-documented Plano sites, a credit to those investigators willing to invest the necessary time to meticulously excavate, map the finds, analyze the data, and publish the results.

The Hell Gap Complex: Jones-Miller

During the summer of 1972, Wray-area rancher Robert Jones, Jr., bladed off a ridge near his home, exposing some bones in the process. Following a good rain that afternoon, Jones noticed what looked like spearpoints, freshly washed and gleaming, among the bones. Realizing that the remains were of something other than cattle, he called a local anthropologist, Jack Miller, who conducted test excavations on the site. It was quickly obvious that this bone bed was an important Paleo-Indian site, and Miller was soon in contact with Dennis Stanford at the Smithsonian. This led to a full-scale excavation, between 1973 and 1978, of what came to be called the Jones-Miller site.

The bones of about 300 bison were found in a shallow draw above the Arikaree River floodplain. Analysis of the tooth eruption patterns indi-

Figure 5-9   Crew member recording part of the bison bone bed at the Jones-Miller site. (S. Cassells photo.)

cated that the animals had been killed during three episodes of one or more winters. The spearheads lying within the dense bed of bones were Hell Gap points, named for the style originally found at Hell Gap, Wyoming. Hell Gap points can be distinguished by a convex blade and a long stem that is well ground on the edges and contracts toward the base. The projectile point from Jones-Miller in Figure 5-8 had been broken and was resharpened to its present form. Some unmodified Hell Gap points are known to be at least twice as long as this specimen. Dates for Hell Gap sites range from 9,600 to 10,060 B.P. Jones-Miller has been dated from carbon at 10,020 ± 320 B.P. and is the only documented Hell Gap site in Colorado.

One of the more interesting discoveries at Jones-Miller was a single post mold 22 centimeters in diameter and 46 centimeters deep. Close to it were three finds unusual for a kill or butchering site: a miniature Hell Gap point, less than an inch in length; a bone flute; and the butchered remains of a dog. Putting together the evidence of the post mold and the possible ceremonial remnants, Stanford has suggested that the actual kill may have resembled the bison-hunting practices of the historic Assiniboine and Cree. Ethnographic documentation of these groups indicated that they often placed a medicine pole in the middle of an area intented to impound bison for slaughter. Offerings were attached to the pole. The pound area, lower than the surrounding terrain, had an entry ramp slickened with water and manure-soaked snow in order to hasten the bison's entrance into the depression and assure their entrapment. The basin itself would be deep with snow. The medicine man might be mounted on the post to aid in the magic of the event. Once driven into the snow-filled pound, the struggling bison would be killed by spears hurled from the sides.

Such a reconstruction is reasonable in light of the lack of other topographic features that could have assisted in the mass bison killings. Stanford's work at Jones-Miller supports the hypothesis of a cultural continuum that extends 10,000 years from the Paleo-Indians to the ethnographic present of the Assiniboine and Cree.

Some negative evidence at Jones-Miller may be indicative of another ceremonial activity. There were very few skulls at the kill, even of a fragmentary nature. It is possible that they were used in something similar to the Sun Dance, a significant ritual of many Plains Indian groups, even today.

The Agate Basin Complex: Frazier

Another of the older Plano sites in Colorado is the Frazier site. It was discovered in 1965 along the South Platte River by Frank Frazier. At that time, both bison bones and distinctive Agate Basin projectile points were eroding out of the Kersey Terrace. At present, Frazier is the only documented Agate Basin site in Colorado.

Agate Basin points, named for the type station in Wyoming, have a straight or slightly bi-convex outline that gently expands toward the center from both ends. No shoulder is present, but the lower lateral edges can be heavily ground. As with Hell Gap points, the Agate Basin points can be quite long and were thus often broken and reworked (while still hafted) into shorter but equally functional spearheads. The Frazier site specimen in Fig. 5-8 was resharpened after being snapped.

Frazier reported the site to Marie Wormington, and in 1965 she undertook a limited test, discovering an Agate Basin point *in situ*, along with chipping debris and bison bone. This led to a major excavation for the next two field seasons.

Wormington recovered the partial remains of at least 43 bison, and the lack of certain skeletal elements suggested to her that this was not the actual kill site but rather the butchering and processing area. The large number of bones probably indicates that the kill was not very far away, however. In place with the bones were five complete and five fragmentary Agate Basin points.

Dates elsewhere for Agate Basin sites range from 10,850 ± 500 B.P. to 9,350 ± 450 B.P. The Frazier site was dated 9,550 ± 130 B.P. and 9,000 ± 130 B.P., with the datable material being a humic acid derived from a gray organic soil horizon immediately *overlying* the gray sandy clay that contained the cultural remains. Thus, the date of Frazier should be considered only a *minimum* age.

The Cody Complex: Olsen-Chubbuck, Jurgens, and Others

Stirred by the finds at Folsom, New Mexico, in 1926-27, arrowhead collectors in northeastern Colorado soon began scouring their local rangeland for comparable artifacts. With the onset of the Dust Bowl drought, vegetation became increasingly sparse, accelerating the deflation of the sandhills and creating or expanding many blowouts for the relic hunters to search. Yuma County seems to have been a center for this collection activity.

In the early 1930s, E. B. Renaud was allowed to study some of the collections, and he published a typology of early unfluted, unnotched, parallel-flaked projectile points, naming them "Yuma points." In 1941 Paul Gebhard conducted his Ph.D. research on Yuma County blowouts, further refining the provenience of Paleo-Indian artifacts in eastern Colorado. Through time, the "Yuma" terminology became entrenched, but because the type included so many point styles, it was meaningless.

This led Marie Wormington and Betty Holmes to undertake a reclassification program in order to sort out the variety of projectile points lumped under the "Yuma" umbrella. As a result of their work, and following a 1941 conference in Santa Fe, the terms Eden Yuma and Scottsbluff Yuma emerged as two of the types. Eden was named for a kind found at the Finley site near Eden, Wyoming, and Scottsbluff for projectile points excavated near Scottsbluff, Nebraska. This was the beginning of the clarification of later Plano cultures, but terms such as Folsom-Yuma were still in use in the late 1940s. In 1948 Wormington published a call for the total elimination of the term "Yuma" from archaeological use. Her suggestion has been largely honored ever since, but in 1960 E. B. Renaud wrote a final paper defending his early typology and decrying what he saw as the confusing new names for the projectile points.

The term Cody Complex came into use following the 1950 excavations of the Horner site near Cody, Wyoming. This was the first site discovered with Eden points, Scottsbluff points, and Cody knives (the latter a distinctive hafted knive with an angled stem). Since then sites with *any* of these three tool types are generally considered to be in the Cody Complex.

As a group the Cody Complex appears to be younger than Hell Gap and Agate Basin sites, with dates clustering between 9,000 and 7,000 years ago. Numerous examples exist on the plains and elsewhere. Out of at least 14 documented Plano sites in Colorado, eight appear to be the Cody Complex. These include the plains sites at Jurgens, Frasca, Nelson, Claypool, Wetzel, Lamb Spring, and Olsen-Chubbuck. The high altitude site at Caribou Lake also seems to be Cody. Just over the border, on the Utah side of Dinosaur National Monument is Deluge Shelter with a probable Cody level.

On the plains, Cody Complex remains have been found as camps, kills, and butchering/processing sites.

The Claypool site is a camp situated in a sand dune. Deflation has apparently disturbed the cultural deposits to a great degree. Fragmentary bison remains suggest a distant kill, and a variety of domestic artifacts, such as scrapers, drills, and Cody knives, support the conclusion that Claypool is a camp.

The Cody level at Lamb Spring is a kill site, with the bones and Cody Complex projectile points embedded in a boggy channel. Two bone

Figure 5-10   An *in situ* projectile point in association with bison bone at the Olsen-Chubbuck site. (University of Colorado Museum.)

samples were dated at 8,870 ± 350 B.P. and 7,870 ± 240 ± B.P. The investigators (Rancier, Haynes, and Stanford) suspect that the younger sample has been contaminated and have rejected the date.

Another interesting kill on the Colorado plains is Olsen-Chubbuck. It was excavated from 1958 to 1960 by Joe Ben Wheat (C.U. Museum). The results of the investigation were spectacular, and the site has gained national recognition.

Wheat found about 200 bison that had been driven into a narrow arroyo, immobilized by the drop and the press of the herd, and the survivors then dispatched with Plano projectile points. Wheat did a masterful job of reconstructing the kill scene, analyzing the butchering techniques and estimating the quantity of butchered meat and the numbers of people it would have sustained. He set a standard of analytical excellence that has stood ever since, providing a pattern to be used in many subsequent Paleo-Indian studies.

Wheat has termed the culture at Olsen-Chubbuck the Firstview Complex, separating it from Cody. Others have questioned the distinctions, but Wheat has countered with an old date of 10,150 ± 500 B.P. as evidence

Figure 5-11   The Area 3 bone bed at the Jurgens site. (University of Colorado Museum.)

beyond projectile point differences. Agreement by all will have to wait until other research clarifies the data.

The Frasca site, excavated by Tommy Fulgham and Dennis Stanford, and the Jurgens site, excavated by Joe Ben Wheat and Marie Wormington, are two excellent examples of Plano butchering/processing locales. A butchering station is usually separate from the actual kill site and is a place to which portions of the carcasses were moved prior to final disarticulation and meat removal. The discarded bones were then often piled around the butchering center.

The investigators at Jurgens had the added good fortune of uncovering both a short-term and a long-term camp of the same age as the main bone bed. Area 1 at Jurgens, the long-term camp, contained elements of at least 31 bison, along with some bone from deer, moose, pronghorn, elk, rabbit, beaver, muskrat, canid (dog family), reptiles, and fish. Stone and bone tools used in butchering, preparing hides, making tools, and grinding seeds and other plant resources were all found in this long-term camp.

The short-term camp, Area 2, had remnants of two bison, five pronghorns, and a smaller but similar inventory of the tool types found at Area 1.

Area 3 held a large number of bones from a minimum of 35 bison. Based on the presence of some skull fragments and articulated legs, the actual kill site was considered to be somewhere near this butchering/processing station.

In addition to the unusual occurence of grinding slabs in all three areas, other interesting and unexpected artifacts at Jurgens included a nicotine-coated pipe and two atlatl hooks. One hook was made of antler and one from a modified bison tooth. Each would have been tied to the end of a stick and inserted into the basal end of a spear shaft, propelling the shaft forward as the atlatl was "flicked" forward by the hunter's wrist and arm.

The projectile points from Jurgens resemble Eden and Scottsbluff points at Frasca and other Cody Complex sites. However, Wheat saw enough differences in their manufacture to cause him to name a new culture, the Kersey Complex. As with Olsen-Chubbuck and the Firstview Complex, not everyone agrees with this new classification, and unanimity of opinion will have to await further research.

Regardless of the ultimate typological classification of the site, Jurgens is certainly an outstanding example of Plano culture. Linked with the kill site at Olsen-Chubbuck, it provides a wide view of the Plano hunter's life — from the kill, to the butchering/processing site, to the short-term camp, and finally the long-term camp.

Dennis Stanford has examined two recently discovered Cody Complex sites, Nelson and Wetzel. Nelson, ten miles upstream from Frasca, appears to retain *in situ* material and should provide interesting comparisons to the Frasca data. At present, access to the site is denied. A bone sample dates at 7,995 ± 80 B.P.. Wetzel, along the Kansas border, was almost completely destroyed by the time Stanford observed it. However, he did recover some Cody Complex artifacts and bison bone. A date of 7,160 ± 135 B.P. was obtained from bone. Wetzel's greatest value is in documenting the easternmost presence of the Cody Complex in Colorado.

James Benedict has found evidence of a Cody Complex occupation at the Caribou Lake site, a camp over 11,000 feet above sea level. Charcoal from the Paleo-Indian level was dated at 8,460 ± 140 B.P. and was associated with a projectile point fragment having a concave basal edge and lateral edge grinding. This point appears to have snapped at the shoulder. Also in the Caribou Lake assemblage were a number of waste flakes and a large bifacial knife.

Caribou Lake is located near Arapaho Pass and could represent a stopping point for hunters moving between the plains and the intermountain valleys. Use of the camp would have been confined primarily to summers and fall during years of normal weather patterns. From an archaeological standpoint, the greatest value of the Caribou Lake site is the *in situ* documentation of Paleo-Indian seasonal use of highly divergent ecosystems within Colorado.

Far to the west, on the Utah side of Dinosaur National Monument, Larry Leach excavated the deeply stratified Deluge Shelter. Found beneath the Archaic and Fremont levels was what appears to be a Scottsbluff point fragment, unassociated with younger artifacts. There is no date to accompany the find, and it is possible it was brought in by later peoples, but because no younger tools were in the zone, there is at least an equal chance it is a legitimate Plano component, forming the baseline of a long cultural continuum at the site.

Western Slope Plano Sites

Bill Buckles, during extensive surveying and excavating of sites on the Uncompahgre Plateau near Montrose (see Chapter 6), uncovered a deep horizon at the Christmas rock shelter. There he found the base of a Paleo-Indian point. As at Deluge, no date has been obtained, but since the level contained no evidence of younger peoples, there is a great likelihood it is of true Paleo-Indian age.

In examining the Paleo-Indian sites plotted in Figure 5-2, one gains the impression that the earliest hunters and gatherers of Colorado were primarily distributed across the plains, with only limited movement across the Continental Divide. The Western Slope plateaus and basins appear nearly devoid of their presence. This may be misleading.

Several Folsom and Plano points have been collected as surface finds near Montrose, on the Uncompahgre Plateau, in Dinosaur National Monument, and in Tabeguache Canyon, adding some credibility to the *in situ* evidence from the Deluge and Christmas rockshelters.

Western Slope ecosystems vary significantly from those on the plains, but there is no reason to suspect that Paleo-Indians were not actively engaged in foraging there anyway. Considering the low density of Paleo-Indian sites everywhere and the differing erosional processes that could have influenced the visibility of early sites, it is reasonable to expect a scarcity of Western Slope evidence. Given intensive surveys and excavations in the future, the problem of a lack of good Paleo-Indian sites on the Western Slope should be remedied.

Late Plano

Near the end of Paleo-Indian times, a flintknapping technique that produced transverse-oblique flake scars seems to have come into vogue. The flake scars are usually oriented from upper left to lower right across the projectile point face, giving the appearance that a single flake was removed across the entire width of the point. In reality, a flake was struck from both sides, but their junction at the center is often hard to see. It was obviously a masterful skill, and perhaps its degree of difficulty was in part responsible for the fact that it was not carried on to any extent in the Archaic. In Wyoming this flaking style is observable on concave-based lanceolate projectile points known as Jimmy Allen and Frederick points, whose dates range from 7,800 to 8,600 years ago.

Three sites in Colorado contain this style of projectile point: LoDaisKa, 5 PA 158, and the Fourth of July Valley.

The LoDaisKa site, in the hogback valley just west of Denver, had a single transverse-oblique flaked projectile point at a low level, apparently unassociated with post-Paleo-Indian occupations. The investigators, Henry and Cynthia Irwin, suspected it was true evidence of Lithic-age occupation at the rockshelter.

At 5 PA 158, a site at 12,010 feet above sea level, a buried level contained a number of undated transverse-oblique flaked projectile points that, though somewhat crude, appear to be Paleo-Indian age.

The greatest enigma concerning this point style in Colorado comes from

Benedict's high altitude Fourth of July Valley site. He recovered a number of projectile points there, including some that resemble the Middle Archaic-age McKean Lanceolate and Duncan point styles (ca. 4,000 B.P.). Also in the site was what appears to be a classic Jimmy Allen point, a type dated elsewhere at 7,900 B.P. Difficulties in interpreting Fourth of July come from a carbon date of 5,960 ± 85 B.P., midway between the expected age ranges for the McKean and the late Plano point styles. One might argue for a multicomponent site, with late Plano (based on the Jimmy Allen point), Early Archaic (based solely on the C14 date), and Middle Archaic (based on the Duncan and McKean Lanceolate points). Benedict has countered such an interpretation with his observation that *all* of the projectile points are made of the same raw material, a quartzite probably derived from the Spanish Diggings, a well-known quarry near the Black Hills in Wyoming. Benedict suggests that the site is a single component and that the date is accurate. He explains the presence of divergent point styles in a single component as indicating a transition between Paleo-Indian and Middle Archaic complexes. This development took place in the high altitude refuge during a major drought on the plains (see Chapter 6 for discussion of this drought).

The Fourth of July Valley site cannot now be placed in the scheme of Colorado prehistory with any degree of certainty, but data from future investigations should help clarify its position.

The Gordon Creek Burial

A very unusual Plano site in northern Colorado has gained national attention. Known as the Gordon Creek burial, it was found northwest of Fort Collins, less than 25 miles from Lindenmeier, in 1963 by U. S. Forest Service personnel during watershed improvement activities and was then reported to the University of Colorado. A salvage excavation was undertaken immediately, revealing a human burial partially slumped out of the gully wall of a Gordon Creek tributary. The individual, determined to be a female, stood approximately 4 feet 11 inches and was about 26 to 30 years of age.

No good diagnostic artifacts that might identify a particular cultural affiliation were found with the body, but the assemblage was interesting. A large and a small biface, both unused, were interpreted as having been made specifically as grave offerings. Another biface, resembling a small projectile point, was shown by the analysis of wear (polish) on its edges to have been used as a knife. Other grave goods included a hammerstone, a smoothed stone, an end scraper, utilized flakes, cut or incised animal bone, and elk

Figure 5-12 Arroyo where the Gordon Creek burial was discovered. The dashed line indicates the location of the find. (University of Colorado Museum.)

incisors that had been perforated and broken. These elk teeth were possibly part of a dress decoration and may have been torn off at the time of the burial as part of the mourning process. Red ocher covered the flexed body, and a fire had been started in or near the grave, damaging some of the artifacts. Red ocher is a typical ceremonial inclusion on many Archaic burials in the Eastern Woodlands, but this is one of the first occurrences so far west.

A pelvic bone was submitted for C14 dating, and it provided an age of 9,700 ± 250 B.P. If this date is accurate, the Gordon Creek burial is undoubtedly Paleo-Indian, one of only a few known in the New World.

It has been argued that since the burial contained no diagnostic Paleo-Indian projectile points, it is probably more recent. But such artifacts would not necessarily be expected with the burial of a female. Non-weapons, such as the items included with the Gordon Creek body, would be more likely. Unfortunately, they are also culturally undiagnostic. Taken with the C14 date, however, the artifacts and red ocher augment our growing knowledge of Paleo-Indian material culture and ceremonial practices. It is unfortunate that two additional artifacts were apparently stolen by a workman/relic collector, as these may have revealed a good deal more about this period.

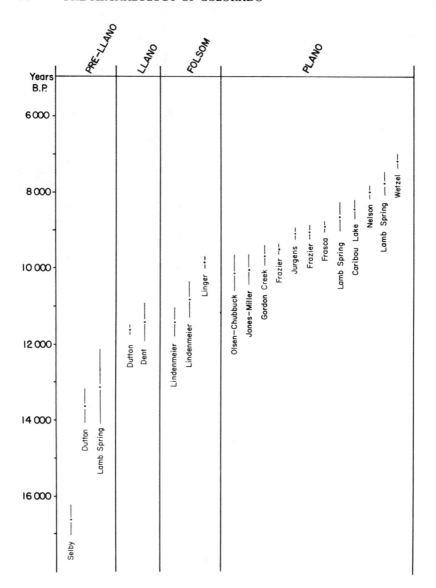

Figure 5-13   Sequence of C14 dated Paleo-Indian sites in Colorado.

Summary

The Lithic or Paleo-Indian Stage in Colorado is relatively well-represented by a range of complexes. There appears to be an increase in site density through time (Clovis - 3; Folsom - 8; Plano - 14). Most of the sites are east of the Front Range and north of the Arkansas River, but limited evidence from the Continental Divide and west suggests that Paleo-Indians were not restricted to plains environments.

All of the Paleo-Indian complexes shared a big game hunting tradition with roots in eastern Asia. Depending on herds of large animals for food, sinew (for sewing and for hafting weapons), hides (for clothing and shelter), and bones (for tools), these early nomads entered the New World and spread out across its unoccupied terrain.

Clovis and Folsom hunters sought to trap their prey in arroyo headcuts (e.g. Folsom, N.M.), sand dunes (e.g. Linger) or bogs (e.g. Lehner, Arizona). The numbers of mammoths and bison killed at any one time were generally small. The extinction of mammoth, horse, ground sloth, and camel during Clovis times, although perhaps related to climatic changes in the waning Pleistocene, may have been at least aided by human hunting pressures. During the Plano, greater social organization seems to have developed, as evidenced by more massive and complex kills that would have required a large number of coordinated drivers and hunters. Prepared traps (e.g. Jones-Miller) or arroyo drives (e.g. Olsen-Chubbuck) became part of their techniques, undoubtedly contributing to the extinction of some bison species.

The exploitation of plant resources during the Plano, is documented through the presence of grinding slabs (e.g. Jurgens). Hunting and gathering parties were moving across massive physical barriers like the Continental Divide, making use of diverse Colorado ecosystems. By the time of the Archaic, groundwork had been laid for efficiently exploiting nearly everything edible.

References

On potential Old World tool kit brought to New World:
Wormington 1962.
On the Hrdlička critiques of early man studies:
Roberts 1940b; Willey and Sabloff 1974.
On the Folsom, New Mexico, site:
Steen 1955; Figgins 1927; Wormington 1957, in prep; Anderson 1975.

On the Dutton and Selby sites:
Stanford 1979a, 1982, 1983; Stanford, Bonnichsen, and Morlan 1981; Graham 1981.

On the Lamb Spring site:
Stanford, Wedel, and Scott 1981; Rancier, Haynes, and Stanford 1982.

On the Llano Complex:
Sellards 1952.

On the Dent site:
Spikard 1972; Bilgery n.d., 1935; Trautman and Willis 1966; Figgins 1933; Wormington 1957, in prep; Haynes 1974; Agogino 1963, 1968.

On the Escapule, Arizona, site:
Hemmings and Haynes 1969.

On the early Blackwater Draw, New Mexico, excavations:
Cotter 1937, 1938.

On the Claypool site:
Dick and Mountain 1960; Malde 1960; Stanford and Albanese 1975.

On the San Luis Valley mammoths:
Hurst 1943a.

On the Sandia controversy:
Stevens and Agogino 1975; Hibben 1941.

On the Lindenmeier site:
Renaud 1931, 1932a; Roberts 1935a; Wilmsen and Roberts 1978; Wormington 1957, in prep; Cotter 1978; Haynes and Agogino 1960.

On Folsom point production:
Frison and Bradley 1980; Frison and Stanford 1982; Wormington in prep.

On the Powars site:
Roberts 1937a; Wormington 1957, in prep.

On the Fowler-Parrish site:
Agogino and Parrish 1971; Wormington in prep.

On the Johnson site:
Galloway and Agogino 1961.

On the Linger site:
Hurst 1941, 1943a; Dawson and Stanford 1975.

On the Zapata skull:
Patterson and Agogino 1976.

On the Zapata site:
Wormington 1957.

On the Cattle Guard site:
Emery and Stanford 1982.

On the Jones-Miller site and Hell Gap points:
Stanford 1974, 1975, 1979b; Agogino 1961.

On the Hell Gap, Wyoming, site:
Irwin-Williams, et al 1973; Agogino 1961.

On the Frazier site:
Wormington in prep.

On the Agate Basin, Wyoming, site:
Roberts 1951, 1961; Frison 1978; Frison and Stanford 1982.

On the Cody Complex and Yuma typology:
Renaud 1931, 1932b, 1960; Barbour and Schultz 1932; Gebhard 1949;
Moss, et al. 1951; Wormington 1948, 1957, in prep; Jepsen 1953; Frison
1978; Agogino and Duguid 1963; Agogino 1964.

On the Olsen-Chubbuck site:
Wheat 1967, 1972; Fulgham and Stanford 1982; Agogino, Patterson, and
Patterson 1976; Wormington in prep; Stanford 1981.

On the Frasca site:
Fulgham and Stanford 1982.

On the Jurgens site:
Wheat 1979.

On the Caribou Lake site:
Benedict 1974, n.d.

On the Fourth of July Valley site:
Benedict 1981a.

On Jimmy Allen and Fredrick points:
Frison 1978; Mulloy 1959; Irwin-Williams, et al. 1973.

On the LoDaiska site:
Irwin and Irwin 1959.

On 5 PA 158:
Schubert, et al. 1981.

On the Christmas rock shelter:
Buckles 1967, 1971.

On the Deluge Shelter:
Leach 1980.

On Western Slope Paleo-Indian surface finds:
Wormington 1957; Steward 1933; Huscher 1939; Breternitz 1970; Hurst
1944.

On the Gordon Creek burial:
Anderson 1966; Gillio 1970; Breternitz, Swenlund, and Anderson 1971.

6 The Archaic

For several thousand years, Paleo-Indians moved throughout Colorado with what appears to have been a steadfast focus upon herds of late Pleistocene big game. In time these first Americans gained a solid foothold in the New World, increasing their numbers and density. They left an indelible imprint that is observable in all those that followed.

By about seven thousand years ago, in what is termed the Archaic Stage, archaeological evidence begins to provide clues that cultures on the plains were changing. These indicators are more than just subtle variations in flint knapping techniques or stylistic differences in projectile point outlines. The large *Bison antiquus*, the mammoth, and other Ice Age fauna were extinct, probably due in part to human hunting. Such a drastic, though perhaps gradual, loss of a primary food source must have created considerable cultural stress. It was probably this that shifted attention to previously unexploited plants and animals. The people of the post-Pleistocene Archaic appear to have learned the harsh lesson of focusing too tightly on a specific food source.

Grinding tools—the handstone (mano) and grinding slab (metate)—are some of the best indicators that diet was changing. It is true that a few such implements have been found at Paleo-Indian sites like Jurgens, but for the most part, the use of plants is only hinted at in the archaeological record of the pre-Archaic. However, this significant element of the foraging life comes to the fore during the Archaic. Also, the recovered bone assemblage suggests the addition of many small game species to the diet.

Such a wide exploitation of niches appears to have begun earlier in the major riverine systems east of the Missouri and Mississippi than on the plains. The Eastern Woodlands, teeming with a myriad of life forms,

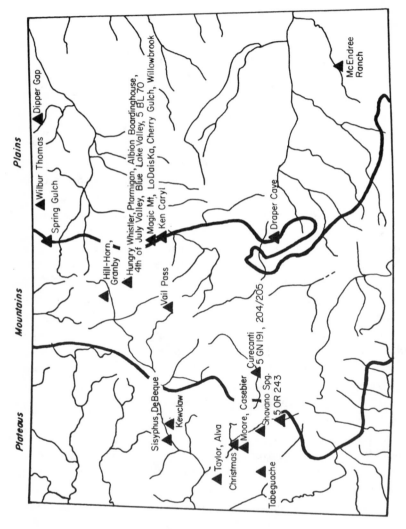

Figure 6-1   Selected Archaic sites in Colorado.

provided ample opportunity for hunters and gatherers to make a good living. Eastern archaeologist Joe Caldwell sees these groups as expanding their environmental utilization to the point where a large number of people were able to exist comfortably in a relatively high density, supported by the surrounding riches of plants and animals. Caldwell terms this optimum adaptation the *Primary Forest Efficiency*.

The existence in the East of large sites with deep refuse deposits of fish bones, shellfish, seeds, nuts, and animal bones, provides ample testimony to increasing population density and a trend toward greater locational permanence. Smaller contemporary sites found there have been interpreted as seasonal camps or procurement areas away from the larger base camps. The strategies for gathering certain foods or other resources may have included periodic forays by small parties or temporary scatterings of the entire group, with a subsequent reunion (perhaps months later) at the main camp.

Throughout the New World, the Archaic was a time of increasing technological (and probably social) complexity. Tools kits became larger, and through time the many regional differences slowly coalesced into more homogeneous forms. Caldwell sees the increasing sameness as evidence that interaction between groups was taking place on a large scale and terms this social contact the *Archaic Diffusion Sphere*.

Improvements in technology during the Archaic included the use of plant fibers for the construction of coiled baskets and cords. The baskets would have been useful in the increased gathering of seeds and nuts. The cordage was woven into nets and lines for fishing and for making snares and animal netting. Bone fish hooks, net sinkers, and other accessories were used in concert with the fiber innovations. Pounding and grinding stones are more common in Archaic sites and are present in a variety of forms, suggestive of special processing techniques for different types of wild crops. Projectile points changed stylistically. Instead of hafting a smoothed lanceolate stem as in Paleo times, the Archaic peoples began notching their points to provide more security when the point, propelled by an atlatl, met a solid object such as the rib cage of a deer. Surprisingly, for all of the technological improvements the Archaic foragers seemed to have developed, their skills in flaking stone tools declined from Paleo-Indian standards. Does this reflect a decline in the importance of hunting? Though we may never know, it sounds reasonable.

In parts of the United States, the Archaic was a time of great stability, due no doubt to a state of optimum balance between humans and the environment. At the Koster site in the Illinois River Valley, there is good evidence for *permanent* villages by 7,000 years ago. This is an especially significant finding, because the aboriginals at Koster were still hunter-gatherers and did not rely on domesticated crops. They had apparently found an ecosystem within easy reach that was rich enough to preclude the need to uproot the entire band in seasonal migrations.

Cultures in other parts of North America also achieved environmental harmony, though not as early as at Koster. For instance, many of the Northwest Coast Indians lived in permanent villages near sources of abundant marine and riverine foodstuffs. They never found it necessary to advance beyond the foraging stage into the farming of domesticates and were still at the food gathering level when first encountered by non-Indian explorers.

Colorado was different. Here the ample plant and animal populations of the Eastern woodlands or the Pacific Northwest were never available. Although Colorado has a far greater number of ecological zones and attendant climatic and biological variability than most other areas, a critical factor known as *environmental resistance* prevented the growth of large populations of most edible species. Environmental resistance creates what is known as *carrying capacity*, the maximum population that an area can support. In animals, this resistance comes primarily from the amount of food and water available. If a population overshoots its food and water supply, it will crash (through massive deaths) to a point below the carrying capacity. A rebuilding will then usually occur, though extinction is possible when minimal reproductive limits of a species are approached. Maintaining game herds below the carrying capacity of the land has long been the ecological justification for modern sport hunting.

The Colorado carrying capacity is principally controlled by rainfall in prairie and basin-plateau country and by temperature, snowfall, and soils in the mountains. Considering the limits placed on animal and plant life in the state, it is not surprising that when the first European explorers penetrated the Central Plains they encountered a relatively small population of foragers and incipient horticulturalists.

The Archaic population density west of the mountains was even lower than on the plains, because the more arid climate of Colorado's plateaus and the Great Basin puts correspondingly greater pressure on the environment. People of the Desert Culture, as the desert version of the Archaic is called, exploited life zones from the low elevation Sonoran Desert to the treeless Alpine. Evidence from sites like Utah's Danger Cave reveals that the Desert Culture was in existence as early as 10,000 years ago, overlapping the Paleo-Indians and surviving into historic times in groups such as the

Paiute. Based on the small number of true Paleo-Indian sites in this part of the West, it has been argued that the Desert Culture was the earliest level of cultural development here.

Perhaps the best evidence for Archaic cultures in Colorado has come from rock shelters. Nomadic groups found these sites to be excellent habitations, warm in winter and cool in summer (if they faced south) and providing protection from wind, rain, and snow. Luckily for archaeologists, rock shelters have also protected the debris left by the inhabitants, preserving an extensive material culture in deep, largely undisturbed stratigraphy. Successive occupations can be observed, conveniently separated by layers of sterile soil. Developmental sequences can be documented and compared to other sites for the purpose of filling in gaps and identifying regional idiosyncrasies and influences. Examples of such sites include the Western Slope shelters of Deluge, Sisyphus, Taylor, Alva, Moore, Casebier, Tabeguache, and Christmas; the Denver Foothills shelters at Willowbrook, Ken Caryl Ranch, and LoDaisKa; the Wilbur Thomas shelter to the northeast; and Draper Cave, far to the south.

If all we knew about the Archaic peoples came from rock shelters, our ability to interpret their lifestyles would be limited, but fortunately, Archaic remains have also been found in open land. In addition to other data from these sites, the locations themselves can reveal something of prehistoric thought processes. For example, camps near bighorn sheep trails or in a piñon forest shed welcome light on hunting and food gathering strategies.

Although the superimposed cultural levels in rock shelters can reveal developmental sequences, problems often arise in the analysis of data obtained from them. Burrowing rodents can mix strata; a nearly continuous human presence can preclude the deposition of sterile soil between cultural levels; complex geological processes can cause confusion. Open sites with only one occupational episode (single component) will often permit a clearer recognition of specific cultural periods, thus providing a good base for comparison in sorting out sequences in stratified, multi-component sites.

Archaic Architecture

Granby and Hill Horn

In 1981 national attention was drawn to some high altitude Archaic structures found in the sagebrush of Middle Park. A major water project was about to commence, and contract archaeologists were called in to survey the property that would be disturbed by the dam and pipeline. Forty-two prehistoric sites were subsequently discovered within the right-of-way. Because some of the sites were considered potentially significant, heavy equipment operations were monitored, and on a ridgetop near the town of Granby an observant archaeologist noted some small fragments of burned clay being brought to the surface by the blade. The construction was quickly halted at that location, and excavations were begun.

Careful examination of the clay revealed impressions of tree trunks, branches, pine needles, and other plant remains, some of which would had to have been carried uphill from the nearby valley. Based on this and other data, the Granby site was thought to contain houses. This conclusion has since forced the archaeological community to rethink the standard model of Archaic foragers in high altitude regions.

The Archaic hunter-gatherers were formerly thought to have been highly mobile, exploiting all available niches but not remaining in one place very long. That they would have passed relatively quickly through harsh, high-altitude terrain like that around Granby, harvesting local food sources on the way, has been assumed, but now there is evidence that they built substantial huts, indicating that they probably lived in one spot for extended periods of time.

Many concentrations of the impressed clay but no actual house outlines were found during the fieldwork. The assumed construction technique was that known as wattle and daub (or jacal), in which a superstructure was built of upright posts and interwoven branches and then plastered over with wet clay. Upon hardening, the walls of the hut could protect its inhabitants in most weather conditions, though excessive rain would begin to erode the clay off the outside. Periodic replastering would be required. Fortunately for the investigative team, the structures (perhaps up to 20 or more) at Granby and the nearby Hill-Horn site burned, firing and hardening the clay and thus preventing it from melting back into the soil.

Artifacts from these sites were all undiagnostic, being general sorts of flaked tools found in a number of different cultures. They were also not very useful in determining what kinds of domestic activities took place there. However, C14 dates of 7,170 ± 200 B.P. from a hearth, and 4,160 ± 110 B.P. and 3,750 ± 70 B.P. from two of the structures, place the occupation deep within the Archaic. Goosefoot (*Chenopdium*) seeds and burned rabbit-sized bones, along with numerous firepits, are further evidence that the sites were camps. A nearby jasper quarry was used to replenish tool supplies, and the headwaters of the Colorado River would have attracted

Figure 6-2   An oblique aerial view of the Granby site (arrow). (Jim Gensheimer photo; Western Cultural Resource Management.)

Figure 6-3   Fragment of daub from the Granby site, showing a portion of a post mold (left) with a diameter of approximately 21 cm. and ponderosa pine needle impressions (right). (Jim Grady photo; Western Cultural Resource Management.)

wild game and nourished riparian plant communities. The scanty deposits of tools and discarded foodstuffs are indicative of short-term habitations, as would be expected in an intermontain valley over 8,000 feet above sea level. This is what makes the presence of substantial structures so puzzling. The evidence is suggestive of some unexpected Archaic lifeways, and hopefully future research at the basically undisturbed Hill-Horn site will resolve the questions.

The shapes of the Granby and Hill-Horn structures cannot be determined with certainty, but investigations farther to the south and west have helped fill in the gaps in our knowledge.

The Curecanti Sites

National Park Service excavations in the Curecanti National Recreation Area (Blue Mesa Reservoir) have revealed a variety of Archaic hearths along the old Gunnison River bank. Dates from hearths at 5 GN 191 cluster around 6,000 years ago. Work nearby at site 5 GN 204/205 brought to light a circular charcoal stain nearly two meters in diameter. It was incorporated in a shallow basin and underlain by pole-impressed burned clay of wattle and daub origin. This feature, dated to about 4,500 years ago, is thought to represent an Early or Middle Archaic structure.

Figure 6-4   A charcoal-stained oval, underlain by pole-impressed burned clay at Curecanti (5 GN 204/205), a probable Early or Middle Archaic structure. (Midwest Archeological Center, National Park Service.)

Figure 6-5   Hearths along the Gunnison River at Curecanti (Blue Mesa Reservoir), dating to Early Archaic times, around 6,000 years ago (site 5 GN 191). (Midwest Archeological Center, National Park Service.)

Kewclaw

To the northwest of Curecanti, in the Colorado River Valley, are the Kewclaw and Sisyphus sites, two good Archaic habitations that have retained architectural elements.

The Kewclaw site is near the town of Parachute and was discovered during archaeological surveys around Battlement Mesa in advance of the ill-fated oil shale development there. Of all the Archaic structures in Colorado, Kewclaw is the best preserved. The structure is a classic pithouse, similar in many ways to those built by subsequent Southwestern horticulturalists. The house had a basin-shaped depression 65 centimeters deep and about 4.5 meters in diameter. It appears to have had at least eight posts that would have supported a superstructure, probably of wattle and daub construction. A slab-covered fire hearth was discovered in the central floor, suggestive of year-round, or perhaps winter, occupation. Associated artifacts included a distinctive loaf-shaped, one-handed mano, a bone awl, and several medium to small corner-notched projectile points. Two C14 dates, $2,900 \pm 60$ B.P. and $2,770 \pm 60$ B.P., place this structure within the Late Archaic. Further confirmation of its early date came from an exterior hearth ($2,590 \pm 70$ B.P.).

Figure 6-6   Feature 5, an Archaic pithouse at the Kewclaw site near Battlement Mesa. (Grand River Institute.)

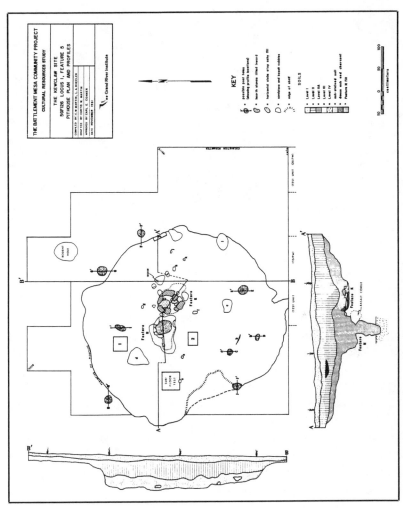

Figure 6-7   Plan and profile map of pithouse at the Kewclaw site. (Grand River Institute.)

Figure 6-8   Feature 9, a slab-lined floor of a probable Archaic structure in the Sisyphus rock shelter. (Colorado Highway Department.)

Sisyphus

Sisyphus, located downstream near DeBeque, had to be excavated, as it was marked for destruction. It was unfortunately in the path of the westwardly-expanding Interstate-70. Sisyphus differs from the other Archaic sites with architectural remains in that it was a rock shelter. It faced south toward the river and would have gathered precious winter sunlight to warm the people who lived there. During excavations in 1979 and 1980, John Gooding and other Colorado Highway Department archaeologists came down on what was designated Level IV and began to expose a rectangular floor (2 by 3 meters) composed of flat-lying slabs. It was later dated at 2,410 ± 70 B.P. No actual post molds were discovered, but the investigators have suggested that some sort of superstructure covered the slab floor during its use. There are some hints that clay may have been plastered on the rock. The rectangular shape is unexpected for this period, as nomadic peoples, for whatever reason, more typically preferred circular structures. An enclosure beneath the overhang would have helped retain heat in the winter and should not be considered an improbable addition to a rock shelter.

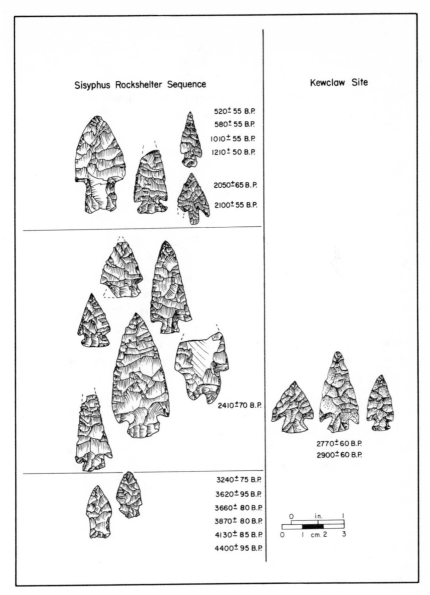

Sisyphus Rockshelter Sequence

Kewclaw Site

520 ± 55 B.P.
580 ± 55 B.P.
1010 ± 55 B.P.
1210 ± 50 B.P.

2050 ± 65 B.P.
2100 ± 55 B.P.

2410 ± 70 B.P.

2770 ± 60 B.P.
2900 ± 60 B.P.

3240 ± 75 B.P.
3620 ± 95 B.P.
3660 ± 80 B.P.
3870 ± 80 B.P.
4130 ± 85 B.P.
4400 ± 95 B.P.

0   in.   1
0   1   cm. 2   3

Figure 6-9   Projectile point sequence from the Sisyphus site, correlated to the points from the Kewclaw site.

McEndree Ranch

On the southeastern Colorado plains, a charcoal-stained, heavily compacted house floor with a ramp entrance was recently discovered at the McEndree Ranch site. It was dated at 2,350 ± 65 B.P., within the Late Archaic, and had similarities to structures near Kansas City. Ramps into semi-subterranian houses were widely used during the Plains Village Tradition of the more easterly plains around A.D. 500 to 1450, but this early occurrence at McEndree, along with abundant floral and faunal remains and some limited lithics, provides an interesting picture of Late Archaic camping on the plains of Colorado.

Summary

These five Colorado Archaic sites are unusual. Evidence of Archaic structures is scarce, and in the open it is generally quite poorly preserved. Typically, what an archaeologist finds in an unsheltered Archaic site is termed a *lithic scatter*, just a number of discarded flakes and perhaps a few broken or lost stone tools. If one is lucky, a firepit or two might be found. To recognize remnants of clay that had been pressed by hand into a cribbing of branches and poles many thousands of years ago, or to pick out the subtle soil discolorations that hint at a pit outline, is a tribute to the skill of the field archaeologists involved, as well as to those who trained them.

From these sites, we can see that Archaic families and bands not only traversed our highest elevations, but *settled* at times, constructing small, mostly circular huts as buffers between themselves and the elements. These earliest Colorado houses do bear a resemblance to the habitations of subsequent groups who perfected sedentary life here. The continuum between the Archaic foragers and the later village-centered horticulturalists is obvious.

The Western Slope Archaic

Tabeguache Caves

In the late 1930s, the first concentrated efforts were made to identify Western Slope prehistoric occupations.

C. T. Hurst excavated several caves south and west of the Uncompahgre Plateau. Known collectively as the Tabeguache Caves, they yielded several discrete artifact assemblages and called attention to some of the less spectacular sites in the Southwest. The best of the finds, Tabeguache Cave

Figure 6-10   Excavations at the Moore shelter, Uncompahgre Plateau, in 1938-39. Denver archaeologist H. Marie Wormington is operating the shaker screen, and Grand Junction journalist and avocational archaeologist Al Look is shoveling. (Gil Bucknum photo; H. M. Wormington.)

II, was featured on the cover of the Colorado Archaeological Society's journal, *Southwestern Lore*, from 1945 through 1951 (during most of which time Hurst was its editor).

The Wormington and Lister Excavations

In 1938 and 1939, Marie Wormington (then Curator of Archaeology at the Denver Museum of Natural History) excavated the Moore and Casebier rock shelters in a canyon near Montrose. In 1951 she conducted work on another nearby rock shelter, the Taylor site, and she was joined in 1952 by Robert Lister of the University of Colorado. That season, Taylor was completed, as was the adjacent Alva site. Of these four, the Taylor site held the longest record of human use, a buildup of soils and rocks 17 feet deep beneath the shallow, south-facing overhang. The work at Taylor provided the first well-controlled projectile point sequence in the area. In addition to points, many other artifacts were recovered, including an interesting shaft wrench made from a bighorn sheep horn and several Uncompahgre scrapers. It is unfortunate that carbon samples were later discarded by some

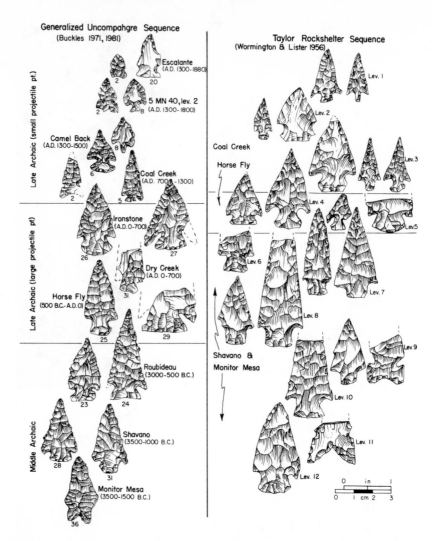

Figure 6-11 Projectile point sequences from the Uncompahgre Plateau. (Right) Types from the Taylor rock shelter. (Left) Generalized sequence from numerous sites examined by Buckles (1971, 1981). The Buckles sequence includes Archaic divisions (periods), phase names, rough dates, and tool type numbers. The Taylor sequence is organized by stratigraphic level, and the Buckles phase names are applied for rough correlation.

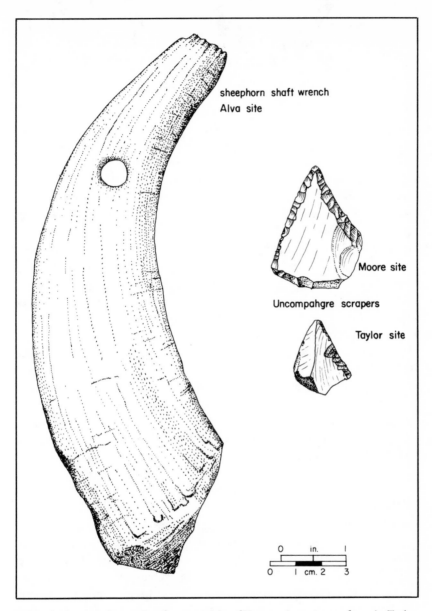

sheephorn shaft wrench
Alva site

Moore site

Uncompahgre scrapers

Taylor site

Figure 6-12   A shaft wrench and two examples of Uncompahgre scrapers from the Taylor, Alva, and Moore sites. (After Wormington and Lister 1951.)

unknown person at the museum. Based on the findings at these four sites, the Uncompahgre Complex was named. It was considered a regional variant of the Desert Culture, which was centered in the Great Basin.

The Ute Prehistory Project

In 1961 a major effort was launched toward understanding the prehistory of the Uncompahgre Plateau. Robert Lister conceived this "Ute Prehistory Project," an undertaking with the goal of clarifying the local archaeological sequence. Since no historic ethnic group other than the Utes are known to have lived on the Plateau, it was hoped that a continuum could be discovered between the historic Utes and their prehistoric counterparts. Soon after the project began, C. U. graduate student Bill Buckles took over the responsibilities of directing the field and laboratory work and completed two more field seasons. The results were the basis for his doctoral dissertation, probably the most often cited research on the area. Seventy-five archaeological sites were investigated, perhaps the most spectacular being the Christmas rock shelter and the open-air site of Shavano Spring. Through his controlled excavations, Buckles established an Uncompahgre Plateau sequence that may reach from Paleo-Indian times to the A.D. 1800s. A trend from corner-notching and stemming in the Monitor Mesa and Shavano Phases progresses toward smaller points with side-notches in the Coal Creek through Escalante Phases. Buckles applied his more complete sequence to the Taylor site artifacts, providing a rough correlation.

Although most archaeologists make a break from the Archaic stage by A.D. 1 - 500, with the advent of the bow and arrow and the introduction of ceramics, Buckles has proposed that the Uncompahgre peoples remained essentially Archaic in both the technological and cultural sense until the 1800s. He divides the Late Archaic into large projectile point (pre-bow-and-arrow) and small projectile point (post bow-and-arrow) divisions.

Ultimately, Buckles did not succeed in delineating the prehistoric Ute to historic Ute continuum, due primarily to difficulties in matching up cultural groups through mostly lithic artifacts. However, he did provide chronological information on the Uncompahgre Complex and filled out the incomplete prehistoric sequence there. He came to the conclusion that there were no unique tools in the complex (e.g. Uncompahgre scrapers), but that when the assemblage was taken as a whole, it did have some quantitative attributes that set the Uncompahgre Complex apart from other Desert Culture adaptations. In the Plateau area, the Uncompahgre Complex follows the earlier Paleo-Indians. The horticulturally-based puebloan groups that appear farther south around A.D. 1 do not appear to have had much influence on these Uncompahgre peoples who had by then settled into a successful foraging pattern.

Sisyphus, DeBeque, Deluge Shelter, and 5 OR 243

A few other representative multi-component sites from the Western Slope are the aforementioned Sisyphus shelter near DeBeque, with C14 dates as early as 4,400 ± 95 B.P. and projectile point styles having similarities to the Great Basin; the DeBeque shelter, with seven components dating between 6,150 ± 190 and 2,440 ± 120 B.P.; and the Deluge shelter in the Utah part of Dinosaur National Monument, having at least a Middle Archaic component and several overlying zones. One of the more puzzling Archaic finds on the Western Slope is 5 OR 243, a deeply buried open-air site along the Uncompahgre River. Discovered and test excavated during the Dallas project in 1980, it may contain a structure, although more work will be required to make certain. The strange part of the find was the presence of *Curcurbita* seeds, possibly a cultivated variety of squash or a wild gourd. Neither plant occurs in the region today, and there is little likelihood that they could have grown at such a high elevation at any time. It seems possible that they were carried in, perhaps as part of an Archaic trade network around 2,060 ± 60 B.P., the date of the seeds.

Summary

Taken as a whole, the Western Slope Archaic is clearly a cultural entity. The Archaic peoples maintained a continuity in lifestyle over many thousands of years, apparently overlapping the Paleo-Indian hunters, persisting while the Anasazi and Fremont horticulturalists flourished on the peripheries of the Archaic territory, and remaining to be encountered by Europeans in historic times. The explanation for this extraordinary longevity must lie in the early striking of an optimum balance with the arid environment. The Archaic peoples' cultural assimilation was so complete that there was never a need to develop new technologies or lifeways.

The Mountain and Plains Archaic

Before delving too deeply into the culture of the Archaic from the mountain and plains provinces, a word of caution is needed. Chronologies and artifact sequences have been published, based on excavated remains

In a valley high in the Colorado Rockies, two Archaic hunters are trying to bring down some mule deer. The man in the foreground has his spear seated in the hook of the atlatl (throwing

from sites concentrated in a restricted region centered on the hogback valley west of Denver and from some alpine sites in the Indian Peaks area west of Boulder. Although some of the components have been dated and the sequences documented in well-controlled research, inter-site comparisons have been difficult. Geologic processes and pot hunting have apparently mixed some of the strata, reducing the usefulness of the data. Comparing projectile point types is difficult, because many of the investigators have applied their own naming or numbering systems to the same points. And finally, it is impossible to compare artifacts from a satisfactory range of locations, since few Archaic sites east of the foothills have been excavated. Of all the work to be done in Colorado by future generations of archaeologists, delineating the Archaic of the mountains and plains will probably be the most challenging. That said, let us consider the evidence.

stick) and is about to launch the shaft. The other hunter has already launched his feathered spear, the atlatl being fully extended in front of his body.

The Early Archaic

Interpretation of Archaic data, especially from the plains, has been influenced by the writings of geologist Ernst Antevs. In 1948 and 1955 he published papers on former environments of the American West, proposing that the past 10,000 years be divided into three climatic episodes. The *Anathermal*, from 10,000 to 7,000 B.P., was thought to be cooler and wetter than now. From ca. 7,000 to 4,500 B.P. was the *Altithermal*, a time drier and warmer than the present. Finally, the *Medithermal* extends from about 4,500 B.P. up to the present, with moisture increasing and temperatures diminishing to current conditions. The Antevs model is based on evidence of erosional and depositional cycles, as seen in strata throughout the western U.S. Of greatest interest to most archaeologists is the Al-

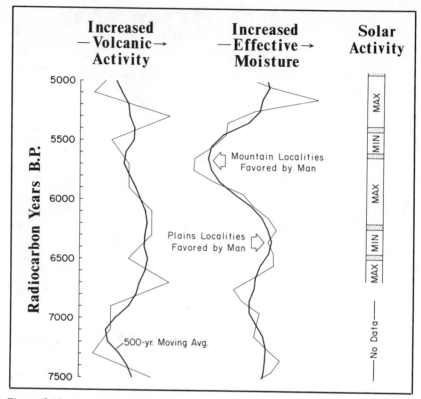

Figure 6-13   Correlation of volcanic activity to moisture changes and shifts in location of human populations. (From Benedict 1981.)

tithermal, because in an area like the plains that often seems to teeter on the brink of climatic disaster, a significant desiccation could dramatically alter the scope of life.

With the Altithermal concept in mind, archaeologists have for many years looked for evidence of human presence on the plains in the 7,500 to 4,500 B.P. range. They found little, and this seemed to confirm the Antevs hypothesis. With such adverse climatic conditions, Early Archaic hunters and gatherers seem to have been forced to move to adjacent areas. Mulloy went so far as to term the period the "Altithermal Hiatus."

If the Altithermal did directly affect foragers living in the rain shadow of the Rocky Mountains (as well as other areas), one problem is to find out what happened to them.

The best evidence for Early Archaic presence in Colorado and Wyoming seems to be in or alongside the mountains. Recognition of this has taken James Benedict to the Continental Divide region west of Boulder. There he has engaged in extended research at numerous archaeological sites, many of which date to the Early Archaic Altithermal. These include Hungry Whistler, 5 BL 70, Ptarmigan, Fourth of July Valley, and perhaps Albion Boardinghouse. A wealth of geological and cultural data has been gleaned from these sites, including a projectile point sequence tied solidly to C14 dates. These data have led him to hypothesize an Altithermal "mountain refugium." In this model, foragers retreated from the drought-stricken plains and plateaus into the cool and moist Rocky Mountains. Benedict has derived population curves based on radiocarbon dates from known Altithermal sites in a large area of the western United States, Canada, and Mexico. He thinks that, based on these curves, there were probably *two* major Altithermal droughts, 7,000 - 6,500 B.P. and 6,000-5,500 B.P., separated by an interval of increased moisture and local mountain glaciation. This interval would have allowed a successful habitation of the lower peripheral plains, plateaus, and basins.

The Ptarmigan site is his oldest, at 6,450 ± 100 B.P., and it is associated with side-notched projectile points.

The next oldest, Fourth of July Valley, contains evidence that is difficult to interpret. Along with an apparently classic Jimmy Allen point of late Plano age (ca. 7,900 B.P.) are points that resemble Middle Archaic Duncan and McKean Lanceolate points (ca. 4,000 B.P.), except that they are transverse oblique-flaked. Benedict's average date of 5,960 ± 85 B.P., however, places the site intermediate to the Plano and the Middle Archaic, well within the Early Archaic. Benedict believes that the date is accurate, that the tools were all manufactured by the same cultural group, and that the Fourth of July Valley site provides evidence of the transition from the Plano to the Middle Archaic (see Chapter 5 for additional discussion of the site). For the time being, I will have to reserve judgement on the Fourth of July Valley site and what it means in the archaeology of the Altithermal.

The Hungry Whistler site and 5 BL 70 have yielded a projectile point style Benedict named the Albion Corner-Notched point. Dated from 5,800 ± 125 to 5,350 ± 130 B.P., it has broad notches and a ground, convex base. Similarities can be seen in points of about the same age from the hogback valley sites of Magic Mountain and Cherry Gulch and from the Wilbur Thomas shelter on the plains. Benedict has suggested that the Mount Albion Complex peoples had a limited occupation during seasonal rounds of hunting and gathering activities, restricted by the Altithermal pressures on the shortgrass prairies.

Within the archaeological community, opinions on the *existence* of the Altithermal, much less its extent and severity, are strongly divided. Some think that the climatic details are oversimplified, while others argue for the total elimination of the Altithermal from the literature. Geologists and paleoclimatologists lean more toward its acceptance. At present, one should be aware that the Altithermal is not something regarded as fact by all. Its final disposition awaits further research.

The "cultural hiatus" seen by those such as Mulloy may, in fact, be only a sampling bias. Open sites along the drainages of the plains (areas of highest site location probability) could have either been destroyed or covered with alluvium. The firm proof of their existence would thus now be beyond recovery.

Benedict's work has come under a certain amount of criticism, but it has also forced many archaeologists to rethink the entire problem of Altithermal population movements. His studies are suggestive, with hypotheses that will merit testing for years to come.

Figure 6-14   The Fourth of July Valley site. (James Benedict and *Plains Anthropologist*.)

The Middle Archaic

The Middle Archaic, beginning about 4,000 B.P., is characterized by an increase in milling stones and a change in projectile point styles. Perhaps the points most often associated with this period are those of the McKean Complex, first named for their presence in stratified sites in Wyoming. These include the McKean Lanceolate in Fig. 6-15 (LoDaisKa type B and 4th of July unshouldered), Duncan in Fig. 6-15 (LoDaisKa type A and 4th of July shouldered), and Hanna (somewhat resembling type MM 17 of Magic Mountain).

In addition to the enigmatic finds at Fourth of July Valley, there have been a number of other Middle Archaic discoveries in Colorado. Both the Wilbur Thomas shelter and the Dipper Gap site of the northeastern plains have good McKean horizons, with dates from Dipper Gap of 3,520 ± 85 to 3,180 ± 90 B.P. Spring Gulch, in the foothills near Lindenmeier, contained all three point types of the McKean Complex. Farther south, in the hogback valley west of Denver, there is evidence of McKean in stratified deposits at LoDaisKa, Cherry Gulch, and perhaps Magic Mountain. LoDaisKa provided dates in the McKean zone (Complex C) of 3,400 ± 200 to 3,150 ± 200 B.P. Draper Cave, far to the south near Pueblo, held substantial evidence for a Middle Archaic McKean occupation, dated from 3,520 ± 70 to 3,480 ± 65 B.P.

The concentration of Middle Archaic sites in the eastern foothills of the Rocky Mountains may indicate a preferred habitat for McKean peoples in Colorado. But rock shelters along the hogback are conspicious and have undergone extensive investigations in the past; open-air sites to the east are far more difficult to find. This can at least partly account for the smaller number of reported discoveries on the plains. In Wyoming, many McKean sites have been found away from the mountains, perhaps indicative of post-Altithermal movements on the shortgrass prairie.

The Late Archaic

The Late Archaic, beginning about 3,000 years ago, can be recognized by the increase in side-notched and corner-notched projectile points.

Interesting Late Archaic sites in the mountains and plains include the aforementioned McEndree Ranch site, with its ramp-entry house, and the high altitude Blue Lake Valley site.

At McEndree, in addition to the structure, several charcoal lenses, a slab-lined hearth, and a probable boiling pit for bone grease rendering were found. Numerous bison bones at this camp are suggestive of a nearby, yet

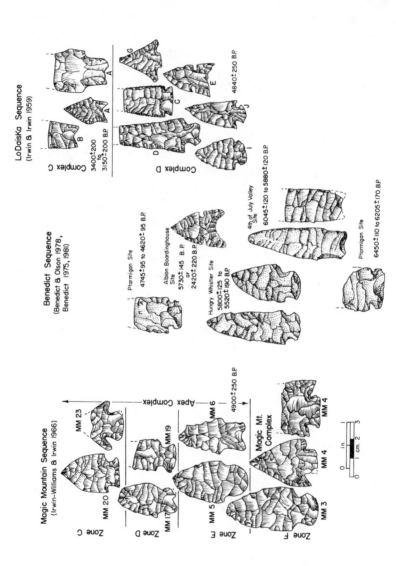

Figure 6-15   Uncorrelated Archaic projectile point sequences from sites along the foothills and the Front Range.

Figure 6-16   The Vail Pass site. (Colorado Highway Department.)

undiscovered, kill site. Camp-associated cutting tools and flakes, but unfortunately no diagnostic projectile points, were recovered. Pollen and fiber analysis of the site indicates that the inhabitants used pine and juniper (for house construction?) and flax and yucca for cordage, matting, and/or basketry.

The Blue Lake Valley site contained an unusual stone circle about two meters in diameter that was dated at $3,215 \pm 90$ B.P. Stone circles are increasingly common from Middle Archaic times on and typically would not be considered out of the ordinary here. However, the location of this feature seems to preclude its use as a dwelling. It is an area that appears to be saturated at most times with meltwater seepage and subject to a cold air drainage from a large snowbank. Far better campsites could be found nearby. Benedict has thus interpreted this circle as a hunting blind. Its center had been deepened artificially, something not generally associated with similar circles on the plains, but could be expected if concealment, rather than shelter, was the principal intent of the occupant. A corner-notched point that appears to be within the Late Archaic range of variation was found at the site, further confirming its age.

In dealing with the Archaic, one final site should be mentioned. Known as the Vail Pass site, it was discovered prior to construction of a rest area along Interstate-70 east of Vail. Located at an elevation of about 10,000 feet above sea level, just below the crest of Vail Pass on its leeward side, it was an extensive multicomponent site with extreme time depth.

The findings suggest seasonal use there from at least Early Archaic times into the historic period. Unfortunately, the site was shallow and had undergone considerable disturbance through frost heaving and rodent activity. Stratigraphic separation was not possible, and thus actual association between the numerous hearths, ceramics, scrapers, and over 100 projectile points could not be demonstrated with any certainty. From a provenience standpoint, the Vail Pass site has only limited utility. However, the documentation of at least seven separate aboriginal occupations extending from over 7,000 years ago to A.D. 1760 does add to our knowledge of cultural distributions and site selection patterns.

Summary

Colorado contains a wealth of archaeological data of Archaic age from the arid Western Slope basins and plateaus, across the cool, pine-covered, well-watered Rocky Mountains, and onto the thirsty shortgrass prairies. These data indicate an increased efficiency in foraging over the preceeding Paleo-Indians. This broader use of plants and animals was at least partially in response to the changing post-Pleistocene environment.

Archaeologists have generated many questions about the Archaic in the course of their investigations. Projectile point styles, although often distinctive, only tantalize the observer with hints of cultural connections between geographic areas. And when a connection can be made, the interpretations can vary dramatically. Would a similar artifact from Colorado's San Luis Valley, the High Plains of Nebraska, and the mountains of Montana indicate a migration of peoples, an ideological influence, trade patterns, or perhaps independent inventions of the same style? Artifact indentification is only a first step in lengthy research efforts aimed at understanding the past.

One of the thorniest problems concerning the Archaic is the nature of the climate and its effects on the resident hunters and gatherers. Clues have been found, but much remains to be discovered before the case can be considered closed. Was there a "mountain refugium" or are we only looking at an incomplete site record?

Whatever the answer, by the dawning of the Christian Era, the way of life was changing. New influences were filtering west up the stream systems of the plains and north from Mexico, New Mexico, and Arizona. Revolution was in the air.

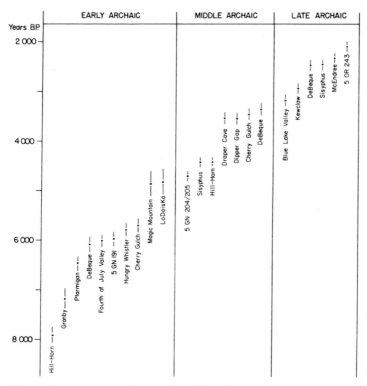

Figure 6-17   Sequence of selected C14 dates from Colorado Archaic sites.

References

On Primary Forest Efficiency:
Caldwell 1958.

On the Koster site:
Struever and Holton 1979.

On the Desert Culture:
Jennings 1957.

On the Granby and Hill-Horn sites:
Huse 1977; Wheeler and Martin 1982.

On the Curecanti area sites:
Euler and Stiger 1981; Jones 1982.

On the Sisyphus site:
Gooding, Kihm, and Shields in preparation.

On the Kewclaw site:
Conner and Langdon 1983.

On the McEndree Ranch site:
Shields 1980; Scott 1982.

On the Uncompahgre Complex sites:
Wormington and Lister 1956; Buckles 1971, 1981; Reed and Scott 1982; Toll 1971.

On the Deluge Shelter:
Leach 1967, 1980.

On the Tabeguache Cave sites:
Hurst 1940b, 1943b, 1944, 1945, 1946.

On 5 OR 243:
Buckles 1981; Lawrence and Muceus 1981.

On the DeBeque shelter:
Reed and Nickens 1981.

On the Altithermal:
Antevs, 1948, 1955; Martin and Mehringer 1965; Bryson, Baerreis, and Wendlund 1970; Bryan and Gruhn 1964; Benedict 1979a.

On the Mount Albion-area sites:
Benedict 1975c, 1979a, 1979b, 1981a; Benedict and Olson 1973, 1978; Lischka 1980; Kay 1979.

On the Magic Mountain and LoDaisKa sites:
Irwin and Irwin 1959; Irwin-Williams and Irwin 1966.

On the Wilbur Thomas and the Dipper Gap sites:
Breternitz 1971; Metcalf 1973.

On the Cherry Gulch site:
Nelson 1981.

On the Willowbrook site:
Leach 1966a.

On the McKean Complex:
Mulloy 1954; Wheeler 1952, 1954; Frison 1978.

On the Spring Gulch site:
Kainer 1974.

On Draper Cave:
Hagar 1976.

On the Wyoming Archaic:
Frison 1978.

On the Blue Lake Valley site:
Benedict 1979b

On the Vail Pass site:
Gooding 1981; Hester 1982; Hoffman, Johnson, and Butler 1982.

7 The Anasazi

In the town of Cambridge, Massachusetts, tucked into a corner of Harvard University on Divinity Avenue, stands a stately brick building, the Peabody Museum of Archaeology and Ethnology. Down in the basement, embedded in the floor of a laboratory, is a brassheaded nail. It identifies the spot where young Alfred Kidder and Samuel Guernsey shook hands and said, "Let's do the Southwest." The pact lead to some of the most productive archaeological work ever done there.

Few areas of the New World have undergone so extensive and intensive a probing as has the American Southwest, and when Kidder first set his sights on that region with a career in mind, others tried to dissuade him. He wrote:

> . . . I was not nearly as wrong as was he who advised me, just 50 years ago, to take up work in another field because, he said, 'The Southwest is a sucked orange.'
>
> I only wish I could return to that wonderful country and wet my aged lips once again on the rich juice of a fruit which a half-century of research has little more than begun to tap.

Early Explorations

The ruins of southwest Colorado were first seen by Europeans in 1765, when Juan Maria Antonio Rivera entered Colorado from the south in quest of silver. He recorded in his diary that ancient ruins could be seen along several of the rivers. Then in 1776, two Franciscans, Fray Silvestre Velez de

103

Figure 7-1   Two Story House in Mancos Canyon, as captured by Hayden Survey photographer, W. H. Jackson, in 1874. (Colorado Historical Society.)

Escalante and Fray Antanasio Dominguez, led an expedition through Southwestern Colorado in search of a practical route from Santa Fe to Monterey, California. They noted several prehistoric sites, including one along the Dolores River that has since been named the Escalante Ruin. This pueblo has now been partially excavated and is open to the public.

In the years following the travels of Escalante and Dominguez, other non-Indians came into contact with these vestiges of early cultures. The Old Spanish Trail led many "49ers" through the heartland of the prehistoric pueblos, although these would-be miners had their hearts set on the golden treasures in the streams of California. Railroads followed, along with Mormon explorers and settlers, but with few exceptions, the outside world was oblivious to the relics of the past in the San Juan country.

During the mid-1870s, following a purchase of land from the Ute Indians, the federal government sent an expedition under the command of F.V. Hayden to explore the Four Corners area. The Hayden Survey examined and mapped portions of the Mesa Verde, McElmo, and Yellowjacket areas, along with adjacent lands outside of Colorado. Two outstanding members of the party, geologist W.H. Holmes and photographer W.H. Jackson, helped interpret the archaeological wonders of the Southwest to the public at large. The Hayden expedition marked the beginning of serious archaeological interest in Colorado's prehistoric pueblos. It

Figure 7-2   The Wetherill brothers at Alamo Ranch about 1893. (Left to right) Al, Win, Richard, Clayton, and John. (Mesa Verde National Park.)

would be another decade, however, before national attention was drawn to the region.

The Alamo Ranch, homesteaded near Mancos, Colorado, in the early 1880s, was the abode of Benjamin Wetherill and his family, which included five sons—Richard, Alfred, John, Clayton, and Win. The Wetherills had originally moved west from Missouri, lured by the talk of silver in Colorado. With little success in the mining camp at Rico, they came out of the mountains and for a time worked a ranch near Bluff City, Utah. Fortune again failed them, and within a few months a torrential rain washed their buildings away. Discouraged, they turned back to the east, traversed the tilted alluvial slopes below the looming northern escarpment of the Mesa Verde, and ended their odyssey in its shadow, deep in the grasses of the Mancos Valley. The scarred but unbeaten family began to pick up the pieces and within a few years had developed a solid agricultural operation. They cultivated wheat and oats and were on good enough terms with the Utes to be allowed to graze their cattle unmolested in the canyons alongside Mesa Verde.

Figure 7-3   Cliff Palace, looking much as it must have when Richard Wetherill and Charlie Mason first saw it in December of 1888. (S. Cassells photo.)

In the course of herding their livestock, they discovered something the Utes and Navajos had long known of: cliff dwellings of the Anasazi (a Navajo term meaning "ancient ones"), perched along and under the towering walls of the mesas. They explored a few ruins and collected artifacts in their spare time. Then, in a snowstorm on 18 December 1888, Richard Wetherill and his brother-in-law, Charles Mason, found something that was to dramatically change their lives. Some of their cattle had strayed off and joined a wild herd. Their tracks led the two cowboys up onto the top of Mesa Verde into an area that was new to them. While resting their horses near a canyon, they walked out to the rim and scanned the terrain. They soon forgot the lost cattle. There, through the haze of falling snow, they made out the form of a massive cliff dwelling unlike any they had seen before. Rooms were stacked on top of rooms, filling the overhang from end to end. Towers rose out of the plaza, standing like turrets of a medieval castle. They later named it Cliff Palace, and in many ways, it is still considered among the most regal of Anasazi villages.

Inspired by these dwellings, the Wetherills began an intensive exploration of Mesa Verde and adjoining areas—Utah's Grand Gulch, Arizona's Tsegi Canyon and Canyon de Chelly, and New Mexico's Chaco Canyon, to name a few. The residents of Denver, and then Chicago, were treated to displays of Anasazi mummies and artifacts, and from then on, the Mesa Verde region would act as a magnet, drawing the curious into its deep recesses.

One of the early visitors captured by the lure of Mesa Verde was Gustaf Eric Adolf Nordenskiöld, a twenty-two year-old Swedish scholar who saw the Wetherill collection in Denver in 1891 and came to the Alamo Ranch to see the Wetherills and secure a guide onto the Mesa. His short sightseeing vacation turned into an entire summer of excavating numerous ruins. Nordenskiöld encouraged the Wetherills to excavate with greater care, and through conversations about the sites began to direct them toward more analytical thinking. By the time he departed for Sweden in September, he had permanently influenced the brothers.

At the Durango depot, Nordenskiöld's collection of relics was detained by a committee of angry citizens who felt it inappropriate that a foreigner remove American artifacts to another land. After two weeks, the court dismissed the case, since no law could be found prohibiting the removal of relics from Colorado or from any other state. The collection toured Europe and now resides in the National Museum of Helsinki, Finland. Nordenskiöld's book on the summer's work, *The Cliff Dwellers of the Mesa Verde*, was a magnificent treatise, documenting the prehistoric pueblo architecture and artifacts of southwestern Colorado with text and numerous maps and photos. This publication became a major stimulus to the increasing interest in archaeology of the region.

Nordenskiöld, at Step House, had noticed a type of crude, undecorated pottery in a part of the cave devoid of pueblo architecture, and he suspected that it represented an earlier age than the flashier painted pottery found in most ruins. John Wetherill further investigated Step House the next year (1892), again noting the lack of refinement in some of the pottery in the open cave area. In 1893, Richard Wetherill identified a pre-ceramic culture in some southeastern Utah sites and named the people "Basket Makers," a name that would stick. The Step House occupations, suspected as early by both Nordenskiöld and the Wetherills, were eventually confirmed as Basketmaker III age.

Although the Wetherills were to continue their excavation of Anasazi sites for over another decade, the creation of Mesa Verde National Park in 1906 and the passage of the Antiquities Act that same year protected significant portions of land from unauthorized investigations. The era of the Wetherill work was drawing to a close.

In the wake of the Wetherills came a parade of archaeologists, from the great and near-great to some approaching the other extreme.

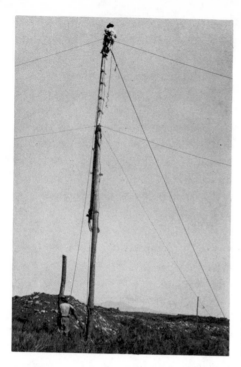

Figure 7-4   Earl Morris at the top of a pole photographing a La Plata Valley ruin from a high angle. (University of Colorado Museum.)

Edgar Lee Hewett of the Archaeological Institute of America—who was largely responsible for the passage of the 1906 Antiquities Act and the establishment of Mesa Verde National Park and many national monuments in the region—led a party of three fledgling Harvard undergraduates into the McElmo Canyon area in 1907 with the purpose of surveying for prehistoric sites. The lure of the archaeology there captured at least two of them: Sylvanus (Vay) Griswold Morley and Alfred (Ted) Vincent Kidder. In 1908 Morley excavated Cannonball Ruin, but both went on to conduct most of their work outside of Colorado.

Jesse Walter Fewkes came to Mesa Verde in 1908. He served as Park Superintendent for the next 12 years while clearing, excavating, and stabilizing many ruins. It appears that his romantic perspectives on archaeology were at least partially responsible for substandard results in data collection.

Earl Morris began his professional career in the Mesa Verde area, digging there from 1913 until 1940. He chased the Anasazi across northern Arizona and New Mexico but made many of his most significant finds along the Animas and La Plata Rivers. Under his hand, the culture of the Basketmakers began to take shape.

In the company of Morris in 1913 was a young Swarthmore student named Ralph Linton. His summer adventure included being trapped alone in a high Johnson Canyon cliff dwelling overnight, where the cold compelled him to strip the ruin of support beams to burn for heat. Linton went on to become a much acclaimed ethnologist, although he first returned to Mesa Verde to excavate and stabilize ruins in 1920.

Jean Jeançon of the Colorado Historical Society excavated in the Piedra Basin during 1921, working on the now-famous Chimney Rock ruins. He was joined in 1922 by Frank H. H. Roberts, Jr., more than ten years before Robert's excavations at Lindenmeier.

In 1921, Jesse Nusbaum replaced Fewkes as Mesa Verde Park Superintendent, and from then until 1929, a significant upgrading in archaeological research took place at the Park. One of the more notable achievements was to follow up Nordenskiöld's observations of early pottery in Step House. Nusbaum went back with a crew that he had trained and exposed a number of Basketmaker III pithouses, thus expanding the known cultural range at Mesa Verde.

Tree-ring research was in full swing during the early 1920s, and many ruins contributed portions of their posts and beams to the growing collections at the Laboratory of Tree-Ring Research in Tucson. The astronomer A. E. Douglass personally made collecting trips into southwest Colorado in the formative days of dendrochronology (see Chapter 4).

In August of 1927, having worked on Pecos Pueblo (near Santa Fe) since 1915, Ted Kidder invited a number of archaeologists to Pecos. His aim in calling the conference was to somehow sort out the data being collected across the region and make some sense out of it through the formulation of a chronologically-based developmental scheme. Ultimately, he was not successful in merging the Mogollon and Hohokam to the south and west with the more northern Anasazi, but his terminology for the Anasazi found general acceptance and is still in use by many today. Basically, the communal-living horticulturalists of the Four Corners were divided into three Basketmaker and five Pueblo categories, extending during Pueblo V times into the historic pueblo villages along the Rio Grande of New Mexico and the Hopi settlements in northern Arizona. Many subsequent workers in the area have broken these periods down into phases, but the Pecos Classification still has utility in comparing data across a broad region. Its development was a definite milestone in Southwestern archaeology.

In 1928, Paul S. Martin replaced Jean Jeançon at the Colorado Historical Society, and he began excavating an Anasazi ruin near Ackmen. He was lured away the next year to the Field Museum of Natural History in

Chicago, but he returned to conduct fieldwork in the same locale through 1938. The best known of the sites he dug is the Lowry Ruin. His analytical approach to the sites set a new standard in Anasazi research.

Many careers of notable archaeologists were launched or perpetuated in the shadows of the southwestern Colorado mesas since the 1920s. Al Lancaster, Al Hayes, Don Watson, Erik Reed, Gil Wenger, and Jack Rudy are a few of the many National Park Service personnel who contributed to the growing body of knowledge about the Anasazi within the borders of Mesa Verde National Park. The University of Colorado made special contributions to the discipline through the work of faculty such as Joe Ben Wheat, Robert Lister, Jack Smith, Dave Breternitz, and Frank Eddy. Dissertations and theses, too numerous to mention, were based on Anasazi investigations, and many of their authors can be found today as valuable members of the archaeological community.

As can be seen, southwestern Colorado has been the setting for myriad archaeological studies since Holmes and Jackson first glimpsed its wealth of prehistoric resources. The contributions of thousands have resulted in a good picture of Anasazi culture over the past 2,000 years but have failed to exhaust the information available in the soil of the Four Corners. Yet nearly 80 years have passed since the region was declared to be as a "sucked orange." With analytical techniques continuing to improve, our under-standing of the past lifeways will correspondingly increase. The genera-tions of archaeologists to come will be up to the challenge.

Terminology

Before examining the development sequence of the Anasazi in south-western Colorado, it seems appropriate to deal here with the terminology used by various researchers.

The Anasazi are considered to fall within the continent-wide Formative Stage, as outlined by Willey and Phillips. They had achieved a communal, sedentary lifestyle and the utilization of horticulture or agriculture compar-able to groups in the Mississippi Valley at about the same time.

Kidder's Pecos Classification distinguishes Basketmaker I - III and Pueblo I - V periods, with P-III being the final developmental period in Colorado prior to abandonment.

Subsequent to Kidder's classification have come a variety of other sys-tems, from that of Roberts in 1935 to the Dolores Archaeological Project's classification in 1979. Most often, the developmental sequence has been

(years)	PECOS SYSTEM (Kidder 1927)	ROBERTS' SYSTEM (Roberts 1935)	GILA PUEBLO SYSTEM (O'Bryan 1950)	MANCOS CANYON SEQUENCE (Reed 1958)	ALKALI RIDGE SEQUENCE (Brew 1946)	WETHERILL MESA SEQUENCE (Hayes 1946)	CHAPIN MESA SEQUENCE (Rohn 1977)	OSHARA TRADITION (Irwin-Williams 1973)	NAVAJO RESERVOIR DISTRICT (Eddy 1972)	CHIMNEY ROCK DISTRICT (Eddy 1977)	DOLORES RIVER PROJECT (Kane 1979)
1900	Pueblo V	Historic Pueblo Period							Lucero Phase		Beaver Point Phase (Shoshonean-/Athabascan Trad.)
1800											
1700											
1600	Pueblo IV	Regressive Pueblo Period							Goberna Phase (Navajo Tradition)		Sundial Phase
1500											?
1400											McPhee Ph.
1300	Pueblo III	Great Pueblo Period	Montezuma Phase	Mesa Verde Focus / McElmo Focus(?)	Montezuma Focus	Mesa Verde Phase	Cliff Palace Ph. / Far View Phase			Chimney Rock Phase	Sagehen Phase (Anasazi Tradition)
1200			McElmo Phase		McElmo Focus	McElmo Phase	Mummy Lake Ph.		Arboles Ph. / Piedra Ph.		?
1100	Pueblo II	Developmental Pueblo Period	Mancos Mesa Phase	Mancos Focus	Mancos Focus	Mancos Phase / Ackmen Phase	Glades Phase		Rosa Phase		
1000								Loma Alta Phase	Sambrito Phase		Great Cut Phase (Four Corners Desert Tradition)
900	Pueblo I	Pueblo Period	Chapin Mesa Phase	Piedra Focus	Ackmen Focus	Piedra Phase	Spruce Mesa Ph.	Sky Village Phase			
800			Four Corners Phase	La Plata Focus	Abajo Focus	La Plata Phase	Twin Trees Phase	Trujillo Phase	Los Pinos Phase (Pueblo Tradition)		
700	Basketmaker III	Modified Basketmaker Period									
600											
500								En Medio Phase			
400											
300	Basketmaker II	Basketmaker Period							Desert Culture Tradition		
200											
100											
A.D. 1								Armijo Phase			
1000	Basketmaker I							San Jose Phase			
2000								Bajada Phase			
3000								Jay Phase			
4000											
5000								Cody Complex			
6000											
7000											Four Corners Paleo-Indian Tradition
8000								Clovis/Folsom Complexes			
9000											
10000 BC											

Figure 7-5   Cultural classifications for southwestern Colorado. (Nickens and Hull 1982:158.)

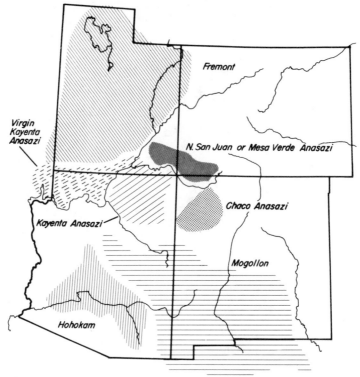

Figure 7-6   Distribution of Formative Stage cultures in the Southwest.

broken down further into phases, with differentiations made generally for groups in various drainage systems.

The Pecos Classification is regarded by many as too gross a system to be of much value in delineating cultural change, and they prefer to use phase systems tailored to specific localized developments within the geographical boundaries of the Anasazi. However, such a level of refinement would be inappropriate for the purposes of this book, and so a broad-brush treatment with the Pecos system will be used. Those interested in the differences in local sequences may refer to Figure 7-5 and the literature citations for the various schemes.

Regional Perspectives

The Anasazi are but one of three major prehistoric horticulturalist groups that existed in the American Southwest. The other two, the Mogollon (pronounced mō-gē-ōn′) and the Hohokam (pronounced hō′-hō-kom), are located to the south and west of the Anasazi. In addition, there is a Great Basin culture to the north of the Anasazi that is known as the Fremont, dealt with in Chapter 8. All of the groups appear to have emerged from the Desert Culture Archaic, with the Mogollon probably the first to have cultivated plants, pithouses, and ceramics (ca. 300 B.C. at the latest). These cultural attributes then appear to have spread west to the Hohokam by 100 B.C. and north to the Anasazi by A.D. 1.

The Mogollons are thought to be the ancestors of the Zuni puebloans of northwestern New Mexico. The Hohokam can now be seen as the Pima and Papago near Phoenix and Tucson, while the Anasazi are thought to be represented in the Rio Grande puebloans of New Mexico, from Albuquerque to Taos, and the Hopi of northern Arizona. What happened to the Fremont is problematical, but some probably melted into the non-horticultural Utes who were moving through much of the same territory.

The primary stimulus behind the great change from a nomadic to a sedentary lifestyle was the introduction of corn, a crop presumably developed in the highlands of Mexico several thousand years earlier. Once incorporated in the cultures of the Archaic, it brought about a variety of effects. Crops could be raised near settlements, and surplus food could be stored, increasing the stability of the social unit.

However, raising corn would have forced the Anasazi to give up their accustomed nomadic patterns to a significant degree. Some members of the family could still seasonally exploit the wild resources of distant areas, but they would have soon returned to the settlements where the remainder of the family had stayed to tend the crops. Also, as sedentary life began to develop, the accumulation of material goods would have militated against the ease of mobility to which the Archaic foragers had been so accustomed. Pottery, for example, is heavy and breakable and therefore inappropriate for nomads. However, when one lives permanently in one place, ceramics quickly become indispensible.

With greater stability in food supply and a probable drop in mortality rate through increased sedentism, the population would have begun to increase, leading to adjustments in social organization and cooperation. It is possible that somewhere in this transition, patrilineal descent (tracing one's ancestry through the father's side) and patrilocal post-marital residence (the new wife living in the husband's group), both practices generally associated with foragers, changed to matrilineal descent and matrilocal residence. It is difficult to sort out cause and effect but it is clear that the importance of the male hunter diminished with the increasing dependence on crops.

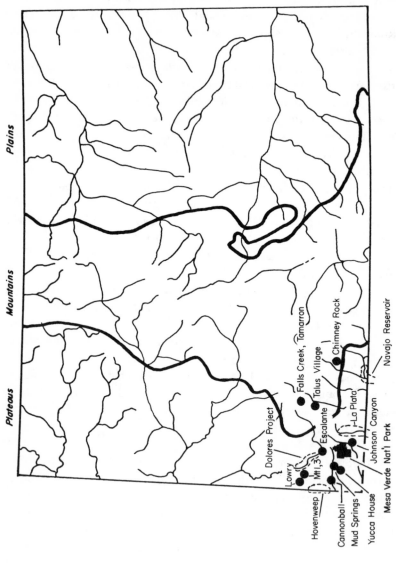

Figure 7-7   Selected Anasazi sites in Colorado.

Within the territory occupied by the Anasazi, several variants of the culture have been identified. Of greatest interest to us in Colorado are the Northern San Juan or Mesa Verde Anasazi. To the south, primarily from Farmington to Gallup, New Mexico, are the Chaco Anasazi, a culture with distinctive pottery and architectural styles and apparently a more intense trade network with Mexico. The Kayenta Anasazi, in the canyons of Arizona south of the San Juan River, also had some unique ceramic and architectural styles that distinguished them from the Northern San Juan groups. Far to the west were the Virgin Kayenta Anasazi, showing Archaic influences from the Great Basin. For the most part, our discussion will center on the Northern San Juan Anasazi, who made southwestern Colorado their home.

The Basketmakers

When Kidder set up the Pecos Classification, he included Basketmaker I, because he assumed that predecessors to known Basketmakers II groups would be found, perhaps having only slight cultural variations. Since then, it has become apparent that Basketmaker II is the first of the Anasazi farming groups. As a result, the Basketmaker I category has generally been dropped and its place usurped by the Archaic.

Basketmaker II

Earl Morris, near the time he finished his active fieldwork in the late 1930s, was drawn to the upper Animas River area north of Durango by Zeke Flora, a local collector who had made remarkable finds there. Accompanied by his laboratory assistant, Bob Burgh, Morris excavated in the two Falls Creek shelters and the Talus Village site, all providing evidence of Basketmaker II occupations. Subsequent to their work, the Colorado Highway Department excavated the nearby Tamarron site. These four sites are the only excavated representatives of BM-II in Colorado, although remains are known in southern Utah and from the Navajo Reservoir Project excavations just south across the Colorado border.

Based on good preservation in the Durango sites, it appears that Basketmaker II builders did not utilize vertical support posts in constructing the walls and roofs of their shallow, rounded houses. Logs were found lying horizontally in a shallow trench surrounding the circular floor, and it is assumed that additional logs were placed in a cribbed fashion above, building up a constricting dome. The house interiors generally contained

Figure 7-8   Earl Morris's Basketmaker II structures at Talus Village in 1940. (University of Colorado Museum.)

manos, metates, a central heating pit, and slab-lined cists. Burials were located in some of these cists. A few samples of crude, poorly-fired pottery are known from this period, so it is evident that some experimentation was going on. However, BM-II people relied mainly on baskets for containers. Other artifacts known to be associated with BM-II include atlatls, bone awls, scrapers, drills, bone gaming pieces, and cordage for nets and snares. Most of these artifact types persist throughout the remaining Anasazi periods.

Tree-ring dates for the BM-II period in the Falls Creek shelters encompass the time between A.D. 46 and A.D. 260. Talus Vilage has been dated to around A.D. 330.

Basketmaker III

The Basketmaker III period is far better represented in Colorado. Tree-ring dates place this occupation roughly between A.D. 450 and A.D. 700. Early BM-III shallow pit structures with four main vertical support posts and surrounding side posts give way in later BM-III times to similar, but deeper, pit structures with benches and crawl holes. An antechamber is generally located to the south, separated from the main room by a slab or adobe partition or by an earthen wall with a crawl hole. These antechambers vary in size and shape. The finding of metates between the hearth and

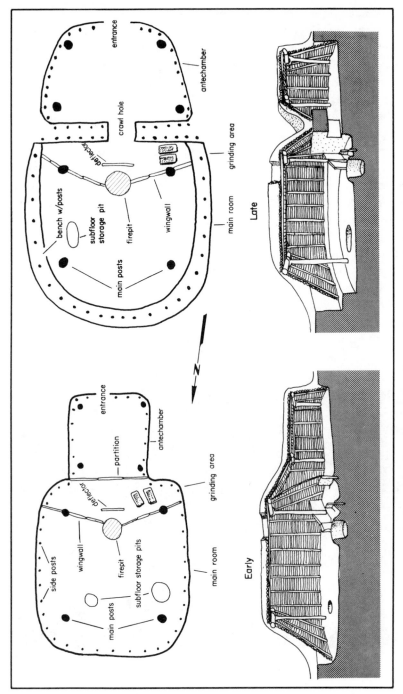

Figure 7-9   Plan and cut-away views of two examples of Basketmaker III pithouse styles.

antechamber (in an area often demarcated on the north by wingwalls) suggests a primary work area. (It should be noted that in *all* Anasazi periods, though certain architectural trends have been identified, there are many "aberrant" styles that do not fit the typical mode.)

Basketmaker III pithouses have been excavated at many locations in Colorado. Step House Cave at Mesa Verde was investigated by Jesse Nusbaum in 1926, and some houses on top of Chapin Mesa have been incorporated into an excellent interpretive sequence for visitors to the national park. A considerable number of pithouses have been found in the Dolores River valley in the course of the major archaeological project currently under way there. Basketmaker remains are also known in the Yellow Jacket area to the west and along many of the southward-flowing drainages between Mesa Verde and the headwaters of the San Juan river to the east.

During Basketmaker III, settlement patterns vary from isolated farmsteads with a single pithouse and perhaps a few surface storage structures made of posts and adobe (jacal), to a cluster of 12 or more houses.

The first good ceramics appear during BM-III. Although typically an undecorated gray ware, some pottery does have decorations—generally a black mineral or vegetable pigment painted in a simple, sometimes assymetrical style on a white surface (black-on-white or B/W).

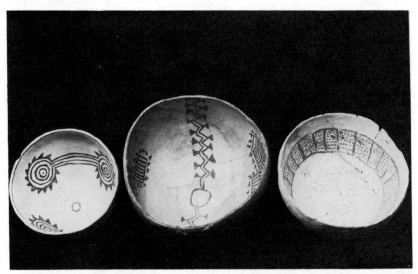

Figure 7-10   Decorated Basketmaker III bowls from the La Plata drainage sites of Morris. (Left to right) C.U. No. 9559, site 19, La Plata B/W; C.U. No. 9555, site 22, La Plata B/W; C.U. No. 3218, site 22, Chapin B/W. (S. Cassells photo.)

Figure 7-11   Jesse Nusbaum's 1926 excavation of Basketmaker III pithouses in Step House Cave. (Western History Department, Denver Public Library.)

Figure 7-12   High angle view of a Basketmaker III pithouse excavated in 1939 by Earl Morris at site Ignacio 7:26 in Hidden Valley, north of Durango. Note crawl hole into long, narrow antechamber, a bench with support beams, the metates in the work area, and the central fire pit. Instead of a four post main support arrangement, there are six main posts embedded in the edge of the bench (outlined in white). (University of Colorado Museum.)

The Puebloans

Pueblo I

The change from Basketmaker III to Pueblo I was gradual, but in the end P-I is quite distinct from BM-III. Rectangular jacal surface rooms become the actual habitations, connected in an apartment-like manner with smaller storage rooms attached behind. The pithouse appears to be in transition from serving as a dwelling to being used for ceremonial purposes. Wingwalls are still incorporated in the pithouse, but the antechamber has been replaced by a narrow ventilator shaft. In anticipation of the succeeding, fully developed ceremonial kiva structures of Pueblo II and III, the P-I pithouse has been termed a "protokiva." Sites of P-I age are often larger than those of earlier stages, with one of Mesa Verde's Badger House clusters a good example of this architectural pattern. Dates for P-I fall generally between A.D. 750 and A.D. 900. Pottery decoration shows some change from BM-III, in the use of neck bands and a greater tendency for decorative symmetry with painted surfaces.

Figure 7-13   Two neck-banded Moccasin Gray vessels of Pueblo I age. (Left to right) C.U. No. 2876, site 13 between the Mancos and La Plata Rivers, cooking pot with loop handle; C.U. No. 3782, site 33 near Johnson Canyon, utility vessel. (S. Cassells photo.)

Figure 7-14   Two Pueblo I Piedra B/W bowls from site 33 of Morris near Johnson Canyon. (Left to right) C.U. No. 3899; C.U. No. 2924. (S. Cassells photo.)

Pueblo II

The subsequent Pueblo II period (ca. A.D. 900 - 1100) is characterized by a development of masonry house construction, generally in rectangular or curved room block arrangements. The fully-developed kiva—with ventilator shaft, a southern recess (altar), deflector, firepit, *sipapu* (hole symbolizing the entrance to the spirit world), bench, wall niches, and pilasters (masonry columns for roof beam support)—appears at this time, generally located south of the room blocks in the "plaza" area. Prehistoric kivas, much like those in modern pueblo settlements, probably served as combination religious and social centers for male members of particular clans. Figures 7-15 through 7-18 show some varieties of kivas.

As was mentioned earlier, standardized settlement models can often prove inadequate when confronted by the reality of specific archaeological data. At site 5 MT 3 near Yellow Jacket, Joe Ben Wheat found good evidence of a P-II village made up of jacal rooms completely encircling a central plaza. A kiva was located in the center of the plaza. Subsequent P-III construction obliterated some of the P-II post holes, and the kiva was modified somewhat, but the early features are still readily apparent. In the Dolores Valley are P-II villages (Grass Mesa Subphase of McPhee Phase) composed of pithouse habitations rather than surface room blocks. It is obvious that pithouse and jacal architecture was functional, and not surprisingly, held an attraction to certain segments of Anasazi society long after they had been replaced by more modern building styles elsewhere.

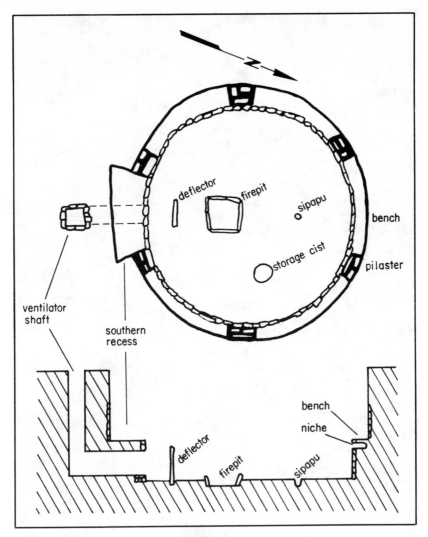

Figure 7-15   Plan view and profile of standard Mesa Verde kiva.

Figure 7-16   Standard kiva form, 5 MT 1, the Porter Pueblo, in the Yellowjacket area. (University of Colorado Museum.)

Figure 7-17   Detail of painted kiva at Lowry Ruin in the early 1930s. Note subfloor ventilator and the poles between the pilasters. (Colorado Historical Society.)

Figure 7-18   The unusual Kokopelli kiva from the Yellow Jacket area. The figure, known also as the "humped-back flute player," is common in Anasazi rock art and on painted pottery. Here the body has been dug into the kiva floor, refilled with other soil, and then plastered over. Probably because of the Kokopelli "power," the builders found no need to put a "sipapu" (spirit hole) in the kiva floor. (University of Colorado Museum.)

Figure 7-19   View of Pueblo II post hole outlines indicating jacal roomblocks, partially obliterated by Pueblo III construction. The kiva at top is P II, with some P III modifications. The site is 5 MT 3 near Yellow Jacket. (University of Colorado Museum.)

Figure 7-20   Mancos corrugated vessels of P II and P III age. (Left to right) C.U. No. 4103; C.U. No. 9596; C.U. No. 23009. (S. Cassells photo.)

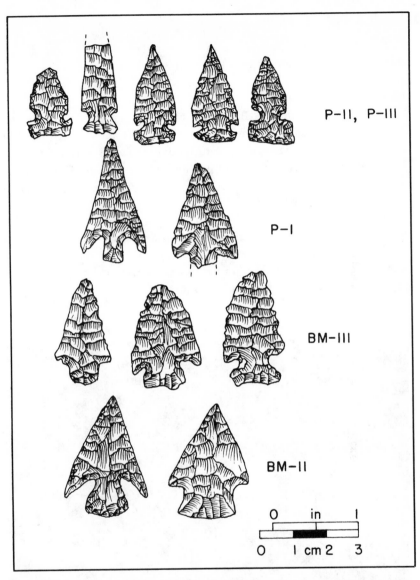

P–II, P–III

P–I

BM–III

BM–II

Figure 7-21 Selected Anasazi projectile point styles, ranging from BM II dart points to smaller side-notched arrow points of P II/III. (Modified from Nickens and Hull 1982:195.)

Pueblo III

The climax of Anasazi culture in southwestern Colorado came during Pueblo III, between about A.D. 1100 and A.D. 1300. The masonry skills acquired during P-II were further honed in the construction of large multi-storied pueblos.

On the Mesa Verde, P-III farmers built their massive communities beneath cliff overhangs. The reasons for this are not totally understood, but proximity to the springs that discharged out of the walls must have been a factor. Also, the overhangs would provide protection from the elements.

P-III fields would still have been on the mesa tops, necessitating an often dangerous climb up sheer cliffs. Most crops were dependent upon available rainfall for survival. However, there is evidence for some water control on the mesas, mostly small check dams to slow the valuable run-off, but larger water impoundments and ditches have also been found. These modifications of the ground surface could reduce the impact of the inevitable dry periods, providing some assurance of a successful crop.

Figure 7-22   Mesa Verde B/W mugs of P III age from 5 MT 3, in the Yellow Jacket vicinity. (Left to right) C.U. No. 13761; C.U. No. 13711; C.U. 13719. (S. Cassells photo.)

Figure 7-23   Mesa Verde B/W vessels of P III age. (Left to right) C.U. No. 4229, Morris site 41 on the La Plata, olla; C.U. No. 9334, bowl. (S. Cassells photo.)

Pottery of the P-III Mesa Verde Anasazi includes a wide variety of styles. Corrugated ware, first found in P-II times, was made by indenting portions of the clay coils to form patterns and sometimes closely resembles the basketry that pottery originally imitated. Other ceramic styles associated with Pueblo III include the distinctive B/W mugs, ladles, bowls, and ollas.

To the north and west of Mesa Verde, in addition to the standard Northern San Juan Anasazi pueblos (open air, not cliff dwellings), are some large P-III communities with dissimilar traits. Instead of room blocks that were enlarged through time as need dictated (Mesa Verde style), some showed forethought in planning and design. Large "great kivas" can be detected in some, and the manner in which many of the kivas were incorporated within large quadrangles provided additional evidence of intrusive traits. These sites have been termed Chacoan "outliers," indicating an expansion of some sort out of the Chaco Canyon center in northwestern New Mexico. Colorado Chaco sites include Lowry Ruin, Escalante Ruin, Yucca House, and Mud Spring Ruin. Far to the east, high above the Piedra River between Pagosa Springs and Durango, is Chimney Rock, an area of intense Anasazi occupation over many periods. Most spectacular of its ruins is another Chacoan outlier, the Chimney Rock Pueblo.

Why Chaco villages are found so far north is not fully understood. We

Figure 7-24   The Chimney Rock Pueblo, a Chacoan outlier in the Northern San Juan region. Note the incorporation of the kiva within a large quadrangle, a Chacoan trait. Also the pueblo has a "preplanned" appearance, as opposed to the more typical "add-on" construction pattern in Mesa Verde sites. (Frank Eddy, University of Colorado.)

know that the Chaco people had extensive connections outside of their population center, based in part on a massive road system that can still be seen radiating out of Chaco Canyon. The Colorado Chaco sites may have been centers for trade with the Northern San Juan Anasazi or storage points for resources obtained in the region. The communities may have been built through the relocation of entire Chaco villages in New Mexico or perhaps were actually Mesa Verde people who were influenced by Chacoan "missionaries." Whatever the case, these villages were beginning to be built about A.D. 1090 and were abandoned by A.D. 1140, an occupation of only 50 years. At about the same time the villages were being depopulated in Colorado, the Chaco culture of New Mexico also was dying out, an indication of intimate ties across a wide region.

What Happened to the Anasazi?

Beginning about A.D. 1200, building activity diminished among the Mesa Verde Anasazi, the last construction taking place at Long House Ruin in A.D. 1280. By then, many settlements appear to have been emptying.

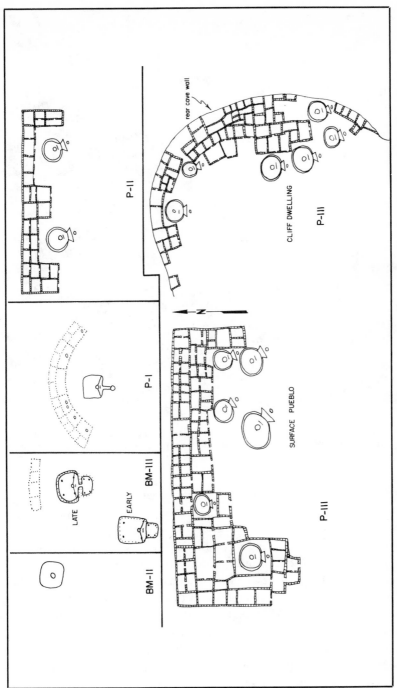

Figure 7-25   Idealized sequence of Anasazi architectural development in the Northern San Juan region by period.

The sun is rising on this southwestern Colorado mesa to find a pithouse engulfed in flames and villagers scrambling to save lives and salvage a few possessions. Given the amount of highly combustible tinder inside such structures, this scene must have been common.

Speculations in the past have centered on Athabascan raiders (ancestors of the Navajo and Apache) driving the Anasazi from their towering apartments. The traditional Hopi-Navajo conflicts in Arizona were used as supportive evidence for such a hypothesis. Archaeological evidence, however, does not indicate the entrance of Athabascans into the Southwest until well over one hundred years *after* the Anasazi left.

Climate change is a much more likely cause of the abandonment of many Anasazi sites. Dendrochronologists, studying the growth rates of trees from the area, have identified a worsening drought, beginning about 1160 and continuing for over 30 years. Later droughts between 1276 and 1299 would have done further damage. In normal years, the climate and soils of southwestern Colorado are sufficient to produce crops of corn, beans, and

squash. However, a late spring cold period or an early fall frost, coupled with a slightly substandard season of rain, would doom the domestic plant growth.

A growing scarcity of trees was perhaps another factor in the abandonment of the pueblos. The dense stands of piñon and juniper on the mesa tops would have been cleared for cornfields and the wood used in construction and for heating, cooking, and firing pottery. As population increased, the decline in the wood supply would have accelerated, leaving the cliff-dwellers with a sense of growing precariousness of life in the country that had been home for centuries.

The entire region was unlikely to have been depopulated through a single or even several mass migrations. The continuation of building at some

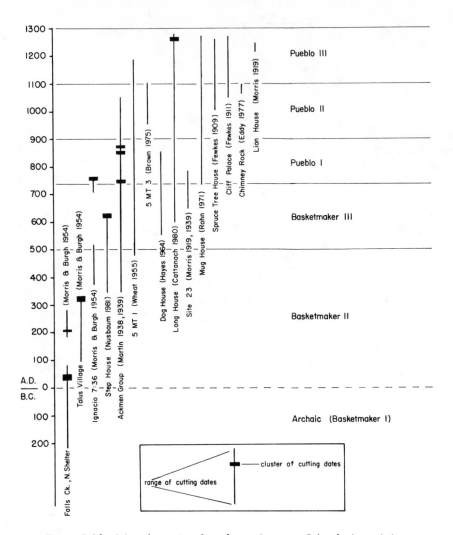

Figure 7-26   Selected tree-ring dates for southwestern Colorado Anasazi sites.

pueblos long after the abandonment of others suggests a slow movement, perhaps a few families at a time, trickling out of the canyons and basins. The people probably headed south toward the warmer and better watered environs of New Mexico. There had always been some Anasazi settlements along the Rio Grande, and the slow influx of northern horticulturalists could easily have been absorbed by the natives.

The Mesa Verde Anasazi of southeast Utah and the Kayenta Anasazi of northern Arizona are most likely the groups that eventually settled near the springs flowing from the south end of Black Mesa in what is now the Hopi Reservation. The Hopi perhaps provide the best analog to the prehistoric puebloans of Colorado. Central in their spiritual life is the control of rainfall, much as it must have been over 1,000 years ago. The ceremonies of the Rio Grande pueblos, on the other hand, seem to be oriented in other directions, such as healing—a testimony to cultural adjustments to the abundant water available through irrigation.

Summary

Southwestern Colorado contains more sites per square mile than any other part of the state, a density that is matched by few other areas of the United States. All of these sites were not occupied at the same time, of course. There is good evidence, in fact, that during some periods entire regions were essentially vacant, only to be repopulated by succeeding generations of Anasazi, perhaps in response to changing environmental conditions.

In all, the development of communal living and horticulture in the Four Corners was gradual, once past the initial cultural changes that brought domesticated crops into their possession. Through time, trade networks intensified, providing the means not only for the movement of goods manufactured or collected at distant points but also for the dissemination of new ideas.

In the end, the agricultural revolution that allowed a massive population explosion began to work against the farmers, as the artificially high carrying capacity of the semi-arid west was reduced through unpredictable weather. The Anasazi packed their most precious and portable belongings and walked out of the towns they and their ancestors had worked so hard to build, leaving them as a legacy to those of us who came later.

References

On early Southwest explorers, Rivera, Escalante and Dominguez:
Cutter 1977; Bolton 1972.

On the Hayden Survey:
Holmes 1878a, 1878b; Jackson 1878.

On the Wetherill brothers:
McNitt 1957; Gillmor and Wetherill 1953.

On the Nordenskiöld explorations at Mesa Verde:
Nordenskiöld 1901; Scott 1972.
On Hewett, Kidder and Morley:
Woodbury 1973; Kidder 1957b.
On Fewkes:
Fewkes 1911, 1919.
On Morris:
Lister and Lister 1968; Morris 1978.
On Linton:
Linton and Wagley 1971.
On early Chimney Rock excavations:
Jeançon 1922; Jeançon and Roberts 1923, 1924a, 1924b, 1924c.
On Nusbaum and Step House:
Smith 1981; Nusbaum 1981.
On the Pecos Conference:
Kidder 1927; Woodbury 1973; Lister and Lister 1968.
On Paul Martin and Lowry Ruin:
Martin 1929, 1930; Martin, Roy, and von Bonin 1936.
On more recent Northern San Juan area excavations and surveys:
Lancaster and Watson 1954; Hayes 1964; Lister 1964; Breternitz 1981.
On Durango-area Basketmaker II sites:
Morris and Burgh 1954; Reed and Kainer 1978; Dean 1975.
On the Navajo Reservoir Project:
Eddy 1961, 1966, 1972.
On southern Utah Basketmaker II:
Nusbaum 1922.
On Basketmaker III sites:
Lancaster and Watson 1954; Martin 1938, 1939; Bullard 1962; Birkedal 1976; Wheat 1955; Gooding 1980; Carlson 1963; Elisha 1968; Nusbaum 1981.
On Anasazi ceramics:
Breternitz, Rohn and Morris 1974; Hayes 1964; Lister and Lister 1978; Colton 1955.
On Pueblo I sites:
Hayes and Lancaster 1975; Hayes 1964; Rohn 1971.
On Pueblo II sites:
Brown 1975; Lancaster and Pinkley 1954.
On Northern San Juan Anasazi Pueblo III sites:
Cattanach 1980; Rohn 1971; Morley 1908; Morris 1919.

On Chaco-influenced sites in Colorado:
Halasi 1979; Martin 1929, 1930; Martin, Roy, and von Bonin 1936; Eddy 1977; Fewkes 1919.

On reconstruction of climate during Anasazi times:
Dean and Robinson 1977; Schoenwetter and Eddy 1964; Weir 1977; Wykoff 1977; Lister 1969.

On the synthesis of Northern San Juan Anasazi archaeology:
Wormington 1956; Nickens 1982; Brew 1946; Kane 1979, 1981.

On tree-ring dating in southwestern Colorado:
Dean 1975; Robinson and Harrill 1974.

On Anasazi classification systems (Fig. 7-5):
Kidder 1927; Roberts 1935d; O'Bryan 1950; Reed 1958; Brew 1946; Irwin-Williams 1973; Eddy 1972, 1977; Kane 1979.

8 The Fremont

In 1928 the area of east-central Utah drained by the Fremont River attracted the attention of Peabody Museum archaeologist Noel Morss. As the result of working there during the next two years, he formulated the definition of the Fremont culture, a ceramic-possessing group that appears to have practiced some horticulture and to have been at least semi-sedentary.

Over 40 years earlier, W. H. Holmes, who had been a member of the Hayden Survey, conducted a study of pottery from Utah, describing the differences he could see within the state. Since then Julian Steward, Marie Wormington, Jesse Jennings, Melvin Aikens, Dick Ambler, and others have refined the Fremont data, attempting to determine both the origins and the ultimate fate of these people.

Compared to Utah, the state of Colorado holds relatively meager evidence of this Great Basin and northern Colorado Plateau culture. Most Fremont sites in Colorado lie in the northwest corner of the state—something of an overflow from Utah.

Five regional variants have been identified within the Fremont culture. Two of these have penetrated the Colorado borders: the Uinta and the San Rafael Fremont.

The Uinta Fremont

The Uinta Fremont in Utah occurs to the north of the San Rafael and is characterized by Uinta Gray pottery; "Fremont blades"; Rose Springs,

139

ROBERT NOEL
FARRINGTON

A pregnant Fremont mother, her two children, and elderly father, on the way home from a wood gathering foray, stop to examine the new rock art figure being pecked onto the sandstone wall of a northwestern Colorado canyon.

Uinta Side-Notched, and Desert Side-Notched projectile points; and shallow pithouses. The near-absence of unfired clay human figurines, a hallmark of Fremont elsewhere, is a negative trait of the Uinta.

Some of the best Uinta Fremont sites have been excavated in Dinosaur National Monument on both the Utah and Colorado sides. Included among these are Deluge Shelter, Mantle's Shelter, Marigold Cave, Hell's Midden, Boundary Village, Wholeplace Village, and Wagon Run, to name a few. The recognition of a pattern in architecture—shallow saucer-shaped pithouses with either a random or a four corner post support arrangement—led to the definition of the Cub Creek Phase of the Uinta Fremont by Dave Breternitz and others at the University of Colorado.

On the Colorado side of the monument, pithouses have yet to be clearly identified, although it is probable they will eventually be found.

The San Rafael Fremont

The core area of the San Rafael Fremont is to the south of the Uinta in Utah and was the type Morss first identified in 1928.

San Rafael characteristics include the presence of Emery Gray pottery and wet-laid (mortar) and dry-laid masonry granaries and habitation structures. San Rafael projectile points are similar to those of the Uinta with the probable addition of Cottonwood points, a triangular style that came into use after the disappearance of the Uinta Fremont but before the end of San Rafael times. Figurines, known in Colorado primarily from private collections, have been found in three instances. A probable figurine base came from Glade Park, while the other two were found at Rat Midden and Marigold Cave in Dinosaur National Monument.

San Rafael sites in Colorado include a number in the Canyon Pintado Historic District along the Douglas Creek drainage south of Rangely. Typically, these Fremont sites are either masonry "promontory" structures high above the canyon floors or are beehive-shaped granaries tucked in along the cliff walls.

Corn has been found in some of these sites, both in the form of pollen and as the actual cobs and kernels. Some of the corn has a closer genetic relationship to types found in Mexico than to those from the Four Corners. A study of the Canyon Pintado area has revealed that the high alkalinity and clay content of the flood plain would have precluded much successful farming there, but the alluvial fans at the mouths of side canyons would have been more productive. It is thus probably not coincidental that Fremont sites in the Douglas Creek vicinity tend to concentrate at these junctions.

Extensive midden deposits are not found at most Fremont sites, suggesting that they were not occupied for long periods of time. This would seem to support the idea that the Fremont were oriented more toward hunting and gathering (and considerable mobility) than toward horticulture.

Along the Colorado River are a few sites that may include Fremont evidence. The Sisyphus shelter and 5 GF 134 both yielded Rose Springs projectile points, and remnants of a probable pithouse was found at 5 GF 134. Radiocarbon dates from both sites fall within the Fremont range. However, no Fremont pottery turned up, and it is tenuous at best to assign Fremont affiliation without ceramics or other stronger evidence.

Fremont sites generally date between A.D. 400 and 1200 (based mostly on C14 samples rather than dendrochronology). The Uinta are thought to range from A.D. 650 to 950, while the San Rafael may extend from A.D. 700 to 1200.

Rock Art

Since the evidence of Fremont habitations is relatively meager, much attention has been drawn to a more visible cultural manifestation: rock art. Colorado's plateau country affords the would-be artist innumerable vertical rock faces on which to paint, peck, or carve. The Fremont appear to have had a predilection toward this form of self-expression, and northwest Colorado is now a massive outdoor art gallery.

Rock art can be pecked into a surface, perhaps removing a patinated surface to expose the unweathered (and contrasting) interior. This technique, as well as incising, produces a type known as a *petroglyph*. The other alternative is to paint on the rock with mineral or plant pigments, producing *pictographs*. The petroglyph, perhaps because of greater permanence, is the more frequently found rock art type here. As a word of explanation, the petroglyphs in the photographs of this chapter may give the misleading impression that they are painted instead of pecked. They have actually only been enhanced with chalk or other non-permanent material for photographic purposes.

A Fremont design can occur as a single, isolated element or as part of a large panel that has been added to over a number of years. By carefully studying the way in which designs have been pecked or painted on top of others, investigators can arrive at a relative dating of various elements and determine the development of style through time.

Common Fremont themes include animals, plants, and human-like figures with trapezoidal or triangular bodies. Headdresses and necklaces can frequently be discerned. Post-Fremont groups that inhabited the area apparently tried to imitate the art they found there, but their skills generally fell far short of the earlier artisans.

Outside Influences

Because the practice of horticulture and the use of pithouse and masonry architecture and ceramics, it has long been suggested that the Fremont derived from a more southern farming society, such as the Anasazi or the Mogollon. At present, although it is clear that the Fremont occupation coincides with the Basketmaker II through Pueblo III periods of the Anasazi, the hard data needed to prove cultural development from any other group is lacking. It is true that connections can be demonstrated with the Anasazi through the finds of Anasazi trade pottery in Fremont sites, especially in the more southern Fremont divisions. The Sevier Fremont of southwest Utah have similarities to the Virgin Kayenta Anasazi, while the San Rafael show affinities to the Anasazi of the Four Corners. However, Fremont peoples were widely distributed across the Great Basin and the Colorado Plateau, and the interaction of Fremont with Anasazi cannot account for all the regional variations.

Fremont rock art figures with shields and horned headdresses have indicated to some that there was a relationship to the Northern Plains of Wyoming and Montana. The "weeping eye" motif, an artistic element of importance to cultures of the southeastern United States, can also be found in some Fremont panels. Perhaps the motif filtered in through Wyoming.

Some of the curvilenear elements, such as spirals, circles, zigzags, and meanders, are known from the Great Basin of Nevada, as well as from Anasazi sites.

Stylistic similarities to many surrounding groups have been noted, something not entirely unexpected. Independent invention is not a reasonable explanation for all of them. Interaction with reciprocal influences must have taken place during Fremont times.

At present, rock art can be dated only by inferences to other data, and it cannot be stated with confidence whether, for example, shields occur first on the Northern Plains or in the Fremont area, or in which direction influences would have been felt. Rock art studies have been quite suggestive but are not yet definitive in terms of detailing cultural diffusion or other processes.

Summary

A variety of Fremont types exists, primarily across the state of Utah. Portions of only two, the Uinta and the San Rafael, appear to have spread into northwest Colorado.

The Fremont were differentiated from the Great Basin Archaic by perhaps A.D. 400, developing viable lifeways that lasted until about A.D. 1200. The ultimate source of the Fremont is still speculative, be it the Archaic foragers themselves or some outside culture or cultures.

Architectural styles have been used to help distinguish between regional variations. The Uinta dug pithouses, while the San Rafael built masonry structures. Both used rock shelters. Ceramic differences —Uinta Gray in the Uinta area and Emery Gray in the San Rafael—have also been recognized. Some rock art styles have been associated with each group, although some elements overlap.

The Fremont practiced horticulture to some extent. A variety of corn types have been found, a few with little similarity to those grown by other Southwestern farming groups but perhaps better suited to the drier and cooler northern regions. Hunting and gathering were still an integral part of the Fremont lifeway. Habitation sites in Colorado show little in the way of extensive midden accumulation, and the stratigraphy in rock shelters indicates primarily intermittent occupations.

Why the Fremont disappeared by about A.D. 1200 is problematical. With their strong hunting and gathering base, any dramatic climatic change would not have had as dramatic an effect on them as it did on the

Anasazi. Since the Fremont occupied such a broad geographical area, it is likely that they dispersed in several directions, perhaps being absorbed back into the Great Basin foraging tradition with the Paiutes and Utes or into the Northern Plains cultures. Whatever happened, the builders of masonry and semi-subterranian structures ceased their long-standing patterns of culture and melted away, abandoning one of the more northern horticultural adaptations in the country.

Figure 8-1   Representative Fremont pottery types. (Modified from Madsen 1977.)

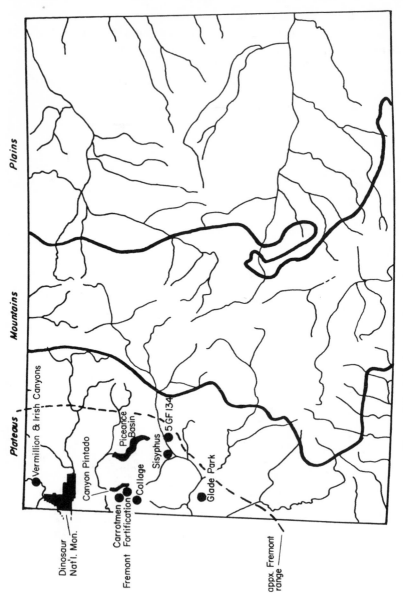

Figure 8-2   Distribution of selected Fremont sites in Colorado.

Figure 8-3   A Fremont vessel in the University of Colorado Museum collection. It was discovered during the 1948 Marigold Cave excavations (Dinosaur National Monument) by Bob Burgh. (S. Cassells photo.)

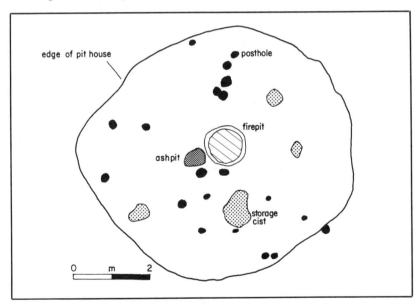

Figure 8-4   Typical Uinta Fremont (Cub Creek Phase) pithouse with randomly-placed post holes. (Modified from Breternitz 1970.)

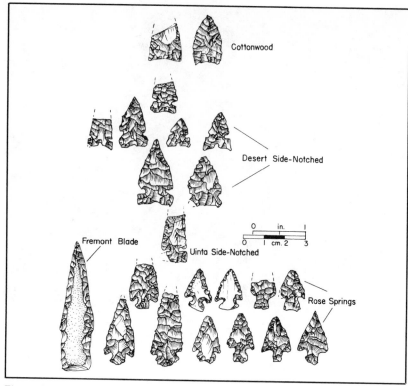

Figure 8-5   Representative types of Fremont stone tools. (All modified from Creasman 1981, except the Fremont blade from Breternitz 1970.)

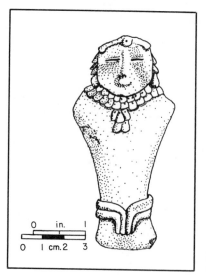

Figure 8-6   Example of typical Fremont figurine. (Modified from Morss 1954.)

Figure 8-7   A Canyon Pintado Fremont granary. (Ray Lyons, Colorado Archaeological Society.)

Figure 8-8   A Fremont masonry promontory structure (5 RB 748) along Canyon Pintado. (Cal Jennings, Colorado State University.)

Figure 8-9 Fremont Lookout Fortification, a National Register site. (Colorado Bureau of Land Management.)

entrance through bedrock

Figure 8-10 Exterior view of the largest Fremont masonry structure known in Colorado. Its name and location are being withheld until excavations are completed by Western Wyoming College. (Dudley Gardner, Western Wyoming College.)

Figure 8-11 Interior view of the Fremont structure in Figure 8-10. The present height of the masonry wall is about nine feet, indicating at least a two story building. (Dudley Gardner, Western Wyoming College.)

Figure 8-12 Bighorn sheep petroglyph at the Raftopoulos site (5 MF 610) near Irish Canyon. Note incorrect joints on rear legs. (James Blinn, Colorado Archaeological Society.)

Figure 8-13   "Bigfoot" petro-glyph with headdress from the Raf-topoulos site (5 MF 610) near Irish Canyon. (Ray Lyons, Colorado Ar-chaeological Society.)

Figure 8-14   Trapezoidal an-thropomorphic figure from 5 MF 353 in Irish Canyon. (James Blinn, Colorado Archaeological Society.)

Figure 8-15   Red pictographs from the Carrotmen Pictograph site, a National Register property. (Colorado Bureau of Land Management.)

Figure 8-16   Post-Fremont petroglyphs from the Raftopoulos site (5 MF 610) near Irish Canyon. The figures may represent dancers. (Ray Lyons, Colorado Archaeological Society.)

Figure 8-17   Fremont pictograph panel at 5 MF 492 in Vermillion Canyon. The largest figure with the necklace and headdress is in the Classic Vernal style of the Uinta Fremont. (Fred Rathbun, Colorado Archaeological Society.)

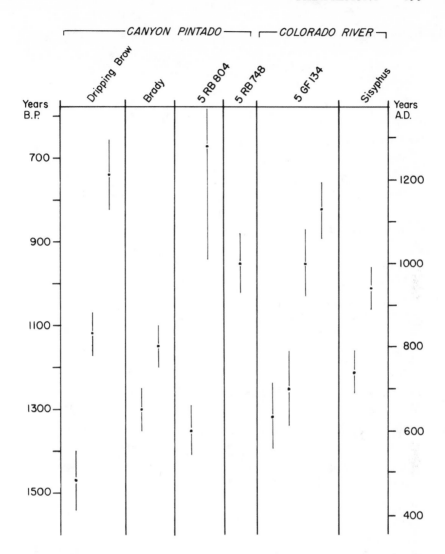

Figure 8-18   Selected range of radiocarbon dates from Canyon Pintado and the Colorado River Valley.

References

On the Morss definition of Fremont:
Morss 1931.

On Fremont regional variants:
Marwitt 1970; Ambler 1966; Schaffsma 1971.

On Fremont pottery:
Madsen 1977; Steward 1936; Rudy 1953; Aikens 1966.

On Colorado Fremont projectile points:
Holmer and Weder 1980; Gordon, et al. 1981; Creasman 1981; Breternitz 1970.

On Uinta Fremont pithouses:
Breternitz 1970.

On Fremont figurines:
Morss 1954, 1957. Lister 1951; Lister and Dick 1952.

On Dinosaur National Monument sites:
Burgh and Scoggin 1948; Dick n.d.; Leach 1966b, 1967, 1980; Lister 1951; Sheets 1969.

On 5 GF 134 and Sisyphus Shelter:
Conner and Langdon 1983; Gooding, Kihm, and Shields in prep.

On the Turner-Look site and reappraisal of the Fremont:
Wormington 1955.

On the Canyon Pintado Historic District:
Wenger 1955, 1956; Creasman 1981; LaPoint, et al. 1981.

On Collage Shelter:
Gordon, Kranzush, and Knox 1979.

On the Piceance Basin:
Grady 1980; Jennings 1974; Hurlbett 1977.

On dating the Fremont:
Marwitt 1970; Creasman 1981; Ambler 1969.

On Fremont rock art:
Schaafsma 1971; Burton 1971; Creasman 1982; LaPoint, et al. 1981; Wormington 1955.

On outside influences:
Jennings 1956; Aikens 1966, 1967; Gunnerson 1960a, 1969; Sharrock 1966; Husted and Mallory 1967.

On Fremont corn:
Cutler 1966a, 1966b; Cutler and Blake 1970.

9 The Post-Archaic of Eastern Colorado

Discussion of cultural development on the plains has been postponed for the last two chapters while the focus was on the sedentary horticulturalists of western Colorado. However, things were not stagnant on the prairies and in the eastern mountains during that time.

The ultimate stimulus of change from the Archaic foraging (Desert Culture) to the Formative in the West came from Mexico with the introduction of domesticated crops and other cultural attributes. The situation was different in eastern Colorado. Routes of diffusion were quite circuitous and came from a variety of sources. One scenario has cultural traits spreading out from the Southeast into the woodlands of the Northeast, eventually spilling onto the plains and into Colorado.

It must be remembered that diffusion is complex and only one of many possible mechanisms of change within a culture. What occurred in Colorado a millenium or more ago may have been the result of numerous influences and migrations which are not by any means fully understood. However, the spreading of ideas out of the Eastern Woodlands and Mexico, by whatever means, is documented and readily apparent.

Pertinent questions to ask when reviewing diffused cultural attributes are why some spread more rapidly than others and why some were accepted *in toto* or in a modified form, while others were not adopted at all. Selectivity in the borrowing of exotic innovations must be related in part to the compatability of the new attributes with the existing culture. The borrowed trait would probably have to satisfy the needs of the new group more quickly and better than the trait it replaced, such as ceramics for basketry.

By about 2500 B.C. evidence of change can be seen in the deep Southeast.

Early crude ceramics are the best horizon marker for those at the forefront of the revolution east of the Continental Divide. By 1000 ± B.C. sites from Illinois to New York had similar pottery. Whether the early ceramics were introduced into the Southeast from somewhere outside or were independently invented, cannot yet be determined. Ceramics appeared later in Mexico, so it does not seem likely that the influence came from that direction. Later, the introduction of corn and other cultigens in the East does provide evidence of connection to Mexico.

Since archaeologists normally consider the Archaic to be pre-ceramic, the acquisition of pottery moves its makers into the Formative Stage and an initial culture known as the Early Woodland. Although this break appears drastic on paper, the transition from the Archaic to the Woodland was apparently not disruptive. Early Woodland peoples retained their hunting and gathering economy and simply added a new skill — making pottery — to their repertoire.

From this Early Woodland base, a culture known as Adena developed in Ohio about 800 B.C. The Adena people built tombs that include both simple conical mounds and elaborate effigy earthworks. The Hopewell, centered in Illinois, arose within the next 500 years, becoming equally complex culturally. Ornaments and other artifacts have been discovered in their log-lined burial vaults. These grave goods include a number of exotic items that originated in such diverse places as Yellowstone Park, the Gulf Coast, and the Appalachian Mountains—ample testimony to a widespread trade network. Corn and other cultigens came into use during the Woodland Tradition, and the sedentary lifestyle became more common.

While this was transpiring far to the east, the dwellers on the western plains continued to go about their long-standing nomadic pursuit of available wild game and wild plants.

The Plains Woodland

By A.D. 1 traits of the Eastern Woodlands had infiltrated Nebraska and Kansas; and in Colorado hints of Plains Woodland culture are documented a little more than 100 years later. It is assumed that movement of Woodland ideas came up the Missouri River and spread west along the Platte, Arikaree, Republican, Smoky Hill, and Arkansas drainages that flow out across the sediment-laden plains of Colorado.

The Woodland Tradition of the Hopewell and Adena—stratified societies dominated by priestly classes, preoccupied to a degree with

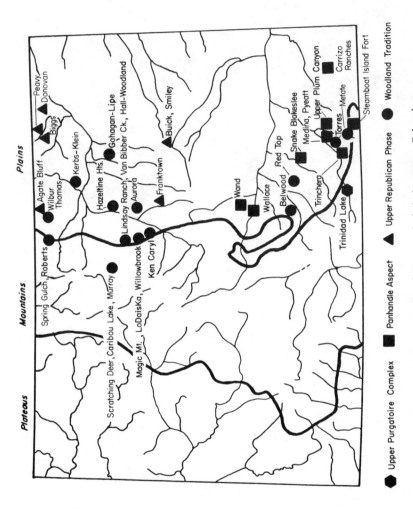

Figure 9-1   Selected sites of the post-Archaic in eastern Colorado.

Figure 9-2   Torres Cave, while under excavation by the Colorado Archaeological Society in 1977. (Ray Lyons, Colorado Archaeological Society.)

mortuary practices, and resplendent with ornate and exotic handicrafts— was not transferred intact onto the Colorado flatlands. As with most diffused traits prior to the advent of instant mass communication, the farther the recipient culture from the nuclear area, the fewer the traits accepted and the less resemblance there is to the donor group. The Plains Woodland of Colorado, dating from about A.D. 100 to A.D. 1000, is then, as expected, an extremely attenuated version of the eastern prototypes.

In Illinois and the surrounding region, Woodland architecture generally took the form of circular surface huts with post supports around the perimeter. Colorado's Woodland inhabitants left few clues to their architectural patterns. Many sites here including the following are in some kind of natural shelter: Wilbur Thomas, Hall-Woodland, LoDaisKa, Willowbrook, Metate Cave, Torres Cave, Medina, Bradford House, Falcon's Nest, and Crescent, the latter four on the Ken Caryl Ranch property. These provide excellent stratigraphic sequences and outstanding preservation but tell us little about the perishable structures that may have been present during the period.

Most of the open sites, such as Magic Mountain, Spring Gulch, Scratching Deer, Caribou Lake, and Van Bibber Creek, retained concentrations of artifacts and other camp debris but no evidence of physical structures.

Figure 9-3   A "metate rock" inside Torres Cave. (Ray Lyons, Colorado Archaeological Society.)

Belwood

At the poorly-reported Belwood site in southeast Colorado, two houses thought to be of Woodland age were discovered. One was a surface structure 18 feet in diameter with eight support posts around the outside and a dry-laid masonry wall forming part of the lower house outline. The other was a shallow pithouse with an eastern entrance. Its discoverer, Arnie Withers, went on to propose these as part of the Graneros Focus, dating A.D. 450-750.

Lindsay Ranch and Red Top Ranch

Charles Nelson excavated two Woodland-age structures at the George W. Lindsay Ranch site, located on a narrow ridge in the foothills north of Golden. Each was a stone enclosure with a diameter of about 13 feet. They were roughly square with rounded corners. The interiors included hearths and storage pits. On the basis of these finds, and in conjunction with numerous other Woodland-age sites along the foothills, Nelson named the Hog Back Phase, dating A.D. 600 to 1000.

Figure 9-4   Stone slab rings at 5 PE 27 on the Red Top Ranch. This site has been interpreted as a probable Woodland-age camp. (Jenny Anderson, Pioneer Archaeological Consultants.)

Sites with circles built of stone slabs and associated with Woodland-type projectile points have been recorded on the Red Top Ranch between the Huerfano and Apishapa rivers of southeast Colorado. No dates or pottery have been used here to confirm the Woodland assignment, but it is likely that it is correct; perhaps the sites are similar to the surface house at the Belwood site.

LoDaisKa and Magic Mountain

Two of the earliest published works on Colorado's Plains Woodland were by Henry and Cynthia Irwin, who excavated in the foothills at LoDaisKa and Magic Mountain. In addition to the lower Archaic zones (discussed in Chapter 6), they identified levels containing smaller corner-notched and often serrated projectile points, along with distinctive pottery generally associated with the Woodland.

The Woodland ceramic tradition is identifiable by its exterior of cord-marking. Sticks or paddles were wrapped with cordage and then pressed into the wet clay on the outside of the vessel. The true paddle and anvil technique employed the use of either a hand or a flat object (perhaps of stone) on the interior of the pot, while paddling or impressing the exterior. Coiling, the method of manufacture preferred by the Anasazi, was not used by Woodland potters. Piece building and/or hand molding accounted for the

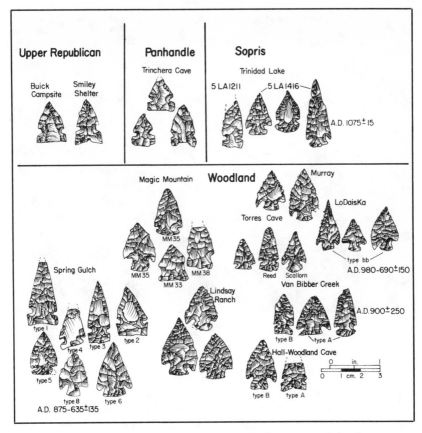

Figure 9-5   Post-Archaic projectile points from eastern Colorado.

basic vessel shape, followed by the refining with the paddling or impressing. Although some cord-marking may have been intended as decoration, the principle function of the cord impressions was to shape and bind the clay together. Woodland pots generally have pointed (conoidal) bottoms with either straight or incurving rims.

In addition to the diagnostic corner-notched projectile points and the conical cord-marked pottery, Woodland artifact assemblages include a full range of scrapers, drills, manos, metates, bone awls, and a variety of ornaments of stone, bone, and shell. Few of these are of value in distinguishing the Woodland from other cultures at earlier or later dates.

Plains Woodland Subsistence

The Plains Woodland peoples in Colorado appear to have subsisted on an

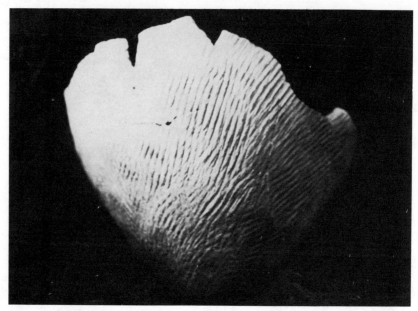

Figure 9-6 Bottom portion of a cord-marked Woodland pottery vessel found near Bethoud, Colorado, and in the C.U. museum collections. (S. Cassells photo.)

assortment of wild plant and animal species. The evidence for domestication is slight. Bison, elk, deer, and rabbit composed the bulk of their meat sources, while wild seeds, such as goosefoot and pigweed, would have been collected for additional sustenance. Evidence from Trinchera Cave suggests that the cultivation of corn may have begun toward the end of the Plains Woodland period. However, in no case would the Woodland people of Colorado have been more than incipient horticulturalists—with a thin veneer of farming over their substantial hunting and gathering base.

Hunting practices during the Woodland would likely have been opportunistic for the most part. Men with atlatls or the newly acquired bow and arrow would always be on the alert for wild game and would seriously attempt to bring down any within range. There were apparently times, however, when large-scale cooperative planning was employed, much as the Plano hunters had done at Olson-Chubbuck and Jones-Miller, collectively driving bison into places where they would become immobilized and easy to kill.

Game Drives

There are vestiges of such practices during the Woodland in eastern

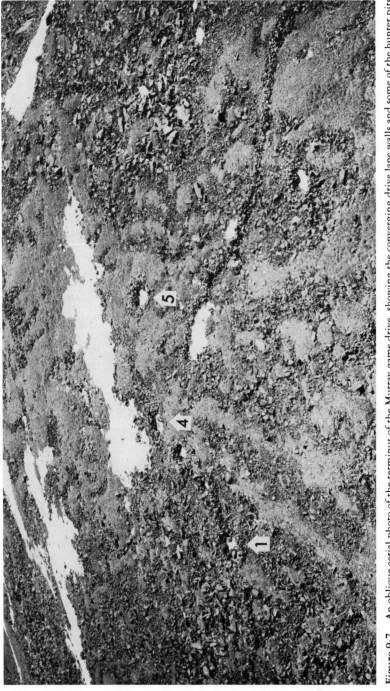

Figure 9-7   An oblique aerial photo of the terminus of the Murray game drive, showing the converging drive lane walls and some of the hunter pits (arrows). (James Benedict and the *Plains Anthropologist.*)

Colorado, the best documented of these being the high altitude game drives along the Continental Divide west of Boulder studied by James Benedict. Murray is one of at least 35 such sites of varying ages recorded in about a 15 mile stretch of the Front Range crest. At Murray there are 13 stone walls, 16 pits of varying shapes and sizes, and 483 cairns. The system is presumed to operate by funneling grazing animals (e.g. bighorn sheep) upslope from the grassy Albion-Kiowa peaks saddle to the crest of Albion Ridge. Many of the cairns along the drive lanes consist of piles of rocks, but some are long slabs jutting up in the air and braced with chinking at their bases. Benedict thinks it possible that these tall rocks were decorated with sticks or hides during the hunt, giving the illusion that additional humans were present and helping to keep the quarry contained and moving along the route. (There is ethnographic evidence for such practices among the Copper Eskimos.) Once the animals reached the constricting walls, hunters concealed in the nearby pits would ambush them.

The nearby Scratching Deer site appears to have been occupied about 300 years earlier than the time Murray was in use and likely served as a camp for

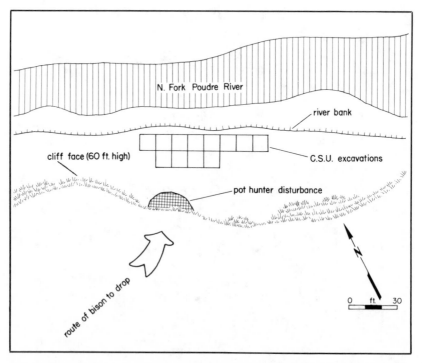

Figure 9-8   Plan view of the Roberts Buffalo Jump. (Modified from Witkind 1971.)

the hunters who used another drive system (5 BL 68) at the east end of the ridge.

Far to the southeast on the Carrizo Ranches in Baca and Las Animas Counties, drive lanes that may fall into the same period have been found. Rock walls or alignments, oriented on flat ground at right angles to distant canyons, probably formed a conduit along which hunters could drive bison to a fatal fall over the edge of a cliff.

Northwest of Fort Collins near the Wyoming border is the Roberts Buffalo Jump, a site with a massive 60 foot cliff below which lay a bed of bison bones and associated camp debris. Assignment of this site to a particular culture or cultures is difficult in that pot hunters disturbed portions of the bone bed, making correlation of artifacts to stratigraphic units difficult in some cases. A flat-bottomed pot of probable Shoshonean origin does suggest a protohistoric use of the jump, but some projectile points recovered there (including some found on the surface) indicate it could be a multi-component site of Woodland and post-Woodland prehistoric hunters. At any rate, Roberts is one of the more southern bison jumps in North America, a representative of a strong tradition throughout Wyoming, Montana, and western Canada that continued into historic times.

Plains Woodland Burials

As was mentioned previously, the Hopewell and Adena had a significant preoccupation with the dead—witness the large number of complex burial mounds built during the peak of the culture. No large-scale mounds have been found much west of the Missouri River, but less elaborate versions of similar interment practices have been observed in Plains Woodland sites in Colorado.

Hazeltine Heights and the Gahagan-Lipe sites are two ossuaries with multiple burials of seven and six individuals respectively. Both sites are primary burials, the bodies being placed in the ground shortly after death (inferred from the articulated nature of the skeletons at time of discovery). The knees were generally bent (flexed) and the legs sometimes drawn up toward the chest. Grave offerings included marine shells (*Olivella* and *Unio*), Woodland projectile points, atlatl weights, and bone beads. In some instances, the grave offerings may have been intentionally broken at the time of burial.

The Kerbs-Klein site is another ossuary, this one with six individuals interred. It differs from the two aforementioned cemeteries, by having all secondary bundle burials. A secondary burial is one that has been placed in

A variety of domestic tasks are being performed in this camp of Woodland people along the eastern foothills of Colorado's Rocky Mountains. (Left to right) A woman grinds seeds with the aid of a mano and grinding slab, another is working with a fresh hide from a deer, while a third is shaping a ceramic vessel by paddling the exterior with a cord-wrapped stick.

the final grave after being "stored" elsewhere for a time. This "storage" could have been on an open scaffold, in a tree, or even in another subterranean grave. At Gahagan-Lipe, the defleshed bones were put into bundles, perhaps tied together with cordage, and then buried. Whether all six individuals were buried at once (in separate graves), as if the deceased were "saved up" for a year or season and interred in one large ceremony, or if they were periodically brought to the same cemetery, is not known. Grave goods included only a few items of ground and chipped stone and a bead. In neither case was Woodland pottery found in the graves, and the assignment of this culture was made on the basis of C14 dates and pattern similarities with Woodland burials elsewhere.

The Aurora burial is a recent discovery that generated considerable media attention in the Denver area. It is an interesting combination of both

ROBERT NOEL
FARRINGTON

In the background, a mother converses with her child. To the right one man is detaching flakes from a core by indirect percussion (hammerstone to antler tine to core), and the other flintknapper is finishing a tool by fine pressure flaking with an antler tip. Skin covered huts, encircled with stones, serve as shelters. The exterior cooking hearth suggests a warm season.

primary and secondary burial practices. The excavation there in 1982 revealed a primary inhumation of an adult male on top of which were the somewhat scattered remains of a five year-old child. That the child's bones were not in a tight bundle may indicate a loose burial or perhaps only that they were subsequently disturbed by something such as rodent burrowing. The excavator of the site, Mark Guthrie, has suggested the possibility that the secondary burial was a mark of status for the adult male, a treatment consistent with stratified societies elsewhere. A broken atlatl weight and a broken pendant were included as grave goods, perhaps intentionally fragmented during the burial ceremony.

Status is not easy to prove, given the available data of Woodland times on the Colorado plains. It has generally been assumed that status and social stratification here would be relatively undeveloped—the egalitarian practices seen in most foraging societies would be more likely. But given the status differentiation observed in the more eastern Woodland, it might be expected that some of these traits made it to Colorado. It certainly merits consideration in future studies of the post-Archaic on the High Plains.

Colorado Woodland Taxonomy

In reviewing the available Woodland data from Colorado, I have personally found it difficult to see much difference across the entire eastern half of the state throughout the period.   Presently, the Parker Focus signifies sites centered in the Denver Basin and to the north; the Hog Back Phase, those in the foothills and mountains west of Denver; and the Graneros Focus, sites in the southeastern part of the state. But there is no discernable difference in the corner-notched projectile points considered diagnostic for the period, and variations in ceramic styles (Parker: cord-marked with straight or slightly incurving rims; Hog Back: cord-marked; Graneros: cord-marked with straight or slightly outcurving rims) are based on such small samples as to make comparisons useful only as suggestions for future study. Taxonomies are needed in the study of prehistory, but in this case progressing beyond the gross level of Plains Woodland seems unjustifiable, given the current data base. If good evidence and adequate samples are accumulated, then significant chronological and regional distinctions can perhaps be made.

The Upper Republican

By about A.D. 400, the southern Hopewell in the Mississippi and Louisiana area began to change dramatically into what has been termed the Mississippian culture, a lifeway that became widespread and highly influential. It flourished at one time across most of the South and extended north into Minnesota. Remnants of the Mississippians still existed in the 1700s when the French observed them in the form of the Natchez and Creek tribes.

The Mississippian pattern included the construction of large metropolitan centers for domestic and religious activities. Massive platform mounds were often built as part of an overall development plan. Community perimeters were usually surrounded by fortifications of wooden palisades and earthen embankments. The communities were generally located near fertile river bottoms where reliable corn crops could be grown.

Some social stratification is observable in the preceeding Hopewell, and the Mississippians appear to have expanded considerably on the principle. Influences from the complex Classic cultures of Mexico seem to have infiltrated the Mississippians. Forced labor was apparently used to maintain the priestly class and their monuments. Human sacrifices were included in some rituals.

By A.D. 900-1000, the Missouri River area of Kansas, Nebraska, and South Dakota began to come under the influence of the expanding Mississippian culture. Here it is termed the Central Plains Tradition or the Plains Village Tradition, which survived as the historic Arikara, Mandan, Pawnee, and other earthlodge villagers in the Missouri River Basin.

The Republican River meanders from its headwaters in eastern Colorado across northwest Kansas, southwest Nebraska, back into north-central Kansas, and eventually joins the Kansas River which flows into the Missouri at Kansas City.

The discovery of small hamlets along the course of the Republican in Nebraska gave rise to the term Upper Republican Phase, a division of the Central Plains Tradition, which began about A.D. 1000. Houses there were generally surface dwellings with square or rectangular floor plans. The perimeter was outlined with posts, and four major posts were emplaced near the room center for main roof support. Upper Republican pottery was produced by paddle and anvil technique and is cord-marked, with some obliteration of the markings especially near the bottom. Instead of the typical conical Woodland shape, Upper Republican wares are usually globular, often with incised rim decorations and sometimes with loop handles. Corn and other cultigens were mainstays in the lives of the Upper Republican people, although bison and deer continued to be hunted to a significant degree. Life was more sedentary than among the more nomadic Woodland people of the plains.

One of the first Upper Republican sites recognized in Colorado was the Buick Campsite near Limon. Arnie Withers excavated there in 1949 and later designated the Buick Focus on the basis of his finds. My criticism of premature taxonomic refinement of the Colorado Plains Woodland also applies here; the Buick Focus is based on an extremely small sample that cannot be adequately separated from Upper Republican elsewhere.

Since Withers worked at Buick, Upper Republican sites have been located at several other places. These include the Smiley Shelter, also near Limon, the Agate Bluff and Peavy rock shelters to the north of the South Platte, and several open sites, like Biggs and the recently discovered (yet unpublished) Donovan site, excavated by Tommy Fulgham and the Colorado Archeological Society. Limited radiocarbon dates for these occupa-

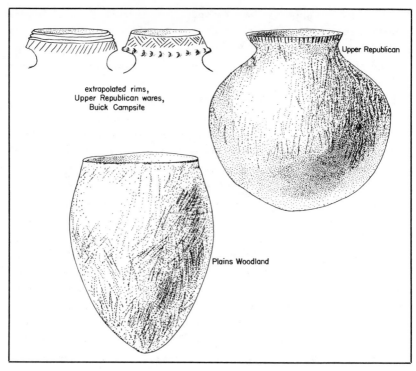

Figure 9-9   Examples of Plains Woodland and Upper Republican vessel shapes.

tions place the people here about A.D. 1100 to 1300, contemporary with those farther east.

Diagnostic Upper Republican pottery and small side-notched projectile points do not differ substantially among Colorado sites or from those in Kansas and Nebraska. The major differences involve the level of permanence and the practice of horticulture. No Upper Republican structures have been identified in Colorado to date, and with the exception of a single kernel of corn from Agate Bluff, no domesticates have been documented in Upper Republican components in the state. Not even corn pollen has been found in stratified rock shelter deposits. Bison scapula (shoulder blade) hoes, common as gardening implements in eastern Upper Republican hamlets, are also lacking in Colorado.

Collectively, this evidence seems to indicate that the Upper Republican peoples in Colorado were engaged in different activities than were their contemporaries farther east. They might have been living here year-round, following the same nomadic foraging patterns present for millenia on the

Colorado plains, but using pure Upper Republican artifacts. Or the Upper Republican sites in the state may be the remnants of camping by Kansas and Nebraska Upper Republican hunters who made only quick forays out onto the western grasslands to procure wild game. At present, the latter hypothesis is generally preferred. That being the case, the Upper Republican populations of Colorado can be considered as only minor participants in the broad trends of the state's prehistory.

As a postscript to the discussion of the Upper Republican, the excavations at Franktown Cave should be mentioned. Over many years a series of variably controlled excavations have produced a good many prehistoric artifacts. Among them are pottery fragments suggestive of vessels with Woodland conical body shapes but having Upper Republican-like rims and obliterated cord-markings. This led Withers to propose the Franktown Focus, a transitional Woodland-Upper Republican culture. Again, this appears to be an unsubstantiated or at least premature classification.

The Panhandle Aspect

Southeastern Colorado is an area of dry tableland. The border with New Mexico is demarcated by the Mesa de Maya, an elevated expanse with basaltic caprock. The Mesa forms an arbitrary line between the Central and Southern Plains. Most of southeastern Colorado is in the Arkansas River basin, and deep canyons have been cut through the sedimentary rocks by tributaries of the Arkansas.

As far back as the 1930s, people like E. B. Renaud recognized substantial prehistoric sites in the area, many with concentrations of rock slabs and pillars arranged in the rounded outlines of house rooms. They were usually located on promontories and appear to be easily defendable. This led to many being characterized as "forts."

Subsequent investigations by others began to shed additional light on the structures' functions and cultural affiliations.

One of the earlier excavations took place in 1949, when Columbia student Hal Chase worked on Snake Blakeslee, a complex site near the Apishapa River. (Incidentally, this particular project, dubbed "The Columbia University High Plains Expedition of 1949," was obliquely referred to in Jack Kerouac's catalytic novel, *On The Road*.)

Many other open-air sites of this type have been reported, including Steamboat Island Fort on the New Mexico border, sites on the Carrizo Ranches, and even a few like the Wand and Wallace sites near Pueblo far to the north. Stratified remains of this culture have been found in a variety of

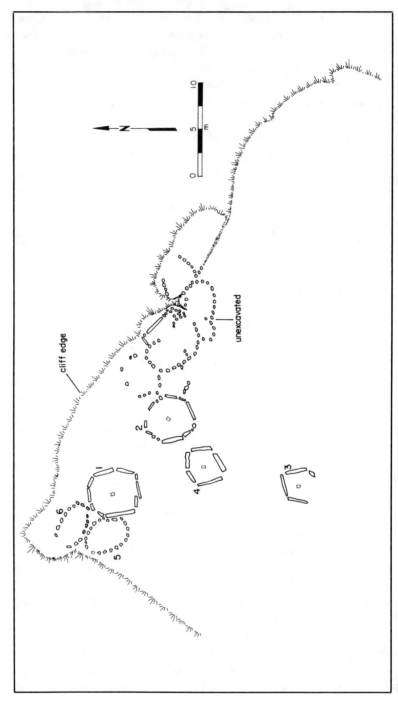

Figure 9-10 A plan view map of the Snake Blakeslee site. (Modified from an unpublished field map by Steve Ireland provided by the University of Denver.)

Figure 9-11 Unexcavated rooms at Snake Blakeslee in 1981. (S. Cassells photo.)

Figure 9-12   A 1949 photo of room 1 at Snake Blakeslee, showing horizontal masonry and the central roof support pillar. (Hal Chase photo; University of Denver.)

Figure 9-13   Chipped stone knife hafted in a bone handle. It was found at the Upper Plum Creek shelter and is probably of Panhandle Aspect age. (Ray Lyons, Colorado Archaeological Society.)

rock shelters, including Medina, Pyeatt, Trinchera, and Upper Plum Canyon (the latter recently completed by the Colorado Archaeological Society and not yet reported).

Artifacts from these sites include small side-notched projectile points and cord-marked pottery with globular shapes and undecorated but out-curved rims. Radiocarbon dates range from about A.D. 1100 to 1450. For the most part, exclusive of the architecture, many similarities to the Upper Republican assemblages to the northeast can be seen.

All of this southeastern Colorado material was put into perspective in 1946 when Alex Krieger defined the Panhandle Aspect in order to cover a group of similar foci that were spread across the Texas Panhandle, western Oklahoma, northeast New Mexico, southwest Kansas, and southeast Colorado. Included in the Panhandle Aspect are the Antelope Creek Focus, Optima Focus, and the Apishapa Focus, the latter term assigned to many of the Panhandle sites in Colorado. Based on the observations of Krieger and others, it seems reasonable that the residents of the Southern Plains, contemporaries of Central Plains Tradition peoples, shared a common background and/or were involved in social interaction.

Unlike the Upper Republican sojourners, the Panhandle occupants obviously came to stay in Colorado. Substantial houses in hamlets and the cultivation of several varieties of corn (probably in valley floor plots) are

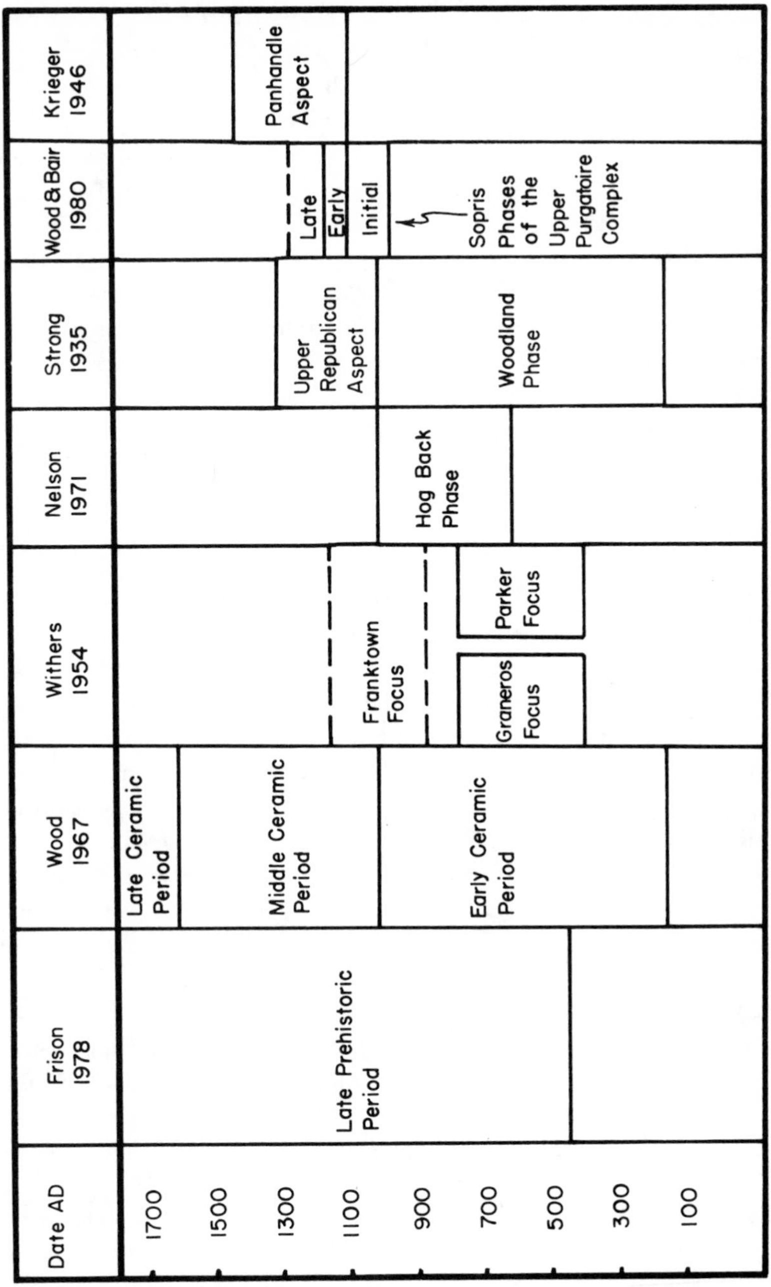

Figure 9-15   Eastern Colorado post-Archaic terminology.

Corn, found to a degree in all phases, could have had a source either to the south or the east. The possibility of an unexpected contributor has been recognized on the basis of skeletal remains there. The first molars on the mandibles (lower jaws) of over 20% of the individuals found had three roots, rather than the usual two. This genetic trait is common in Athabascan populations, late arrivals to the New World. This far south, they are known as Apache or Navajo and would normally not be expected here for a few more centuries.

These data are intriguing, but many questions about the origins and dispersal of the Upper Purgatoire people must remain unanswered for the present time. It could be that their distribution is not as localized as suspected, but more systematic and sustained investigations over a broader area will be required to determine that.

Summary

Eastern Colorado is a good candidate for a homogeneous culture area, with its fairly uniform climate from north to south, and east of the mountains, terrain that is reasonably flat.

During the reign of the Plains Woodland foragers, this may have been the case. However, the data base is limited and such a view could be too simplistic. As some sage remarked, "The fewer the data, the smoother the curve." But I will go ahead and propose such homogeneity, since little regional or chronological variation has been observed so far in the eastern part of the state. Future research may prove this hypothesis is incorrect.

After A.D. 1000 there is a strong possibility of actual migrations into Colorado from several directions. The Upper Republican people, transient as they appear to have been, came in from the northeast. The Panhandle cultures may have entered from the southeast. The Rio Grande Anasazi, although probably not residents this far north, obviously came into contact with peoples along the Colorado border, undoubtedly influencing them in many ways. The southward push of the Athabascans may also have been a contributor to the Native American populations of eastern Colorado at this time.

As the site distribution map for this chapter indicates, the post-Woodland inhabitants of the plains probably did not participate in a great deal of north-south movement across the state. This may have been due to the divide between the drainages of the Arkansas in the south and the South

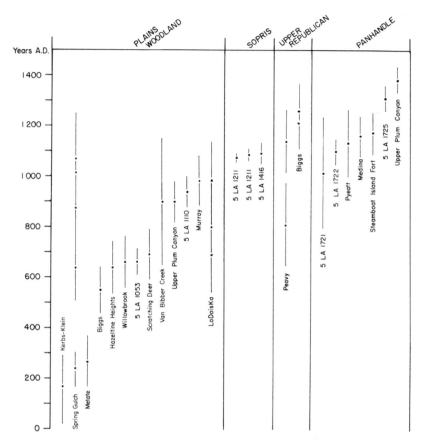

Figure 9-16   Selected range of radiocarbon dates for eastern Colorado during the post-Archaic.

Platte in the north. People and ideas entering Colorado after about A.D. 1000 seem to have come via these two basic river systems (in addition to the Republican tributaries and the overland route from the Rio Grande). None of the immigrants or the residents found it compelling to cross the drainage divide to any significant degree.

All of the cultures described up through this chapter were purely prehistoric. In other words, literate Europeans had yet to penetrate the New World and document the native populations. When they did enter Colorado several centuries later, the groups they saw may have had some of the heritage of Colorado in their blood but in few cases can actual cultural connections be made.

References

On early ceramics in the Southeast:
Stoltman 1966; Jennings 1968.

On Hopewell and Adena:
Griffin 1952; Jennings 1968.

On the Plains Woodland:
Wedel 1961.

On the Wilbur Thomas shelter:
Breternitz 1971.

On the Hall-Woodland Cave:
Nelson 1967.

On LoDaisKa:
Irwin and Irwin 1959.

On the Willowbrook site:
Leach 1966a.

On Metate Cave:
Campbell 1969.

On Torres Cave:
Hoyt 1979; Rathbun 1979; Guthrie 1979; Lyons 1979.

On the Ken Caryl Ranch sites:
Medina 1974, 1975; Horner and Horner 1974; Richardson 1974.

On the Magic Mountain site:
Irwin-Williams and Irwin 1966.

On the Spring Gulch site:
Kainer 1974, 1976.

On the Scratching Deer site:
Benedict 1975b.

On the Murray game drive system:
Benedict 1975a.

On the Van Bibber Creek site:
Nelson 1969.

On the Graneros Focus:
Withers 1954.

On the George W. Lindsay Ranch site:
Nelson 1971.

On the Hog Back Phase:
Nelson 1971.

On the Red Top Ranch sites:
Anderson 1976.

On Trinchera Cave:
Wood 1974; Wood-Simpson 1976.

On the Carrizo Ranches sites:
Kingsbury and Nowak 1980.

On the Roberts Buffalo Jump:
Witkind 1971.

On the Hazeltine Heights burials:
Buckles, et al. 1963; Breternitz 1972.

On the Gahagan-Lipe burials:
Scott and Birkedal 1972.

On Kerbs-Klein burials:
Scott 1979.

On the Aurora burials:
Guthrie 1983.

On a summary of Plains Woodland burials:
Breternitz and Wood 1965.

On the Parker Focus:
Withers 1954.

On the Mississippian culture:
Griffin 1952; Jennings 1968.

On the Plains Village Tradition:
Strong 1935; Wedel 1961; Ludwickson et al. 1981.

On the Upper Republican Phase in Nebraska:
Wedel 1961; Ludwickson et al. 1981.

On the Buick Campsite:
Withers 1954; Wood 1971.

On the Smiley Shelter:
Wood 1971.

On the Agate Bluff shelters:
Irwin and Irwin 1957.

On the Peavy Rock Shelter:
Wood 1967.

On the Biggs site:
Wood 1967.

On Franktown Cave and the Franktown Focus:
Withers 1954; Nelson 1983.

On the Snake Blakeslee site:
Renaud 1942a; Chase n.d.; Ireland 1968.

On the Steamboat Island Fort:
Campbell 1969.

On the Wand and Wallace sites:
Ireland 1968.

On the Medina Rock Shelter:
Campbell 1963, 1969.

On the Pyeatt Rock Shelter:
Campbell 1969.

On Trinchera Cave:
Wood 1974; Wood-Simpson 1976.

On the Panhandle Aspect:
Krieger 1946; Campbell 1969, 1976.

On the Antelope Creek, Optima, and Apishapa Foci:
Campbell 1969, 1976; Lintz 1979; Stuart and Gauthier 1981.

On the Trinidad Reservoir sites and the Upper Purgatoire Complex:
Dick 1963; Ireland 1971; McCabe 1973; Bair 1975; Wood and Bair 1980.

10 The Historic Tribes

The Plains Indians! To many people, just the name can conjure up dramatic visions of fiercely-painted warriors, bedecked with feathers, armed with shields, spears, bows and arrows, swooping down from a ridgetop to attack an isolated caravan of covered wagons. A number of movie moguls have made their fortunes by elaborating on such scenarios for the silver screen.

The opening of the Oregon Trail in 1840, coupled with the establishment of the Mormon Trail in 1847, the California Gold Rush in 1849, the Colorado Gold Rush in 1858, and the railroad crossing the nation in the 1860s, caused tensions with the indigenous inhabitants to reach the breaking point. Misunderstandings abounded and treaties were broken, leading to numerous skirmishes, battles, and massacres which were instigated at various violent times on the plains, with a sustained struggle for land being waged by both the aboriginal societies and the immigrant whites.

Perhaps the most notable and infamous of conflicts in Colorado's past was the Sand Creek Massacre, when, just at dawn on 29 November 1864, Colonel John M. Chivington led his First Colorado Cavalry to the camp of Black Kettle's Cheyenne and Arapaho families. There he and his troops killed many of the inhabitants while they stood around Black Kettle and his fluttering American flag and a white flag of truce.

In reprisal, war broke out along the South Platte River. However in the end, reservation life became the only alternative to death for most of these Native Americans.

But this is only the last part of the story of Colorado's historic Indians. Much went on within the state involving several distinctive tribes since

European explorers first documented their presence in the 1700s. What we see as the mounted warrior is a minor addendum to a lengthy heritage.

The purpose of this book has primarily been to detail prehistoric life in Colorado, not the protohistoric and historic groups, and the following treatment may seem superficial, relative to the massive amounts written on them elsewhere. Those interested in further pursuing this fascinating topic are directed to the references at the end of this chapter.

Before dealing directly with the information available on Colorado's ethnohistoric aboriginals, a few clarifications need to be made on some widespread misconceptions.

To begin with, we generally refer to these groups as "tribes," a term in anthropology that refers to a widespread and stratified societal integration under the leadership of a chief. In reality, most of them operated under organizational principles of a smaller and more temporary scale. It was not until the late 1800s that the federal government imposed "tribal level" social organization on most Native American populations. Prior to Anglo domination, the functioning of the societies was more often at the "band level," where closely related groups operated under the loose authority of a "headman," the position having been earned rather than inherited.

Secondly, this chapter deals with reconstructions of relationships, territories, and other identifications of groups. Although this is a common approach to the subject, it should be understood that such reconstructions are fraught with problems. What we know about these peoples at the dawn of Colorado's recorded history is fragmentary at best: the information comes from early European explorers who ventured into the region only at sporadic intervals. As a result, the territorial boundaries that are described here and the succession of populations across the state should be taken only as general trends. The dates are not to be viewed as firm but are just intended to be used as aids in viewing cultural activities in the state in a sequential manner.

The Plains Apaches

During the early 1930s, archaeologists in Nebraska began recognizing sites with attributes different from the usual Woodland or Central Plains Tradition types. As these were first found along the Dismal River, this culture has come to be known as the Dismal River Aspect. Subsequent research by a number of individuals has led to a fairly complete description of these people's architecture and artifacts.

Figure 10-1 Top and side views of three Dismal River sherds from Nebraska (in the University of Colorado Museum collections). Note the punctation (left) and incisions (center and right) on top view of rims. (S. Cassells photo.)

Surface surveys and examinations of pottery in museum collections have revealed many sites in Colorado which seem to fall within the range of variation normally ascribed to Dismal River. With well-controlled excavations of Dismal River sites in adjacent states, it would not seem unreasonable to expect similar finds here.

Dismal River houses are circular, built either on the unmodified ground surface or in shallow depressions. They are about 25 feet in diameter and generally have five main support posts arranged in a circle with leaners filling in the perimeter.

One of the most interesting Dismal River finds was made at Scott County State Park in Kansas, where a combination of excavations and historic documentation have fairly conclusively tied the Dismal River Aspect to the Apaches. In 1706 the Rio Grande refugee pueblo of El Cuartelejo was visited by the Spaniard Ulibarri. A 1727 map produced as a result of that expedition indicates a nearby Apache camp. The map distinguished this camp as culturally separate from the Comanches, also residents at times in this part of Kansas. Excavations at this camp revealed an undeniable Dismal River affiliation, thus making the connection between the protohistoric Dismal River Aspect and the historic Apache. It is not often that such a confirmation can be made in archaeology, but it is the potential of such discoveries that drives many archaeologists on.

The Plains Apaches are part of the Athabascan language group that is thought to have been a late entrant into the New World. Aligned with the Apaches linguistically are the Navajos, various tribes of the Pacific Northwest, and the Bloods of Canada, among others.

The Athabascan migrations brought several of the groups to their final

Figure 10-2   Excavated pithouse at Cedar Point Village, 1952. Note single post hole on far edge. Judging by ceramics, it *may* be an early Apachean hamlet. (University of Colorado Museum.)

settlement locales in the American Southwest well after the development of the Puebloan societies. Those of the Southwest, such as the Mescalero and Chiricauhua, are the current stereotypes of Apachean life, but plains groups did exist, including the Lipan.

The migration routes taken from the north are problematical. With the presence of Dismal River villages on the plains, along with the historically-documented Lipan, a plains thoroughfare has generally been assumed, but some have proposed an intermountain path, based on the Athabascan people's initial subarctic adaptations.

Excavations in Colorado have not been particularly fruitful in identifying early Apachean campsites. Perhaps the best is Cedar Point Village, a concentration of seven shallow circular to rectangular dwellings associated with pottery quite unlike the nearby Upper Republican sites of Smiley Shelter and the Buick Campsite. Projectile points there included un-notched and side-notched triangular styles (some obsidian), and plainware ceramic types with heavy temper and some indications of stamping on the exterior.

Based on the knowledge of protohistoric and historic groups in this area of eastern Colorado, the assignment of Plains Apache to Cedar Point Village is logical, but Ray Wood, in his reanalysis of the material, does not feel it

Figure 10-3   Stone circle (foreground) of unknown (but possible Apachean) affiliation on the Red Top Ranch, 5 PE 16. (Jenny Anderson, Pioneer Archaeological Consultants.)

can be confidently defended. Radiocarbon dates and perhaps excavation of other portions of the site are needed to at least put the site into a general chronological context.

The plains and mountains in Colorado, as well as in many surrounding states, contain numerous stone rings on or near the ground surface. For many years these have been termed "tipi rings," with the inference that these stones had been used to hold down the outer and/or inner skin coverings of dwellings. Suggestions have been made that diameters of the rings are indicative of age, with the smaller circles used during pre-horse times when larger and heavier skin coverings could not have easily been transported.

It is not a foregone conclusion that all of these circular rock arrangements were used in conjunction with hide-covered frameworks, given the above recognition of difficulties in transporting heavy hides prior to the acquisition of the horse. With some radiocarbon dates from hearths inside these rings indicating occupations up to several thousand years ago, the likelihood of brush or grass-covered superstructures is high in some cases. Only the investigation of individual stone circles can reveal their age and possible cultural affiliations.

The Plains Apaches south of Colorado have been documented with skin-covered tipis as early as 1598, and ethnographic studies have placed Apaches in Colorado shortly thereafter. In 1706 Ulibarri mentions Jicarilla Apaches along the southern Colorado border, while the Penxaye Apaches were to the north, perhaps within the Apishapa drainage. This evidence would then suggest that at least some of the stone circles on the southeastern Colorado plains were the results of Apache occupations.

Work on the Carrizo Ranches by Kingsbury and Nowak has revealed several stone circle sites that they believe were left from Apache camping episodes, although they discount a Dismal River affiliation because of differences in artifact inventories. In direct association with the stone circles were small notched and triangular projectile points and pottery that had been produced and traded in from the Rio Grande Puebloans. Other pottery there may have been manufactured by Jicarilla Apaches. Pueblo pottery types have been dated in the Rio Grande at between A.D. 1490 and 1515. Charred bone from one of the Carizzo sites dated A.D. 1350 ± 55. The likelihood is strong that these rings are from Apacheans, given the architectural departure from the slab and pillar houses of Panhandle peoples and the subsequent documentation of Apaches in this area south of the Arkansas.

When the Colorado Apaches actually obtained horses is not known with any certainty. Only approximations can be made, based on documented observances elsewhere. Logistically, the potential for widespread dispersal of horses capable of reproduction would not have been great until well into the 1600s. Although the Navajos are known to have raided Spanish settlements in the Rio Grande by 1659, taking horses with them, and some sporadic trading of slaves for horses was conducted by Apaches to the east of Santa Fe by 1664, the real momentum for horse distribution across the plains began only after the Pueblo Revolt of 1680, when the Spanish were driven back into Mexico. During the 13 year hiatus that followed, the Indians of the Rio Grande would have had many opportunities to trade the horses to outside tribes of the plains and the Great Basin. By 1720 horses were seen at Middle Missouri villages in South Dakota and at camps in Montana and the surrounding region to the northwest. We can therefore say that the Apaches of Colorado probably did not have horses prior to 1680, or at least 1664, but had many opportunities to gain them over the next 40 years up to 1720. The horse would have been a significant addition to their culture, but probably did not change them in any dramatic way, as it did some other tribes. The Apache had been somewhat mobile anyway, and this would have only served to reinforce a deeply-rooted tradition.

During the early 1700s, an influx of Comanches and their Ute allies

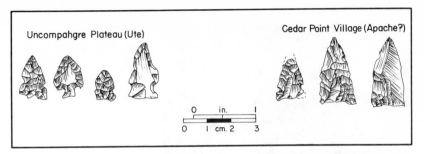

Figure 10-4   Ute and possible Apache projectile points.

appear to have replaced most of the Apaches in Colorado. The Apaches became established farther to the south.

The Utes

The Utes are Numic speakers, related to the Paiutes of Utah. A probable reference to them by the Spanish in 1626 and a treaty in 1680 make them the earliest historically documented aboriginal group in western Colorado. An early history of New Mexico by Fray Pasados places them on the plains with the Apaches and probably in the area north of the San Juan and as far west as the Great Salt Lake. There is little reason to doubt subsequent accounts, including that of Dominquez and Escalante in 1775-76, which portray the Utes as the sole aboriginal inhabitants of western Colorado in historic times.

Upon completing his research for the Ute Prehistory Project, Bill Buckles found that he could not state with certainty how long the Utes had been in Colorado. Because the remains are basically lithic, connecting the historic Utes to the prehistoric Desert Culture is impossible. However, it is suspected that *at least* the later Desert Culture is ancestral Ute, since little difference can be detected in the lifestyles of the two groups.

Some historic Ute sites retain architectural elements today, but it will be only a few decades before these will be gone. Their housing was often built of branches either leaned against each other to form a cone structure or were positioned against the branches of living trees. Known as wickiups, these small huts can still be found, either singly, in pairs, or in clusters of up to ten or more. The Utes also used hide-covered tipis, or even rock shelters, when available.

Ute rock art differs from Anasazi and Fremont depictions and can be

Figure 10-5 Standing wickiup framework at 5 MN 1519 (the Grand Lodge site), a historic Ute encampment. There are 52 probable structures at this site, located during the South Divide Timber Sale survey west of Montrose in 1982. (Hank Deutsch photo; Polly Hammer, United States Forest Service.)

found on panels across western Colorado. Some of their art includes representations of horses, indicating post-Spanish contact times.

Ute pottery is simple, made by coiling and often taking the form of wide-mouth jars with pointed bases, low shoulders, and slightly flared rims. The exteriors of the vessels are generally yellowish-brown or gray in color, and have been finished with a smoothed surface or with rows of fingernail impressions perpendicular to the coil junctures. This impressing technique may have been employed to strengthen the bonding of the coils. Jim Benedict has found what may be a Ute variant at the Caribou Lake site, with rows of punctuations on the pottery surface, impressed with perhaps a stick rather than with fingernails.

Later Ute sites have been found with historic trade goods, such as glass beads and metal items like projectile points.

Seldom reported and fast disappearing remnants of Ute culture in Colorado are scarred trees. The Utes, as well as other groups in parts of

Figure 10-6   A Ute encampment at the Los Pinos Agency in 1874, as photographed by
W. H. Jackson. (Colorado Historical Society.)

North America, would strip bark from trees (in Colorado, principally pine)
for a variety of purposes. Some are said to be "medicine trees." An ill person
would be placed next to the scar during the healing process, somewhat
analogous to Navajo sand painting ceremonies. Medicinal teas are known
to have been brewed from the inner bark, and other peelings were for food.
Such practices have been characterized as associated with "starvation diets"
during hard times. Other reported uses were as materials for cradleboards
and other items.

The Utes were probably one of the more instrumental groups in the
northward spread of horses from the Rio Grande Spanish communities.
Some Utes had been slaves of the Spanish prior to the Pueblo Revolt of
1680, and that contact had provided them with opportunities to learn how
to ride. When the Spanish were driven south, the Utes went home, taking
herds of horses with them. Through trade, they distributed the animals
along the Western Slope, up into Wyoming and beyond. Much as the
Apaches, the Utes were already a mobile, but pedestrian, society, and the
acquisition of the horse, though quite useful in their lifeway, did not
change the qualities that had been maintained for centuries. It only
increased their mobility.

Today they are divided into the Southern Utes and Northern Utes, but
this is a modern distribution based on reservation assignments following

Figure 10-7   A petroglyph of probable Ute origin from the Uncompahgre Plateau. The horse and rider depiction indicates Spanish contact. (Ray Lyons, Colorado Historical Society.)

Figure 10-8   A scarred ponderosa pine near the Continental Divide south of Gunnison. Note the straight edge at the bottom of the scar (original cut) and how the scar tapers in near the top, indicating an upward peeling motion. (Marilyn Martorano.)

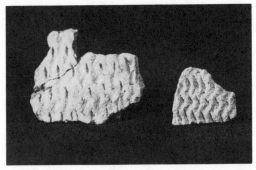

Figure 10-9   Fingernail-impressed Ute pottery collected during the Ute Prehistory Project on the Uncompahgre Plateau and now in the University of Colorado Museum. (S. Cassells photo.)

Figure 10-10   Punctate pottery sherds from the Caribou Lake site. These may be variants of Ute fingernail-impressed wares. (James Benedict.)

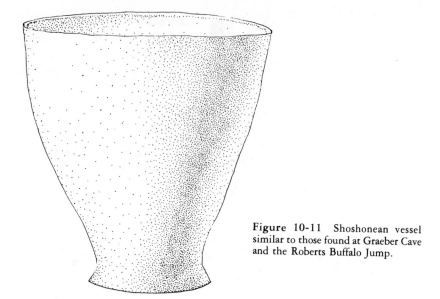

Figure 10-11   Shoshonean vessel similar to those found at Graeber Cave and the Roberts Buffalo Jump.

the removal of some from Colorado after the 1879 Meeker Massacre. Traditionally, the real separation was between the Eastern Utes of Colorado and the Western Utes of Utah. The Utes in Colorado today are concentrated at the Southern Ute Indian Reservation and the Ute Mountain Indian Reservation, both in the southwest corner of the state.

The Comanches

The Comanches were late arrivals to the state, having moved down from the Northern Plains and the Great Basin. The Spanish mentioned that the Comanches had originally been in the Teguayo area (probably the Great Salt Lake) before coming to Colorado.

The language of the Comanches is Shoshonean, with distant ties to the Ute tongue. It is thought that the Comanches had split from the Shoshonis by 1700 and entered the Colorado plains, where they joined with the Utes against the Apaches.

Archaeological evidence for the Comanches in Colorado is scant. Perhaps most suggestive of their presence in aboriginal sites is the rare discovery of a distinctive ceramic vessel style known as Shoshonean or Intermountain Tradition pottery. The wares, more common in Wyoming, have flat bottoms and usually a flowerpot shape with a flanged base. Such vessels have been found in the eastern Colorado foothills at the Roberts Buffalo Jump and at Graeber Cave. Whether these particular pots are actually from a Comanche influx or from some earlier Shoshonean incursions is not known.

The Comanches and Utes became more widely distributed with their newly acquired equestrian mobility. As peoples covered greater expanses of land, they vied for resources with other indigenous groups. With some, alliances were forged, and with others, antagonisms developed.

The Plains Apaches moved over time to more southerly locations in New Mexico, and the plains of Colorado became populated with Comanches, Utes, and other groups who utilized the land as mounted hunters and raiders.

By 1820 the Comanches were known only south of the Arkansas River, with the Arapahos and Cheyennes to their north. Eventually the Comanches moved into Oklahoma and southern Kansas, near the Kiowas and Kiowa-Apaches.

The Arapahos and Cheyennes

From the early to the late 1800s, much of eastern Colorado was occupied by the Arapahos and their allies, the Cheyennes. Both tribes are part of the Algonkian language stock, and it is not surprising that they joined forces.

The prehistoric movements of the Arapahos are not known with any degree of certainty, but it is thought that they came into Colorado from the north, possibly via Canada, North Dakota, Montana, and Wyoming, having broken with the Atsina in North Dakota.

The Cheyennes were on the North Dakota-Minnesota border perhaps as early as 1700. Within the next 40 years some had moved to the Missouri River, where they adopted the sedentary Plains Village lifestyle, complete with farming. Then, around 1760, the horse was introduced into their villages, and this brought about a freedom that dramatically altered the remainder of their lives. They became mounted hunters, turning their backs forever on the village horticulturalists along the Missouri. Their primary territory for many years was in the area from South Dakota's Black Hills to the Big Horns of Wyoming. Then, when Bent's Fort began operations in southeastern Colorado, the Cheyennes were invited by the Bents to come to the vicinity and be part of their trade system. In 1837 the Cheyennes split, some permanently joining the Arapahos near the Arkansas, and the remainder becoming affiliated with the Arapahos in Wyoming

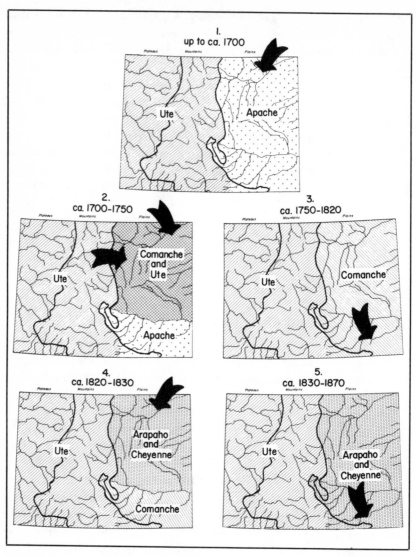

Figure 10-12   Idealized sequence of cultural succession in Colorado from before A.D. 1700 to ca. 1870.

and Nebraska. Thus began the divisions of Northern and Southern Cheyennes.

Some of these Southern Cheyennes were part of Black Kettle's Arapaho camp decimated by Chivington and his troops at Sand Creek in 1864. By the late 1870s, all the Arapaho and Cheyenne survivors of the plains warfare were confined principally to Oklahoma reservations.

With the final aboriginal societies removed from most of Colorado by the 1870s, the land was opened for total settlement by those of Euro-American descent. These latest immigrants could not have realized then how great a heritage was contained in the soils of the newly emerging Centennial State. Before them had come 12,000 years or more of struggles and successes, innumerable innovations, adaptations, and acquisitions that had contributed to the thriving of humankind in a diverse environment.

References

On the Sand Creek massacre:
Hoig 1961; Brown 1970.

On the Dismal River Aspect (Apache):
Gunnerson 1960b, 1968; Wedel 1961; Champe 1946, 1949.

On the Scott County State Park site:
Champe 1949.

On the Ulibarri expedition to El Cuartelejo:
Thomas 1935.

On an intermountain migration route of the Apache:
Perry 1980; Huscher and Huscher 1942.

On the Apaches in Colorado:
Buckles 1968; Kingsbury and Gabel 1981.

On Cedar Point Village:
Wood 1971.

On the Carrizo Ranches sites:
Kingsbury and Nowak 1980; Kingsbury and Gabel 1981.

On the Red Top Ranch sites:
Anderson 1976.

On the dispersion of horses across the plains:
Wissler 1914; Haines 1938a, 1938b.

On Spanish references to the Utes:
Schroeder 1965; Tyler 1951; Hackett 1931, 1934; Bolton 1972; Hill 1930; Buckles 1968.

On ethnographies of the Utes:
Stewart 1941, 1942, 1948, 1966, 1971, 1982.

On archaeological investigations of the Utes:
Buckles 1968, 1971; Huscher and Huscher 1939, 1940a, 1940b, 1940c, 1941; Wormington 1955, Wormington and Lister 1956; Wenger 1956; Nykamp 1982.

On the Caribou Lake site:
Benedict n.d.

On scarred trees:
Martorano 1981; Doll 1977; White 1952; Cassells 1979.

On the role of the Utes in the dispersion of horses to the north:
Stewart 1982:

On the Utes and Comanches against the Apaches:
Forbes 1960; Thomas 1935.

On the separation of the Utes and Comanches:
Tyler 1951.

On the Comanches on the plains:
Crouse 1956; Tyrell 1916; Coues 1965; Thomas 1935; Buckles 1968.

On the Roberts Buffalo Jump:
Witkind 1971.

On Graeber Cave:
Nelson and Graeber 1966.

On Wyoming Shoshonean pottery:
Frison 1971, 1978; Wedel 1954.

On the Arapahos on the plains:
Haines 1976; Strong 1940; Buckles 1968.

On the Cheyennes on the plains:
Grinnel 1915, 1923; Powell 1969, 1980; Berthrong 1963; Buckles 1968.

12 Colorado Archaeology Today

Professionals in Government and Academia

Up until about a decade ago, professional archaeologists in Colorado were primarily working for the National Park Service at Mesa Verde National Park, were curators at museums, or more commonly, were college professors who taught during the school terms and excavated in the summer. Funding for fieldwork generally came from the National Science Foundation or similar sources. Gathering at annual meetings of the Society for American Archaeology, the Pecos Conference, or the Plains Conference, they would visit with colleagues and present their latest findings. Eventually the results of their excavations would be published in scholarly journals, such as *American Antiquity, Plains Anthropologist, Southwestern Lore, El Palacio,* or *The Kiva.*

Contract Archaeology

"Cultural resource management," a concept originating in the 1960s and vastly increasing its influence in the 1970s, has moved archaeological fieldwork in an additional, very important direction. Several significant pieces of federal legislation were passed that require archaeologists to become involved in early stages of projects on federal land or in federally-funded projects in which alteration of the ground surface is to take place. Primary tasks of these archaeologists, conducting what was earlier known as "salvage archaeology" and now termed "contract archaeology," is to survey the surface of land that might be "adversely impacted," and record any sites present. Once found, all sites are mapped, photographed, and recorded on site forms. They are evaluated to see if they meet federally-stipulated criteria for inclusion on the National Register of Historic Places. If so, recommendations (e.g. avoidance, preservation or excavation) and final decisions about the disposition of the significant sites are made by the land managing agencies involved and by the final authority, the Keeper of the Register. The current attitude in cultural resource management tends toward avoidance and thus the conservation of prehistoric and historic resources whenever possible. This trend promises to continue for some time.

One of the results of the legislative mandates and their implementation by federal agencies has been a proliferation of jobs in the archaeological realm, primarily those in surveying land in advance of oil drilling, mineral exploration, timber harvesting, highway construction, and a variety of other ground-disturbing activities.

This in turn has required additional archaeological personnel in the land managing agencies (National Park Service, Bureau of Land Management, Bureau of Reclamation, United States Forest Service) to oversee all of the contract work.

Since 1973 Colorado has had a State Archaeologist, a position created through a great deal of effort by members of the Colorado Archaeological Society and various archaeologists from the state's colleges and universities. Working in tandem with the State Archaeologist is another individual with the position of State Historic Preservation Officer (SHPO). Between them, they maintain the ever increasing site files and help review and comment on archaeological work in the state.

Avocationals

In addition to those employed by government, academia, and through contracts, there is a large heterogeneous body collectively known as "avocationals." These are individuals whose professional ties are in other fields, although their love for prehistory involves them in archaeology to some degree during their spare time.

In 1935 a zoology professor and Dean at Western State College, C. T. Hurst, saw a need to channel avocational drives and provide an opportunity for interchange between professonals and amateurs. He established the

Colorado Archaeological Society (CAS) and its journal, *Southwestern Lore.* Both the organization and the journal are still flourishing today.

Through the Colorado Archaeological Society, avocational archaeologists have an ideal outlet for their energies. They have regular local and statewide meetings, conduct surveys and excavations under the direction of professionals, and in the process, contribute a great deal to the knowledge of state prehistory.

In 1979 a program was established by the Office of the State Archaeologist and the Colorado Archaeological Society to train avocationals in various aspects of the archaeological discipline. Entitled the Program for Avocational Archaeological Cerification (PAAC), its goals are to equip avocationals with survey, excavation, and analytical skills. Woven into the fabric of the courses are healthy doses of behavioral and ethical standards, reinforcing the already strict Code of Ethics subscribed to by the Society.

Pothunters and Vandals

Regardless of the exemplary efforts of the Colorado Archaeological Society and the positive opportunities they offer for archaeological pursuit, there are those who have chosen other routes to self-fulfillment. These are the pothunters and vandals. Their motives vary, but the final results on the cultural resource base are about the same.

Former State Archaeologist Bruce Rippeteau has classified them into three partially overlapping groups. These are "Weekend Citizens," "Vicious Vandals," and "Commercial Miners."

The "Weekend Citizens" are seen as recreational collectors who might involve the whole family on brief picnic-like outings which would include scouting out archaeological sites, collecting their surfaces, and perhaps probing the ground with shovels. They may resent professional archaeologists and legal prohibitions, although they will often profess ignorance of antiquities laws. Those items they recover from archaeological sites usually remain their personal possessions, perhaps being framed behind glass and hung on their walls. They are primarily curio hunters and collectors, like antiquarians of old. They do not understand that the true value of artifacts is in their context in the sites, not the objects themselves.

The "Vicious Vandals" are an entirely different group. Rather than finding inherent value in prehistoric or historic remains and wanting to possess them, these individuals seek to damage or destroy remnants of the

Figure 12-1   Pictograph of bear along the Purgatoire River near Las Animas, ca. 1900. (Western History Department, Denver Public Library.)

Figure 12-2   A 1929 photograph of the bear in Figure 12-1. Note the vandalism that has taken place in just a few decades. (Western History Department, Denver Public Library.)

past, thus depriving future visitors any pleasure in their discovery. This may involve such things as pushing over masonry walls in free-standing pueblos or removing 1,000 year-old support beams and burning them in campfires. Vandalism to rock art has been extremely prevalent, taking the form of painting or carving names across panels, firing weapons at the artistic representations of animals, or even applying chemicals to the walls to obliterate the designs. This type of behavior is senseless and quite difficult for enforcement officers to stop.

The "Commercial Miners" form a particularly despicable, though at least understandable, group. They have discovered that certain prehistoric artifacts (in Colorado, primarily Anasazi pottery) have great monetary value, and they seek to discover these "treasures" and then sell them to antiquarians who do not care how they were obtained. Knowing that ceramics can accompany burials, they often use heavy equipment (backhoes, bulldozers) to expose the skeletons and gain access to the grave goods. Such ill-gotten pottery from Colorado has been sold throughout the nation and has even wound up in collections overseas.

Private land in Colorado is exempt from antiquities laws, and pothunters can "mine" sites on such property without any fear of personal liability. However, greed often drives them out onto the abundant federal and state lands where they can be arrested and prosecuted under both the 1906 Antiquities Act and the Archaeological Resources Protection Act of 1979 (ARPA).

Enforcement officers have been hired by various land managing agencies, and civil authorities, such as county sheriffs, have also become involved in trying to stem this tide of depredation on Colorado's heritage. They are meeting with increasing success.

At the time of this writing, two individuals have been arrested and charged with three counts each of violating the Archaeological Resources Protection Act by allegedly digging more than three sites on U.S. Forest Service land near Chimney Rock. If convicted, they face maximum penalties of two years in jail and a $20,000 fine *for each count*. Although these will be the first convictions in Colorado under ARPA, the 1906 Antiquities Act has been successfully used before, with less severe penalties.

Public education is the first line of defense against pothunting and vandalism. The potential of winning-over the "Weekend Citizen" to the side of site conservation is perhaps the greatest. This is being accomplished through such activities as public-oriented articles and books, television programs, the Program for Avocational Archaeological Certification, and media publicity of antiquities violations, trials, and convictions. The year

Figure 12-3 Detail of pueblo wall at 5 MT 697, showing a hole dug by pothunters. Note the moisture on the wall caused by the digging. This can help undermine the masonry and cause a collapse. Two individuals were convicted for this crime in 1978 under the 1906 Antiquities Act. (Colorado Bureau of Land Management.)

1983 was designated Colorado Archaeological Awareness Year, with many associated educational activities taking place. Avocationals are continually encouraged to become involved with the Colorado Archaeological Society, hopefully absorbing in the process high ethical standards in their dealings with archaeological resources.

Education will be less successful with the "Vicious Vandals" and the "Commercial Miners." Economic reccession and increasing pottery values will only spur pothunters on to greater and more clandestine efforts. Law enforcement officers, spread quite thin across the vast tracts of federal and state land, benefit greatly when citizens report suspected vandalism and pothunting to them.

Another avenue that would seem reasonable to follow is that of shutting off the market at the other end. If art dealers, museums, and collectors did not buy these items, the commercially-oriented pothunters might begin

Figure 12-4   A Bureau of Land Management archaeologist examines the scattered human bones at a looted site in southwestern Colorado. (Colorado Bureau of Land Management.)

seeking other means of income. In 1970 the General Conference of the United Nations Educational, Scientific and Cultural Organization (UNESCO) held a conference in Paris, ultimately producing the "Convention on the Means of Prohibiting and Preventing the Illicit Import, Export and Transfer of Ownership of Cultural Property" as an attempt to reduce international antiquities trafficking.

The United States Senate voted unanimously to ratify the UNESCO Convention, but there is as yet no binding U. S. legislation to accompany the initial ratification, and so, after ten years, the ratification is legally meaningless. Congressional committees have yet to move on S. 1723, *The Cultural Property Implementation Act*, because of pressure from a powerful collector and art dealer lobby. Although this particular piece of legislation might not bring the pillaging of Colorado sites to a halt, its passage could be the falling domino eventually leading to the collapse of the entire illegal antiquities trafficking industry.

Summary

Archaeological activity in Colorado is very high, given the current demands for compliance work by contract archaeology. Parts of the state that have held little interest for researchers in the past are now being surveyed intensively, and the files of the State Archaeologist are growing rapidly with information on newly-recorded sites.

Public interest in archaeological sites is also great. Mesa Verde National Park recorded 602,698 visitors to their ruins in 1982, as compared with 546,300 just 10 years earlier.

Involvement in the Colorado Archaeological Society and the Program for Avocational Archaeological Certification is strong, and the future of this organization looks secure.

Unfortunately, exploitation of archaeological resources for personal gain is also on the rise as more people journey off asphalt highways in four-wheel drive vehicles.

Whether or not remnants of Colorado's prehistory will survive the coming years is difficult to say. Given adequate educational efforts directed at individuals at all age levels, a fair percentage of our population may become sensitized to the fragility of this non-renewable resource. Perhaps these people will join with the rest of us as stewards of the physical remains of our heritage, seeking to contribute to its preservation. Hopefully, a stepped-up program of law enforcement will be able to deal with the others who have consciously chosen to operate outside the law.

Let us hope that future generations will be able to share the same wonder and appreciation of the past that we have been fortunate enough to experience.

References

On Cultural Resource Management:
McGimsey and Davis 1977; Schiffer and Gumerman 1977.

On the origin of the Colorado State Archaeologist position:
Lyons 1973.

On C.T. Hurst and the formation of the Colorado Archaeological Society:
Stewart 1949; Borland 1949.

On pothunting, vandalism and illicit antiquities trafficking:
Rippeteau 1979; Nickens 1977; Nickens, Larralde and Tucker 1981; Meyer 1973; Vitelli 1982; Brinkley-Rogers 1981; Hothem 1978; Reyman 1979; Scott 1977, 1980; Sheets 1973; Williams 1977; Thompson 1982.

On the UNESCO Convention and the Cultural Property Implementation Act:
Vitelli 1982; Coggins 1979.

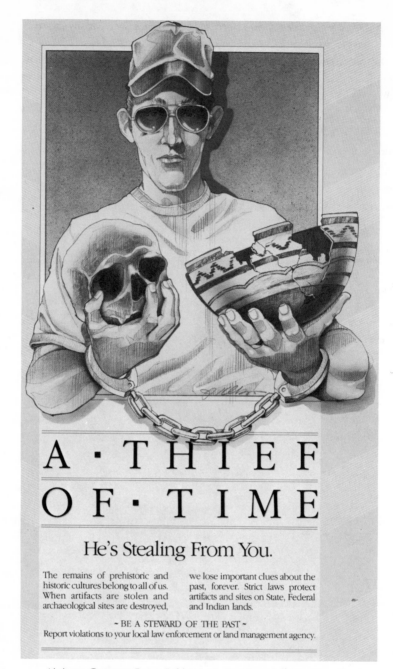

(Arizona Governor Bruce Babbitt's Archaeology Advisory Group)

13 Scrapbook of Colorado Archaeologists

Fieldwork in Colorado has been pivotal in the development of American archaeology. Since the late 1800s, a remarkable collection of individuals has been involved in the discipline within the state's boundaries. As I researched and wrote this book, I found it frustrating to pass by most of these men and women with a mere mention in the text or a listing in the bibliography. Yet including their biographies in the course of the main discussion would have been distracting. In the end, this "scrapbook" became the solution to my problem.

Today well over 100 professional archaeologists and a large contingent of worthy avocationals are working in the state. Lack of space prevents my including them all, and the chapter would probably be out of date before the book saw print if I did. To select those to be included on the basis of my subjective judgment of their importance would be unsatisfactory on several counts. So, in order to dance my way out of these self-created difficulties, I have decided to treat only those individuals who began working in the state no later than the 1950s and/or who are not active in fieldwork in Colorado now.

This solution is not completely satisfactory either, and I sincerely regret not being able to recognize many worthy Colorado archaeologists. Perhaps a future edition of this book can pay tribute to them.

For those familiar with the individuals included here, perhaps seeing their photos and reading the brief biographies will help close the gaps in time between their earlier publications and the present. I hope that the reader who has not consulted the works of these individuals and to whom the names mean little will gain some sense of the richness of early Colorado archaeology and of the character of the people who shaped it.

215

Figure 13-1   George Agogino removing preservative from the Dent mammoth bone before running a radiocarbon date. (George Agogino.)

George Allen Agogino (b. 1920)

George Agogino was born 18 November 1920 in West Palm Beach, Florida. He received a B.A. in anthropology (1949) and an M.A. in sociology (1951) from the University of New Mexico and went on to Syracuse University to earn a Ph.D. in anthropology in 1958. In 1961-62 he attended Harvard on a Wenner-Gren post-doctoral fellowship.

Agogino's archeological work has been varied, with experience throughout the plains. In addition to expertise in Paleo-Indian culture, he has demonstrated skills in the analysis of human skeletal material, as well as maintaining an interest in witchcraft, primitive religion, and Southwest ethnology. In 1954 he began his teaching career at Nasson College (Maine), remaining there for two years. He was at Syracuse University from 1956-58, then spent 1958-59 at South Dakota State University, 1959-62 at the University of Wyoming, 1962-63 at Baylor University, and has been a professor at Eastern New Mexico University in Portales since 1963, serving concurrently as director of the Blackwater Draw Museum, the Anthropology Museum, Miles Museum, and the Paleo-Indian Institute.

Outside of Colorado, he has been involved in many significant projects, from Hell Gap, Wyoming, to Blackwater Draw, New Mexico. His contributions to the knowledge of Colorado prehistory began in 1959 when he and Vance Haynes collected charcoal samples from Lindenmeier for dating purposes. He also dated bone from the Dent site after experimenting with an extremely laborious process to remove preservative applied by Figgins in the 1930s. During the 1960s he took part in excavations at the Johnson site and the Fowler-Parrish site, both significant Folsom sites in northeast Colorado. His analysis of a skull from Zapata has raised the distinct possibility that it is of Folsom age.

Colorado-related publications: Agogino 1960, 1961, 1964, 1968; Haynes and Agogino 1960; Galloway and Agogino 1961; Agogino and Duguid 1963; Agogino and Egan 1965; Agogino and Parrish 1971; Agogino and Folsom 1975; Patterson and Agogino 1976.

Figure 13-2 Galen Baker, ca. 1962. (Trinidad State Junior College.)

Galen Rueluff Baker (b. 1933)

Galen Baker was born 4 October 1933 in Denver. He earned an A.A. from Otero Junior College, La Junta, in 1953, a B.A. in anthropology from the University of Arizona in 1955, and an M.A. in anthropology from the University of Colorado in 1956. He spent 1956-58 and 1961-62 at the University of Arizona, working toward a Ph.D. During 1970-71 and 1974, he was at the University of North Carolina, where he completed all but his dissertation requirements for the Ph.D.

Some of his earliest fieldwork experience came at Mesa Verde in 1956, as part of a University of Colorado project crew. In 1958 he was employed by the National Park Service at Arizona's Tonto National Monument, followed by a year of teaching about American Indians in Scandinavia for the United States Information Service. In the summers of 1961 and 1962 he was Director of Archaeology at Philmont Scout Ranch southwest of Raton, New Mexico, and from 1962 to 1966, was on the Trinidad State Junior College faculty. During that time he was involved in excavations at Ft. Vasquez and Ft. Massachusetts as part of field school experiences in conjunction with both Trinidad College and the Colorado Historical Society. From 1966 to 1978, with time out for the NCU studies, he taught at Otero Junior College and conducted archaeologial investigations in the area. He was also heavily involved as instructor and a guide for the Koshare Indian organization over many years. In 1978, he retired from Otero due to poor health. He lives with his family in La Junta.

Colorado-related publications: Baker 1964, 1965a, 1965b, 1977, n.d.

Figure 13-3 Dave Breternitz working in South Dakota for Wes Hurt in 1951, while a student at the University of Denver. (Dave Breternitz.)

David Alan Breternitz (b. 1929)

Dave Breternitz was born in Fremont, Nebraska, on 12 November 1929 and spent his early years in several different communities, from Gothenburg, Nebraska, to Denver and La Junta, Colorado. He entered the University of Denver, where he earned a B.A. in anthropology in 1952. Following two years in Korea with the U.S. Army, he enrolled at the University of Arizona, completing both M.A. (1956) and Ph.D. (1963) in anthropology.

His archaeological experiences include participation in the University of

Arizona Field School in 1949, 1954, and 1955. In 1950 he worked in eastern Colorado as a surveyor and excavator for Denver University's Arnie Withers. He spent the summer of 1951 in two locales. First he was part of a crew directed by Wes Hurt of the South Dakota State Archaeological Commission and the University of South Dakota. He then went to New Mexico, where he joined a team stabilizing some of the ruins in Chaco Canyon. He was Curator of Anthropology at the Museum of Northern Arizona from 1956 to 1959, worked as a graduate assistant at the Laboratory of Tree-Ring Research in Tucson in 1961-62 and then joined the faculty at the University of Colorado in 1962, where he has remained ever since. Ongoing activity in Colorado since his teaching appointment includes numerous seasons at Dinosaur National Monument and at the Wilbur Thomas Shelter in northeastern Colorado, involvement with the analysis of the Gordon Creek Paleo-Indian burial, and the Directorship of the University of Colorado Mesa Verde (Regional) Research Center. Since 1978 he has been Principal Investigator of the Dolores Archaeological Project, one of the largest continuing mitigation projects in the world. While he still maintains his C.U. faculty position, his work is primarily centered in southwest Colorado, and he lives in Dove Creek.

Colorado-related publications: Breternitz 1966, 1969, 1970, 1971, 1972, 1975, 1979, 1981, 1982; Breternitz and Breternitz 1965; Breternitz and Wood 1965; Breternitz and Lister 1968; Breternitz, Swenlund and Anderson 1971; Breternitz and Norby 1972; Breternitz and Smith 1972; Breternitz, Rohn and Morris 1974; Breternitz, Norby and Nickens 1974; Breternitz and White 1976, 1979; Breternitz, Bye, James, Kane and Knudson 1980; Breternitz and Lucius 1981.

Robert Frederic Burgh (1907-1962)

Bob Burgh was born 23 December 1907 in Denver but spent most of his early years in Three Oaks, Michigan. In 1927 he began undergraduate studies in engineering at Purdue University but left after two years due to poor health. He soon became a general assistant at the Chamberlain Memorial Museum in Three Oaks, where he eventually developed an interest in archaeology. It wasn't until the late 1930s that he went back to college, earning a B.A. from the University of Colorado in 1939.

A chance meeting with Carl Guthe of the University of Michigan Museum inspired Bob to pursue archaeology further. In 1931 Guthe introduced him to Paul Martin, and Bob was able to get on Martin's crew at Lowry Ruin, digging there with Wat Smith, who became his life-long

Figure 13-4   Bob Burgh (left) and Watson Smith in front of Smith's "Peabody West of the Pecos" in 1958. The "institution" name was originally a joke started by Jo Brew but has since stuck in the literature. (Watson Smith.)

friend. In 1932 Burgh was a ranger at Mesa Verde National Park, followed by another season at Lowry. He spent almost three years with the National Park Service, working at Mesa Verde, Chaco Canyon, and Aztec and as a result, became friends with Earl Morris. In 1935 Bob was part of the Awatovi excavations in Arizona. He returned to Three Oaks in 1937 to write a local history of the area but later that year he was hired by the Carnegie Institution of Washington and spent several years working with Earl Morris on various projects such as the Basketmaker sites around Durango. He and Earl published *Anasazi Basketry* about that time, a report still considered the final word on the subject. In 1940-41 he took part in Kidder's excavations at Copan, Honduras, followed by two years in the army. He was discharged in 1944 for health reasons and became a draftsman for a time before accepting the position of Curator of Anthropology at the University of Colorado Museum. While in that position he engaged in research at Dinosaur National Monument, adding to the work of Scoggin several years prior. He completed a report that incorporated Scoggin's findings with his own. There was then brief employment with Gila Pueblo, Arizona, but this too was cut short by poor health. Following recuperation, he moved to Tucson, Arizona, in 1955 and was married in 1957. At that time he renewed his association with Watson Smith at the "Peabody West of the Pecos" and helped write up the ceramic analysis from the earlier Awatovi excavations.

Most of Bob Burgh's life was spent battling respiratory problems, and he finally succumbed on 16 March 1962 in Tucson at the age of 54.

Obituary: Smith 1962.
Colorado-related publications: Burgh 1957; Morris and Burgh 1941, 1954; Burgh and Scoggin 1948.

Figure 13-5 Hal Chase, ca. 1951-53. (Trinidad State Junior College.)

Figure 13-6 (Left to right) Hal Chase, Jack Kerouac, Allen Ginsberg, William Burroughs in New York City, 1944. (Allen Ginsberg.)

Haldon MacNair Chase

Information on Hal Chase has been difficult to obtain, and as a result, this biography is not as complete as others in the chapter.

Hal is a native of Denver. In 1941 he entered Columbia University in New York, earning a B.A. in anthropology in 1947. He then undertook graduate studies there through 1949. Something of a free spirit, he was part of a social group that included Jack Kerouac, the author of *On The Road*, author William Burroughs, and poet Allen Ginsberg.

In 1949 Chase led the Columbia University High Plains Expedition that undertook excavations in southeastern Colorado. The principal site that year was Snake Blakeslee, an Apishapa Focus hamlet on the rimrocks above the Apishapa River. In *On The Road*, Kerouac mentions Hal Chase (under the name Chad King) and his band of anthropologists at this site. In 1951 Chase joined the faculty at Trinidad State Junior College, initiating their program in anthropology. He remained there through 1953.

His trail in recent years is faint, but it appears that he and his wife now live in a somewhat remote location of California, where he builds and repairs musical instruments.

Colorado-related publications: Chase 1949, n.d.; Kerouac 1957; Charters 1973; Gifford and Lee 1978.

Figure 13-7   John Cotter at Lindenmeier in 1935. (John Cotter.)

John Lambert Cotter (b. 1911)

John Cotter was born in Denver on 6 December 1911, graduated from Denver's East High in 1930 (a classmate of Marie Wormington) and received both a B.A. (1934) and M.A. (1935) in anthropology at Denver University. Among his professors there was E.B. Renaud. He received a Ph.D. in anthropology from the University of Pennsylvania in 1959.

His primary field experiences in Colorado were in leading an excavation at Lindenmeier, under the auspices of the Colorado Museum of Natural History in 1934-5, and then with Roberts under the Smithsonian banner in 1935-6. In 1936-7 he was Chief of Party for Edgar Howard during the excavations at Blackwater Draw, New Mexico, that resulted in the recognition of the Clovis projectile point type. From 1940-1977 he was a career archaeologist in the National Park Service, a Professor at the University of Pennsylvania, and a curator at the University of Pennsylvania Museum (Emeritus 1980). He lives in Philadelphia.

Colorado-related publications: Cotter 1978.

Figure 13-8   Herb Dick, ca.
1961, in Trinidad. (Herb
Dick.)

Herbert William Dick (b. 1920)

Herb Dick was born in Chicago on 15 October 1920 but was raised
primarily in New Mexico. He received his B.A. in anthropology from the
University of New Mexico in 1946 and both his M.A. (1948) and Ph.D.
(1957) in anthropology from Harvard.

From 1949 to 1953 he was Curator of Anthropology at the University of
Colorado Museum, excavating in Dinosaur National Monument, the
Claypool site, and at the three Limon-area sites of Cedar Point Village,
Smiley Rockshelter, and Buick Campsite. He is widely recognized for his
work at New Mexico's Bat Cave. From 1952 to 1956 he was Executive
Secretary of the Colorado Archaeological Society. From 1953 to 1962, he
was on staff at Trinidad State Junior College, excavating at Bent's Old Fort,
Trinchera Cave, and Trinidad Reservoir. He was on faculty at Adams State
College in Alamosa from 1963 to 1980, and while there, most of his
fieldwork was conducted in New Mexico. He retired from Adams State and
today resides in Taos, where he runs his company, New Mexico Mining and
Milling Company, Inc.

Colorado-related publications: Dick 1953, 1956, 1963, n.d.; Lister and Dick 1952;
Dick and Mountain 1960.

Figure 13-9   Jesse Walter Fewkes supervising the excavation of Cliff Palace at Mesa Verde in 1909. (Western History Department, Denver Public Library.)

Jesse Walter Fewkes (1850-1930)

Jesse Walter Fewkes was born in Newton, Massachusetts, on 14 November 1850. He entered Harvard at the age of 21, graduating with honors in natural history in 1875. He then went on to Harvard to receive the M.A. and Ph.D. degrees, also in natural history.

He was appointed an assistant in the Museum of Comparative Zoology at Harvard and later became widely known as a marine zoologist. In 1888, while on a trip to California, his interest in ethnology began, and with the support of Mrs. Mary Hemenway undertook studies at Zuni Pueblo. He later worked in the Hopi villages in Arizona, collecting cultural data on ceremonies and other lifeways. In 1895 he excavated the early Hopi ruins at Awatovi and Sikyatki while in the employ of the Bureau of American Ethnology. In 1908, shortly after the establishment of Mesa Verde National Park, he began excavating and stabilizing a number of Anasazi ruins there, along with publishing a number of papers on the work. In 1918 he was appointed Chief of the Bureau of American Ethnology. He retired in 1928 and died 31 May 1930.

Obituary: Hough 1931.

Colorado-related publications: Fewkes 1909, 1911, 1916, 1919, 1920, 1921, 1923.

Figure 13-10   J. D. Figgins, ca. 1934. (Denver Museum of
Natural History.)

Jesse Dade Figgins (1863-1944)

J. D. Figgins was born 17 August 1867 in Frederick County, Maryland.
His early interest was in ornithology, leading first to a position with the
United States National Museum and then with the American Museum of
Natural History, where he became the head of the Department of Prepara-
tion and Exhibition.

In 1910 he became director of the Colorado Museum of Natural History
(now Denver Museum of Natural History), holding that position until
1936. He resigned at that time in order to assist in the building of a
museum in Kentucky for the Bernheim Foundation. The war forced a halt
in that project, and he became affiliated with the University of Kentucky.
He died in Lexington, Kentucky, 10 June 1944.

In addition to directing the construction of many fine exhibits at the
Denver Muesum, he achieved fame for his involvement in the first
documented discovery of human artifacts with extinct bison at Folsom,
New Mexico. That find in 1926 opened up the field of Paleo-Indian
studies. Subsequent work at the Dent site in Colorado revealed fluted
projectile points (later named Clovis) with mammoth remains, extending
the known presence of humans in the New World back an additional
millennium beyond the Folsom culture.

Obituary: Wormington 1946.
Colorado-related publications: Figgins 1927, 1931, 1933, 1934, 1935a, 1935b.

Figure 13-11   Zeke Flora, excavating an Anasazi site, ca. 1936. (Gladys Flora.)

Isaiah Flora (1901-1979)

"Zeke" Flora was born in Ohio 3 April 1901. He married there in 1926 and worked as a machinist. In 1933 he and his wife moved to Durango, Colorado.

Soon after arriving, he developed an interest in local antiquities as a result of prospecting for gold in the area's canyons. In 1934 he dug in some shelters along Falls Creek, unearthing the Basketmaker mummy, 'Esther,' along with numerous artifacts. Earl Morris was later notified of the finds, and he undertook major excavations there. Harold Gladwin, of Gila Pueblo in Arizona, hired Flora to conduct archaeological surveys of the Durango area in the mid-1930s.

In 1935, Flora went to Gila Pueblo, saw how tree-rings could be interpreted in order to date construction periods in early ruins, and set out to amass a considerable collection of wood from sites. From 1938 through 1940, Morris put Flora in charge of collecting, documenting, and distributing tree-ring samples from the Falls Creek shelters and Talus Village. In 1940, after Morris and Flora had a falling-out, Morris came to Durango and retrieved many specimens for curation in Boulder. With the onset of World War II, Flora boxed up the large number of his samples he still had and put them into storage at his home. In 1967 the Laboratory of Tree-Ring Research acquired these documented samples of wood for final curation and study in Tucson.

Flora's mummy, 'Esther,' along with other materials, was ruled to be government property, based on its removal from U.S. Forest Service land.

Ultimately, the National Park Service at Mesa Verde took possession of them, much to Flora's dismay.

From about 1949 to 1959, he operated a shop in Durango, Zeke's Western Jewelry, eventually retiring due to poor health.

Many of his early archaeological explorations around Durango were not conducted in a manner befitting a proper prehistorian, and he could legitimately be characterized as a pothunter. However, his zeal in seeking tree-ring samples, and his care in packaging and storing them, when discarding the bulky packages would have been so much easier, has led to our current knowledge of early Anasazi chronologies. His samples alone extended the known record back several hundred additional years to 322 B.C., the earliest tree-ring dates in the Southwest.

He died 20 March 1979 in Durango.

Obituaries: Anomymous 1979.
Biography: Kaplan 1973.
Other reference: Dean 1975.

Figure 13-12   Paul Gebhard at a campsite in Yuma County in 1941. (Paul Gebhard.)

Paul Henry Gebhard (b. 1917)

Paul Gebhard was born 3 July 1917 in Rocky Ford, Colorado. He received his entire collegiate training in anthropology at Harvard, earning his B.S. in 1940, M.A. in 1942, and Ph.D. in 1947.

In 1934-5, he conducted archaeological surveys for E. B. Renaud in southeastern Colorado and northeastern New Mexico. In 1936 he dug at

Kinishba Pueblo, Arizona, under Dean Byron Cummings. He then excavated in the Aleutians in 1937 with Aleš Hrdlička. In 1940, with sponsorship of the Peabody Museum, he and his wife excavated rock shelters along Colorado's Purgatoire River. The following year, they spent the summer in Yuma County, Colorado, surveying blowouts that had been the source of many Paleo-Indian projectile points.

This was basically the end of work in the West for them. In 1944-5 he was a Psychiatric Research Associate at Massachusetts General Hospital, and in 1946 he joined the faculty in the Department of Anthropology, Indiana University, while holding a joint position in the Institute for Sex Research (Director 1955-82). In 1982 he became Curator of Collections of the Kinsey Institute for Research in Sex, Gender and Reproduction. He remains as Professor of Anthropology at Indiana University, residing in Nashville, Indiana.

Colorado-related publications: Gebhard 1943, 1949.

Figure 13-13 Edgar Lee Hewett (right) with benefactor John D. Rockefeller, Jr., in Santa Fe, ca. 1930. (Neg. No. 7361, Museum of New Mexico.)

Edgar Lee Hewett (1865-1946)

Edgar Hewett was born 23 November 1865 in Warren County, Illinois, attended Tarkio College, Missouri, and from 1884 to 1886, taught at a Missouri country school. In 1886 he was appointed to the chair in literature and history at Tarkio College. He then became superintendent of schools first in Fairfax, Missouri, and later in Florence, Colorado. From 1894 to 1898, he was the superintendent of the training department at Colorado Normal School in Greeley, and while there, undertook his first archaeological work, both on the Pajarito Plateau, west of Santa Fe, and at Pecos Pueblo, east of Santa Fe. He was the President of the newly-established Normal University at Las Vegas, New Mexico from 1898 to 1903, organizing the first college courses in the nation in American archaeology. In 1906, Hewett was chosen as the director of American research for the Archaeological Institute of America. He remained in that position for the next 40 years until his death. His primary goal was to establish an archaeological research institute, which he did.

Hewett was instrumental in the drafting of the 1906 Antiquities Act, and he surveyed the property soon to be designated Mesa Verde National Park. In later years he helped in establishing Chaco Canyon National Monument and other monuments, making him a pivotal individual in the saving of some of the most significant concentrations of prehistoric settlements in the New World.

In 1907, Hewett took three Harvard students out to the McElmo-Yellow Jacket area and told them: "I want you boys to make an archaeological survey of this region. I'll be back in six weeks. You'd better get some horses."

Those three included future poet and writer John Gould Fletcher, and future archaeological greats, A. V. Kidder and Sylvanus Morley.

The School of American Archaeology (later renamed the School of American Research) was established by Hewett at Santa Fe in 1909. The Museum of New Mexico was created at the same time.

Throughout the coming years, he accomplished other significant tasks, such as founding the journal *El Palacio* (1913). He also received many awards and honors. However, one would have to recognize his contributions in writing the 1906 Antiquities Act, helping to set aside significant archaeological properties in the Southwest, and establishing the School of American Research as his greatest contributions to American archaeology.

He died 31 December 1946 in Albuquerque.

Obituary: Walter 1947.
Related publications: Hewett 1906, 1907, 1911; Kidder 1948; Judd 1968.

Figure 13-14   C. T. Hurst. (Western State College.)

Clarence Thomas Hurst (1895-1949)

C. T. Hurst was born 20 June 1895 in Kingston, Kentucky. He was a zoologist by training, receiving both his B.A. (1923) and M.A. (1923) from Western State College, Gunnison, Colorado, and a Ph.D. from the University of California (1926). He taught public school in Colorado from 1916 to 1921, was an Assistant Professor at Wills College, California, and in 1928 began a teaching career at Western State College that would last for the next 21 years until his death 17 January 1949.

Early in his tenure at W.S.C., he accepted the responsibility for organizing and curating a large collection of artifacts from the Southwest. This led him into a detailed study of prehistory, and in time he realized the great potential for damage to archaeological sites by vandals and pothunters. He became the principal force behind the formation in 1935 of the Colorado Archaeological Society and the publication of the Society's official journal, *Southwestern Lore*. This organization has maintained a steadfast stand against pothunting and vandalism ever since, while serving as an educational source, and an outlet for avocational archaeologists in the state.

Hurst was involved in a number of archaeological projects in the state, publishing most of the results in *Southwestern Lore*. Perhaps the best known of his sites are those on the southwest edge of the Uncompaghre Plateau, known as the Tabeguache caves, and which contained evidence of Desert Culture and Ute occupations.

Obituaries: Stewart 1949; Borland 1949.
Colorado-related publications: Hurst 1935a, 1935b, 1936, 1939, 1940a, 1940b, 1940c, 1941, 1943a, 1943b, 1944, 1945, 1946, 1947, 1948; Hurst and Anderson 1949.

Figure 13-15 A passport photo of
Henry Irwin. (Cynthia Irwin-Williams.)

Henry Thomas Johnson Irwin (1938-1978)

Henry Irwin was born 28 March 1938 in Denver and lived there until beginning college. He attended Harvard, receiving his B.A. in 1960, M.A. in 1961, and the Ph.D. in 1968. During 1962-63, he studied at the University of Bordeaux in France, obtaining another M.A. degree.

He and his sister, Cynthia, met Marie Wormington when she came to speak at their school while they were both youngsters. This marked the beginning of a close, life-long, relationship. Marie and her husband, Pete Volk, encouraged their progress and supported them in their activities as they grew up. In Colorado archaeology, when the name Henry Irwin is mentioned, so is his sister's, as they worked as a team on several important excavations from the mid-1950s to 1960. These include the Upper Republican sites at Agate Bluff, and two Denver foothills sites, LoDaisKa and Magic Mountain. Stone typologies developed there are still in use today. Following his study at Harvard, Henry was hired as a faculty member at Washington State University and was involved with his sister, George Agogino, and others at sites like Hell Gap and the U.P. mammoth sites in Wyoming. Henry remained at W.S.U. for 11 years, until his death on 17 April 1978.

Obituaries: Anomymous 1978a; 1978b.
Colorado-related publications: C. Irwin and H. Irwin 1957, 1959, 1961; Irwin-Williams and Irwin 1966; Irwin and Wormington 1970.

Figure 13-16   Cynthia Irwin-Williams, photographed during fieldwork in New Mexico. (A. Burke photo; Cynthia Irwin Williams.)

Cynthia Irwin-Williams (b. 1936)

Cynthia Irwin-Williams was born 14 April 1936 in Denver and was raised there, along with her younger brother, Henry Irwin. She attended Radcliffe College, earning both a B.A. (1957) and an M.A. (1958) in anthropology. She then enrolled at Harvard and was awarded a Ph.D. in anthropology in 1963.

Cynthia and Henry were both encouraged in their pursuits by Denver archaeologist Marie Wormington and her husband, Pete Volk (see Henry Irwin biography). From the mid-1950s until 1960, Cynthia and Henry excavated sites in Colorado that are cited with regularity in the current literature. These were the Upper Republican shelters at Agate Bluff and the Denver foothills sites of LoDaisKa and Magic Mountain. Cynthia's fieldwork experiences outside of Colorado include being research assistant for a Harvard project on the Upper Paleolithic in the Dordogne of France, a director of work at Valsequillo, Mexico, co-director on Paleo-Indian excavations in Wyoming, and numerous projects in New Mexico, the most extensive being at Salmon Ruin near Farmington. From 1964 to 1982, she was on the faculty at Eastern New Mexico University and is now the Executive Director of the Social Sciences Center, Desert Research Institute, Reno, Nevada.

Colorado-related publications: C. Irwin and H. Irwin 1958, 1959, 1961; Irwin-Williams and Irwin 1966.

Figure 13-17   Jean Jeançon, sometime prior to 1929. (Colorado Historical Society.)

Jean Allard Jeançon (1874-1936)

Jean Jeançon was born in Newport, Kentucky, on 14 December 1874, moving to Colorado when he was 20. His educational background has not been well detailed, but it is known that he graduated from the Conservatory of Music in New York. From 1919 to 1921, he served as assistant to Jesse Fewkes at the Smithsonian's Bureau of American Ethnology and in 1921 was hired as the Curator of Archaeology and Ethnology at the Colorado Historical Society in Denver. While at that post, he was involved in numerous projects in and out of the state. In 1921 he began an extended excavation at Chimney Rock and that same year was in charge of the National Geographic Society's Beam Expedition, gathering tree-ring samples across much of the Southwest. Later, his investigations took him as far west in Colorado as Paradox Valley. His interest in music and ethnology led him to extensive study among Indian groups, and he was eventually adopted into Tewa society on the Rio Grande. His publications of Indian music were appreciated by numerous audiences. He resigned from his curator role in 1927 due to health reasons and died 10 April 1936 in Denver.

Obituaries: Anonymous 1936.
Colorado-related publications: Jeançon 1922; Jeançon and Roberts 1923, 1924a, 1924b, 1924c.

Alfred Vincent Kidder (1885-1963)
in photos with Frank H.H. Roberts, Jr., and Jesse Nusbaum

Ted Kidder was born 29 October 1885 in Marquette, Michigan. He attended secondary schools in Cambridge, Massachusetts, and La Villa, Ouchy, Switzerland. In 1904 he entered Harvard, receiving his B.A. (1908), M.A. (1912), and Ph.D. (1914).

Although he intended to study for a career in medicine, he responded to an advertisement in Harvard's newspaper, the *Crimson*, in 1907. As a result, he and fellow students, Sylvanus Morley and John Gould Fletcher, took a summer's job surveying for archaeological sites in southwestern Colorado and southeastern Utah at the behest of Edgar Hewett of the Archaeological Institute of America. Both Kidder and Morley were drawn into the discipline, going on to lifelong careers.

Before Kidder went on to his well-known work at Pecos Pueblo, New Mexico, under the sponsorship of Phillips Academy (initiating the annual Pecos Conference and the classification of Anasazi cultures), he did work at Mesa Verde with Jesse Nusbaum (under Hewett), as well as on Utah's Alkali Ridge and in many other places in New Mexico and Arizona.

In 1928, after Pecos, he expanded his field of knowledge by embarking on what was essentially a second career. With the support of the Carnegie Institution of Washington, and joining Morley, he worked at Maya centers in the Yucatan until his retirement in 1950.

Kidder died 11 June 1963 in Cambridge, Massachusetts, having been a major force in bringing American archaeology into a new, more systematic age.

Obituary: Wauchope 1965.
Biography: Woodbury 1973.
Selected publications: Kidder 1910, 1923, 1924, 1957b; Morley and Kidder 1917.

James Allen Lancaster (b. 1894)

Al Lancaster was born 4 September 1894 in Clifton, Tennessee. He was raised in Beaver County and Fairview, Oklahoma, prior to coming to southwestern Colorado. Although completing neither high school nor college, he has, through personal diligence, risen to the upper echelons of the profession, contributing much, as well as garnering the high esteem of his colleagues.

While farming in the Cortez area during the 1920s, Al began to see evidence of prehistoric cultures, and his interest was generated. During the late 1920s and early 1930s, he became associated with Paul Martin, eventually spending three years on the excavations at Lowry Ruin. He went on to serve eight years with J.O. Brew at Awatovi and Alkali Ridge, along with other stints as a ranger or archaeologist at Hovenweep, Tumacacori, Yucca House, Aztec Ruin, and Chaco Canyon. He spent 25 seasons at Mesa Verde in charge of numerous excavations and stabilization projects. For six years he was affiliated with the staff of the University of Colorado field school at Mesa Verde. In 1962 Al was presented the Distinguished Service Award, the highest award the Department of Interior can bestow. Al resides today in Cortez, within sight of Mesa Verde.

Citation for Distinguished Service: Brew 1963.

Colorado-related publications: Lancaster and Watson 1942, 1954; Lancaster and Pinkley 1954; Lancaster and Van Cleave 1954; Hayes and Lancaster 1975.

Figure 13-10   Robert Lister (left) and Al Lancaster when both were supervising the excavation of site MV-820 on Mesa Verde in 1968. (Jack Smith, Mesa Verde National Park.)

Robert Hill Lister (b. 1915)

Bob Lister was born 7 August 1915 in Las Vegas, New Mexico, was raised in the area, and attended the University of New Mexico, where he earned a B.A. (1937) and M.A. (1938). This was followed by additional study at Harvard, leading to an M.A. (1947) and Ph.D. (1950) in anthropology.

From 1947 to 1970, he was on the faculty at the University of Colorado, teaching numerous students who have gone on to successful careers in archaeology themselves. During those years he conducted many archaeological projects, primarily on the Western Slope. Hell's Midden and Glade Park were two notable areas of investigation, along with his directing the Ute Prehistory Project that resulted in Bill Buckles' well-known dissertation. During the 1960s, much of his fieldwork took place at Mesa Verde for the National Park Service. His wife, Florence, and he wrote a biography of Earl Morris as well. In 1971 he began teaching at the University of New Mexico, combining that with a National Park Service position. He has since retired and lives in Prescott, Arizona.

Colorado-related publications: Lister 1951, 1953 1961, 1964, 1965, 1966, 1967, 1968, 1969; Lister and Dick 1952; Lister and Lister 1968, 1978; Wormington and Lister 1956; Breternitz and Lister 1968.

Figure 13-19   Paul Sidney Martin excavating at Lowry Ruin in 1934 or 1935. (Colorado Historical Society.)

Paul Sidney Martin (1899-1974)

Paul S. Martin was born in Chicago 20 November 1899. He went through both undergraduate (Ph.B. 1923) and graduate (Ph.D. 1929) studies at the University of Chicago. (There is *another* Paul S. [Schultz] Martin in the discipline, but his research interests include the study of fossil pollens, and in order to avoid confusion in conversations, Paul Schultz is commonly known by the moniker "Pollen" Martin).

During the winters of 1926 through 1928, Martin worked with Sylvanus Morley at Chichen Itza in the Yucatan and had it not been for his doctor's recommendation to cease work there following his contraction of malaria and amoebic dysentary, he would probably have finished his career as a Middle American student.

In 1928 he held his first professional position, replacing Jean Jeançon as Curator of Archaeology and Ethnology at the Colorado Historical Society. He began excavating Anasazi sites in the Ackman-Lowry area north of Cortez, the most notable being Lowry Ruin (1934 and 1935). In 1929 he left Denver to accept an Assistant Curator's job at Chicago's Field Museum. He remained in their employ throughout the remainder of his career, along with being a lecturer at the University of Chicago. While at the Field Museum, he continued excavations in the Lowry vicinity until 1939, at which time he redirected his energies to Mogollon sites in New Mexico and Arizona. His work there was innovative, setting high standards in "processual archaeology" by investigating evidences for prehistoric social organization through the testing of hypotheses.

In 1973 he moved to Tucson, Arizona. He died 20 January 1974.

Obituary: Longacre 1976.

Colorado-related publications: Martin 1929, 1930, 1938, 1939; Martin, Roy and von Bonin 1936.

Figure 13-20 Sylvanus Morley at the School of American Archaeology in Santa Fe, ca. 1910. (Neg. No. 10313, Museum of New Mexico.)

Sylvanus Griswold Morley (1883-1948)

Vay Morley was born 7 June 1883 in Chester, Pennsylvania, and was 10 when he and his family moved to Buena Vista, Colorado. Buena Vista and

Colorado Springs were the scenes of his early upbringing. He received a degree in civil engineering at Pennsylvania Military College in 1904, followed by a B.A. (1907) and an M.A. (1908) in anthropology from Harvard.

Compared to most of those in this chapter, Morley's work in Colorado was quite limited. His 1907 survey of the McElmo region with Kidder marked the start of his involvement in archaeology. The following year, he dug at Cannonball Ruin, along the Utah border, the first systematic excavation of an area ruin not on Mesa Verde itself. From then on, the lure of the Yucatan proved too great, and under the sponsorship of the Carnegie Institution of Washington, he excavated many of the major Mayan centers in Central America. In 1947 he was appointed Director of the Museum of New Mexico, planning to fully step into the position in 1948 following his retirement from the Carnegie that year, but he died 2 September 1948 in Santa Fe.

Obituaries: Thompson 1949; Kidder 1948; Roys and Harrison 1948.
Colorado-related publications: Morley 1908; Morley and Kidder 1917.

Earl Halstead Morris (1889-1956)

Earl Morris was born 24 October 1889 in Chama, New Mexico, living, studying and working most of his life in the area of the Four Corners. With a father interested in antiquities and having dug in sites since childhood, he gravitated toward the field in young adulthood. In 1908 he entered the University of Colorado, receiving a B.A. in 1914, and an M.A. in 1915. In 1942 he was awarded an honorary Doctor of Science from C.U. While studying at the University, he was befriended by Junius Henderson, Curator of the University Museum. Henderson was largely responsible for guiding Earl into becoming a scientist.

Some of Earl's earliest professional field experiences came under Edgar Hewett, both in the Southwest and in Guatamala. In 1915 he served an apprenticeship with Nels C. Nelson of the American Museum of Natural History, excavating in the Rio Grande Valley. From 1916 to 1923, he worked at Aztec Ruins near Farmington, as well as in Canyon del Muerto, Arizona.

In 1923 Earl married Ann Axtell, a recent graduate of Smith College and just back in the United States after studying archaeology in Paris under a scholarship from the School of Prehistoric Research. They were married in

Figure 13-21 Earl Morris driving "Old Joe" into Arizona's Canyon del Muerto in 1924. His wife Ann is in the front seat; companion Oscar Tatman is in the back. (University of Colorado Museum.)

Gallup, New Mexico, in the midst of the annual Intertribal Ceremonial and spent a honeymoon visiting excavations near Zuni and in Chaco Canyon. From there they went directly to a season of fieldwork in Canyon del Muerto. Over the ensuing years, Ann was inseparable from Earl, working as an able collaborator in many projects and developing quite a reputation as an artist and author as well. She died at the age of 45 in 1945, being survived by Earl and two daughters, Sarah Lane and Elizabeth Ann. Elizabeth has gone on to an archaeological career herself and is now a professor of anthropology at Colorado State University. In 1946 Earl married Lucile Bowman, a principal in the Boulder school system.

Aztec Ruin is often thought of as Earl's *pièce de résistance*, with his reconstruction of the great kiva being the crown jewel. However, his investigation in Colorado along the La Plata and the upper Animas rivers went a long way toward filling out the known scope of Anasazi occupations in the Southwest.

When he finished digging at Talus Village with Bob Burgh in 1940, Earl hung up his shovel for good. He returned to Boulder and became involved in writing and editing, along with some teaching at the University. In 1954 Earl was presented the Alfred Vincent Kidder Award by the American Anthropological Association for his achievements in archaeology. Then, in 1955, he retired from the Carnegie Institution. He died the following year on 24 June 1956, leaving a valuable legacy of knowledge for all who followed.

Obituaries: Burgh 1957; Kidder 1957a.
Biographies: Lister and Lister 1968; Morris 1978.
Selected Colorado-related publications: Morris 1911, 1919, 1927, 1929, 1931, 1939, 1944, 1949, 1952; Morris and Burgh 1941, 1954.

Figure 13-22   Gustav Nordenskiöld, ca. 1890. (Jack Smith, Mesa Verde National Park.)

Gustav Eric Adolf Nordenskiöld (1868-1895)

Gustav Nordenskiöld was born 29 July 1868 in Stockholm, Sweden, the son of an arctic explorer and scientist. In 1889 he graduated from the University of Uppsala in Sweden with a degree in chemistry and mineralogy.

In 1890, while on an expedition to Spittsbergen, he contracted tuberculosis. The following year he came to the United States, and while passing through Denver, saw a display of Anasazi artifacts collected by the Wetherill brothers. He went to Mancos, met with the Wetherills, and had them take him into the recesses of Mesa Verde to explore the ruins there. He had intended to stay a short time when he arrived in early June, but the summer came and went before Nordenskiöld finally packed up the artifacts they had excavated from various cliff dwellings on the Mesa. After several weeks of waiting while the citizens of Durango fought through the courts (unsuccessfully) to prevent the removal of Anasazi artifacts from the country, Nordenskiöld left for Sweden. The artifacts and photographs from the expedition toured Europe, and he gained honors for them. In 1893 he published his book on Mesa Verde, drawing considerable attention of Anasazi ruins in Colorado.

He died 5 June 1895 in Morsil Station, Sweden, at the age of 27.

Obituary: on file at Mesa Verde National Park.
Colorado-related publications: Nordenskiöld 1901.

Figure 13-23   Jesse Nusbaum (left) and Ted Kidder standing on the rimrock above Mesa Verde's Spruce Tree House in 1908. Both Nusbaum and Kidder have uncharacteristic growths of facial hair this particular summer, with Kidder's beard grown in response to Nusbaum's initiative. (Columbia University Press.)

Jesse Logan Nusbaum (1887-1975)

Jess Nusbaum was born 3 September 1887 in Greeley, Colorado, and raised in the area. He graduated from the State Normal School, Greeley, in 1907.

His earliest archaeological fieldwork took place in 1907, when he was a photographer for Edgar Hewett of the Archaeological Institute of America. As the years passed, he worked on a number of projects in Utah, New Mexico, and Central America. In 1921 Nusbaum became superintendent of Mesa Verde National Park. Being a trained archaeologist, he differed from previous National Park Service personnel there, and thus brought a new dimension to the study and interpretation of the prehistoric remains of the Mesa. In 1924 Nusbaum was instrumental in the building of the park's present museum, through the generosity of John D. Rockefeller, Jr. Between 1924 and 1929, Rockefeller funded Nusbaum and his crews on excavations of various ruins in the area, one of the most notable being the Basketmaker III pithouses at Step House Cave. In 1929 Nusbaum was lured to Santa Fe and the newly-established Laboratory of Anthropology, an institution also sponsored by Rockefeller. Nusbaum served as director of the Laboratory from 1930 to 1935. He went on to become the Departmental Consulting Archeologist for the Department of the Interior, initiating the Pipeline Archeological Salvage Program in 1950, the first of its kind in the nation.

He died 22 December 1975 in Santa Fe.

Obituary: Peckham 1976.
Biographies: Smith 1981; Judd 1968.
Colorado-related publications: Nusbaum 1981.

Figure 13-24   Alan Olson during the 1950s. (University of Denver, Department of Anthropology.)

Alan Peter Olson (1926-1978)

Alan Olson was born 28 December 1926 in Hillrose, Colorado. He was raised in Boulder, served in the United States Army Air Force for one year, and then enrolled at the University of Colorado, where he earned a B.A. in anthropology in 1951. He was awarded a Ph.D. in anthropology from the University of Arizona in 1959.

Early fieldwork included excavations at the Lyons Rock Shelter, as well as serving on crews for Arnie Withers in the southeastern part of Colorado. In 1950 he was a member of Herb Dick's expedition to Bat Cave. While at the University of Arizona, he was a student and then foreman at the Point of Pines archaeological field school. He also served as editor of *The Kiva* during those years. In 1959 he was hired as curator of anthropology at the Museum of Northern Arizona, along with teaching at what is now Northern Arizona University. In 1964, he joined the faculty of the University of Denver. In addition to his teaching at D.U., his research included a number of contract archaeology projects. He died while still on the D.U. faculty, 26 May 1978.

Obituary: Morris 1981.

Colorado-related publications: Olson 1953, 1976; Olson, Rowland and LaFree 1976; Olson, Bridge and LaFree 1976.

Figure 13-25   E. B. Renaud at an eastern Colorado shelter. Upon seeing this photo, Marie Wormington said she was sure someone else was using the shovel, as manual labor was not something he practiced. (University of Denver Department of Anthropology.)

Etienne Bernardeau Renaud (1880-1973)

E.B. Renaud was born in Bellancourt, France (near Paris), on 14 June 1880. He received a bachelor's degree from the University of Paris in 1905. With a three-year fellowship, he came to the United States where he undertook graduate work in physics, chemistry, and mathematics at Catholic University, Washington, D.C. In 1913 he became an American citizen and from 1914 to 1916 was an instructor in romance languages at the University of Colorado while working on an M.A., which he received in 1915. In 1916 he began a similar teaching and study regimen at Denver University, teaching romance languages and anthropology until 1920, when he received his Ph.D. He then became a professor of anthropology and was department head for 28 years.

During World War I, Renaud served in the U.S. Army as a lieutenant and was a director of language studies in the Army Special Training Program at D.U. during World War II. He received the Palmes Academiques from France, was made a commander of the French Legion of Honor while at D.U., and served as the acting French consul for Colorado, Wyoming, and Utah from 1931 to 1937.

In 1920 and 1921, he was part of the Jeançon excavations at Chimney Rock and from 1930 to 1947 was director of D.U.'s Archaeological Survey of the High Western Plains. From the latter work, Renaud published numerous papers on archaelogical finds throughout eastern Colorado and parts of New Mexico, Wyoming, Nebraska, and South Dakota. By today's standards, much of his work appears superficial and inexact. Great difficulty is encountered when relocation of his numerous sites are attempted.

Despite these shortcomings, he was largely responsible for alerting the archaeological community to the richness of sites in what was often treated as a cultural backwater. In addition, he was the principal inspiration for many students entering the discipline, among them Wormington, Cotter, and Roberts. He retired from D.U. in 1948, after teaching there for 32 years.

He died 6 February 1973 at the age of 92, in Denver.

Obituaries: Chapman 1973; Anonymous 1973.

Biography: Anonymous 1948.

Colorado-related publications: Renaud 1931, 1932a, 1932b, 1933, 1934a, 1934b, 1935, 1936a, 1936b, 1937, 1938a, 1938b, 1940, 1942a, 1942b, 1943, 1945, 1946, 1947, 1960.

Figure 13-26   Important visitors at Roberts' excavations at Lindenmeier, ca. 1935. (Left to right) Earl Morris, A. V. Kidder II, Kirk Bryan, Donald Scott, Ted Kidder, and Frank H. H. Roberts, Jr. The youth in the foreground may be crew member Carl F. Miller. (University of Colorado Museum.)

Frank Harold Hanna Roberts, Jr., (1897-1966)

Frank H.H. Roberts was born 11 August 1897 in Centerburg, Ohio. When he was three, his father, Frank Hunt Hurd Roberts, accepted a civics and history position in Laramie, Wyoming, and the family lived there until 1903, when the senior Roberts went on faculty at Denver University. In 1910 his father became president at Las Vegas (N.M.) Normal University, just a few years after the departure of Hewett as president. It was in Las Vegas that young Frank finished his high school education and spent one year of college. He then left for the University of Denver, where he received a B.A. in history and English in 1919 (the year 1918 being spent in the Army). In 1920, after a year as a reporter and city editor of *The Las Vegas* (N.M.) *Daily Optic*, he returned to Denver University, earning an M.A. in political science in 1921. The influence of E.B. Renaud during those years helped to generate an interest in archaeology. In 1924 he entered Harvard, and by 1927 had earned a Ph.D. in anthropology.

His early fieldwork had come at the direction of Renaud and Jeançon. In 1921 he excavated in the Chimney Rock area with Jeançon. This work was to continue into 1924, along with some teaching of Spanish and anthropology at D.U. Then, while in the Harvard program, he worked at Pueblo Bonito under Neil Judd, gathering the material he used to complete his dissertation on Chaco Canyon ceramics. In 1926 he joined the staff at the Smithsonian Institution's Bureau of American Ethnology, an association that was to last the next 38 years until his retirement in 1964. His accomplishments were many during that time. He excavated throughout much of the Southwest and the plains, was one of the founding fathers of the River Basin Surveys and the Society of American Archaeology, and was the recipient of numerous honors, including SAA's Viking Fund Medal and Award in 1951. Colorado was the scene of one of his greatest contributions. In 1934 he began excavations at Lindenmeier, perhaps the most important Folsom site yet discovered. He continued work there through 1940. As a result of this work, our knowledge of Paelo-Indian lithic technology and camping patterns is rich roday.

Following a period of declining health, he died in Washington, D.C., on 23 February 1966.

Obituary: Stephenson 1967.

Colorado-related publications: Jeançon 1922; Jeançon and Roberts 1923, 1924a, 1924b, 1924c; Roberts 1925, 1929, 1930, 1934, 1935a, 1935b, 1935c, 1936a 1936b, 1936c, 1937a, 1937b, 1938, 1940a, 1940b, 1941, 1946a, 1946b.

Charles Romine Scoggin (1914-1944)

"Chili" Scoggin was born 10 July 1914 in Bridgeport, Nebraska, attended elementary school in Chula Vista, California, high school in Ovid, Colorado, and then moved with his parents to Julesburg, Colorado, living there for a few years before entering the University of Colorado in 1935. Due to harsh economic conditions, he had to work a great deal during his undergraduate days, making his attendance irregular, and contributing to the fact that he did not complete the requirements for a degree.

As a young man in the Julesburg area, he became interested in prehistoric artifacts, collecting specimens from local sites. In 1934 he was one of the pioneers in launching the Society of American Amateur Archeologists and editing their journal, *The Arch*. It so happened that the Society for

Figure 13-27   Charles Scoggin in Julesburg, Colorado, ca. 1939. (Charlene Scoggin.)

American Archaeology was beginning at about the same time, and with this group and the fledgling Colorado Archaeological Society also recruiting, membership in the S.A.A.A. did not grow sufficiently. Publication of *The Arch* was suspended after three issues when Scoggin started school at the University of Colorado. Upon the collapse of the organization nationally, Scoggin took it upon himself to pay off all the debts, a little at a time, while working his way through college.

In 1936 he joined the Smithsonian's excavations at Lindenmeier, working with Roberts through 1940. During the 1940 season, he was left in complete charge of the camp and excavations. In the winter and spring of 1939-40, he and Edison Lohr surveyed and tested an extensive area in Dinosaur National Monument, their greatest find was perhaps Mantle's Cave. Over the winter of 1940-41, he analyzed the recovered materials while attending classes and then returned the next summer as a temporary National Park Service ranger to complete fieldwork there. During the 1941-42 school year, he worked entirely on the final analysis and report preparation of the Dinosaur project, as he anticipated being called up for military service and did not want to leave the record incomplete. As a result, he gave up the chance to finish his final two semesters of classes required for a degree. With permission from his draft board, he returned to Dinosaur in the early summer of 1942 in order to accompany National Park Service officials on a tour of the sites there.

He entered the Army in July of 1942 and was later commissioned a 2nd Lieutenant in the Corps of Engineers. On 2 February 1944, he was killed on Anzio beachhead, Italy. He left his wife, Charlene, and an infant son whom he never saw.

Obituary: Roberts 1944.
Colorado-related publications: Scoggin 1939, 1941, 1942; Burgh and Scoggin 1948.

Figure 13-28   Omer Stewart, 1974. (Omer Stewart.)

Omer Call Stewart (b. 1908)

Omer Stewart was born 17 August 1908 in Provo, Utah. He received a B.A. in anthropology from the University of Utah in 1933 and later attended the University of California at Berkeley, where he earned a Ph.D. in 1939.

His training and expertise lie primarily in ethnology, and he is regarded as one of the foremost authorities on the Ute Indians. In 1930 he was a cook for Julian Steward during the Promontory Point and Black Rock Cave excavations and then cooked for Lynn Hargrave in 1933 during the Rainbow Bridge-Monument Valley Expedition. In 1933 he was an instructor at the University of Texas, moved to the University of Minnesota in 1940 on a post-doctorate fellowship and taught there in 1941. At the end of the year, he was inducted into the Army, serving until 1945. Upon discharge, he accepted a faculty appointment at the University of Colorado and has been there ever since. Following the death of C.T. Hurst in 1949, Stewart assumed the position of Executive Secretary of the Colorado Archaeological Society, holding it until 1952. In 1974 he became Emeritus Professor at C.U. and continues to maintain an office there. He has always considered himself an avocational archaeologist and remains a strong supporter of the amateur movement in the state, while continuing to produce publications on ethnohistoric subjects.

Colorado-related publications: Stewart 1941, 1942, 1947a, 1947b, 1948, 1949, 1963, 1966, 1971, 1977, 1979, 1982.

Figure 13-29   Gil Wenger, 1972. (Gil Wenger.)

Gilbert Riley Wenger (b. 1923)

Gil Wenger was born 16 June 1923 in Grand Junction, Colorado, graduated from high school in Salt Lake City, and then entered the University of Denver. During 1943-45 his education was interrupted while he served in the Air Force in the Pacific Theater, where he was awarded the Purple Heart. Returning to Denver University, he received a B.A. in anthropology in 1948 and then was awarded an M.A. in anthropology in 1956. The M.A. degree would have been given several years earlier, but a fire in his home destroyed all six copies of the thesis, requiring a rewriting.

In 1950 Gil conducted a survey in northwestern Colorado, and from that he produced his M.A. thesis primarily on Fremont occupational evidence. He joined the National Park Service in 1951, serving at a variety of stations, including Arizona's Tonto National Monument and Montezuma Castle. He was also at the Western Museum Laboratory in San Francisco, where he designed Southwestern region archaeological museums for the National Park Service. From 1968 to 1981 he was the Chief Park Archeologist at Mesa Verde National Park. He retired from the National Park Service in 1981 and resides in Grand Junction, Colorado.

Colorado-related publications: Wenger 1955, 1956, 1980, 1981.

Figure 13-30 Joe Ben Wheat examines a fragment of bison bone at the Jurgens site in 1970. (Bill Peery photo; Frank Frazier.)

Joe Ben Wheat (b. 1916)

Joe Ben Wheat was born 21 April 1916 in Van Horn, Texas. He studied at the University of California under Kroeber and Lowie, receiving a B.A. in anthropology in 1937. Later graduate work at the University of Arizona earned him an M.A. in 1947 and a Ph.D. in 1953.

His fieldwork has been quite varied. During 1939-41 he was in charge of W.P.A. excavations in Texas, being the first to dig the now well-known Paleo-Indian locality at Lubbock Lake. In 1947 he was involved with salvage operations by the Smithsonian River Basin Surveys, also in Texas. While studying at the University of Arizona, he spent several seasons at the University's field school at Point of Pines, working with Mogollon sites. In the summers of 1952 and 1953 he was in charge of the Tusayan Museum at the Grand Canyon. Upon receiving his Ph.D. he was hired by the University of Colorado Museum to replace the departing Herb Dick as curator of anthropology. While at the museum, Joe Ben has excavated at many sites in the state, including the possible Apachean Cedar Point Village near Limon, the Paleo-Indian sites of Olsen-Chubbock and Jurgens, and several Anasazi sites in the vicinity of Yellow Jacket. Joe Ben began semi-retirement at the museum in 1982 but maintains his office and continues his Yellow Jacket work. He and his wife, Pat, live in Boulder.

Colorado-related publications: Wheat 1955, 1967, 1972, 1979.

Figure 13-31   Arnie Withers (standing, with hat) on a University of Denver fieldtrip to Mesa Verde in 1953.
(Mel Griffiths, University of Denver.)

Arnold Moore Withers (b. 1916)

Arnie Withers was born in Pueblo, Colorado, on 28 May 1916. He was
raised in Rye, Colorado, and continues to maintain a home there now. He
attended the University of Arizona, receiving a B.A. in 1938 and an M.A.
in 1941. He then went to Columbia University, earning a Ph.D. in
anthropology in 1947. Several years between his M.A. and Ph.D. were
spent with the military in the South Pacific during World War II.

He was hired directly from Columbia as a professor at Denver University
and remained there for his entire career. During that time, he excavated
numerous sites on the plains, having special interest in Formative-age
cultures. He worked at the Bellwood site (type site for the Graneros Focus),
at the Limon-area Buick Campsite (Upper Republican), and Franktown
Cave. He was involved with early contract archaeology in the state at
Chatfield Reservoir, the Blue River-South Platte project, and the Pueblo,
Ruedi, Sugarloaf, and Twin Lakes reservoirs. He and Al Schroeder have
retraced much of the early routes of Ulibarri and others who came across
Colorado from New Mexico in the 1700s. He retired from Denver Univer-
sity in 1976 and lives part of the year in Santa Fe and part in Rye.

Biography: Simonich 1980.

Colorado-related publications: Withers 1954, 1964a, 1964b, 1965, 1972, 1981,
1982; Withers and Roberts 1948; Withers and Huffman 1966.

Figure 13-32   Marie Wormington at the Moore shelter near Montrose in 1937. (Marie Wormington.)

Hannah Marie Wormington Volk (b. 1914)

Marie Wormington was born in Denver on 5 September 1914. A classmate of John Cotter, she graduated from Denver's East High School and entered Denver University. There she studied under E.B. Renaud. She earned her B.A. at D.U. in 1935. Following that she attended Radcliffe, where she found that many of her required courses for an anthropology major had to be taken at Harvard. She became the second woman admitted to the Harvard department. Radcliffe awarded her an M.A. in 1950 and a Ph.D. in 1954.

In the year of her graduation from Denver University, she was able to obtain field experience excavating Paleolithic sites in France for Dr. Henri Martin. Upon returning to Denver, she was hired as a staff archaeologist at the Denver Museum of Natural History by J.D. Figgins. In 1937 she was promoted to curator of archaeology. She remained at that position (with time out for graduate studies at Radcliffe) for the next 31 years. She conducted numerous excavations in the region, often accompanied by her husband, the late Pete Volk, a well-known petroleum engineer. Also during that period she wrote several of the most useful syntheses on various cultural stages in North America. Her *Ancient Man in North America* has been a standard reference for decades, and she now has a new book, *Ancient Hunters and Gatherers in the New World*, in the final stages of editing. After leaving the Denver Museum, she accepted various visiting professorships at schools around the nation, as well as here in Colorado. She resides today in Denver.

Just as Margaret Mead did in cultural anthropology, Marie has paved the way for women in archaeology, having persevered despite various degrees of discrimination throughout her career. In 1958 she was recognized by her peers through her election as the first woman president of the Society for American Archaeology and in 1983, as a Society member "whose achievements have been clearly extraordinary in nature and have resulted in a genuine and lasting contribution to the archaeological profession," she was awarded SAA's Distinguished Service Award. She has brought great credit to the state of Colorado and to the discipline as a whole.

Biography: Sudler 1983.
Colorado-related publications: Wormington 1948, 1955, 1956, 1957, 1962, in prep; Wormington and Lister 1956.

Terminology

As prehistoric aboriginals lived out their lives on the prairies, mountains, and plateaus and in the valleys of Colorado, they probably had a feeling of continuity with their ancestors. Generations would pass with little recognition of drastic cultural change. Changes did take place, however, but not at a fixed rate.

When viewed from the perspective of the twentieth century, cultural evolution is readily apparent. The systematic study of prehistoric cultural change is a principal goal of archaeological inquiry. Archaeologists have constructed a variety of frameworks to help organize diverse cultural data into manageable entities by defining the parameters of time and geographical distribution for each culture stage. These frameworks are not designed to be sacrosanct but are working models that allow the testing of hypotheses. As new data are introduced or as faulty components of the classification systems are discovered, modifications can be incorporated and tested. Those that withstand the test of time usually find general acceptance and widespread use. Whether a prehistoric hunter would recognize and agree with the cultural, geographical and chronological distinctions made by archaeologists is debatable. But, an organized approach to the study of past cultures requires a foundation upon which comparative analysis can take place.

Willey and Phillips

As the framework with the greatest scope, the system of Willey and Phillips will be considered first. Building upon the work of Julian Steward,

253

Alex Krieger, and many others, and using numerous local and regional chronologies, Gorden Willey and Phillip Phillips proposed a "Historical-Developmental" interpretation for the New World.

In conjunction with a multi-stage cultural evolution scheme encompassing the Americas, they organized a reasonable integrative system for various archaeological units. They attempted to draw together three significant variables: cultural content, time, and space.

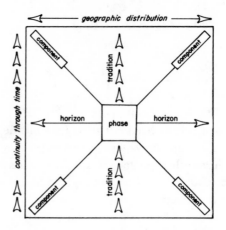

Figure T-1   Model of primary archaeological integrative units. (Modified from Willey and Phillips 1958:41.)

Cultural content is incorporated in the *phase*. A phase has "traits sufficiently characteristic to distinguish it from all other units similarly conceived whether of the same or other cultures . . . ." A phase is an identifiable culture type, represented by specific sites or levels within sites (components) of a region or locality.

STAGE	GENERALIZATION	OLD WORLD EQUIVALENT
Post-Classic	imperialistic states	Civilization
Classic	early urban developments	Civilization
Formative	beginnings of settled village life, horticulture/agriculture, ceramics	Neolithic
Archaic	post-Pleistocene hunting and gathering	Mesolithic
Lithic	terminal Pleistocene hunting and gathering	Upper Paleolithic

Figure T-2   Historical-developmental system of Willey and Phillips. (1958.)

Time in the system is represented by *tradition*. A tradition exists when continuity in cultural characteristics persists through time. This can mean that certain parts of the cultures may undergo change, but other integral features will remain recognizably connected to the original phase.

Space is represented in the *horizon*. A horizon, like a tradition, deals with cultural continuity, but it is across a geographic expanse instead of through time. Units within a horizon are assumed to be approximately contemporaneous.

Using these qualifiers as units of integration, Willey and Phillips proposed five stages that embrace the entire cultural experience of the prehistoric Americas. These stages are the broadest categories generally used to classify prehistoric cultures in the New World and were not intended to be used for chronological purposes, but only to serve on a gross level as a general guide to classifying cultural development.

The first is the *Lithic*, a stage which has a data base composed almost entirely of stone tools. Lithic peoples probably gained their subsistence primarily through big-game hunting, with a lesser emphasis on gathering. The term Paleo-Indian (coined by Roberts 1940), though not preferred by Willey and Phillips, has been in general use with this stage. The environmental context for the Lithic stage was terminal Pleistocene and early post-Pleistocene. Geographic distribution seems to include most, if not all, of the Americas.

The *Archaic* is a continuation of the pre-ceramic Lithic during the post-Pleistocene. Hunting was more balanced with gathering of wild plants. Regional diversity seems to have developed, with a wide variety of edible resources exploited, depending on availability. Archaic peoples were similar to those of the Lithic but without the Ice-Age mammals to rely upon for food. As a result, a more generalized economy was established.

The *Formative* stage is characterized by the cultivation of domesticated crops and by increased sedentism. Hunting and gathering continued, though with less importance than before.

The *Classic* and *Post-Classic* stages are beyond the developmental levels achieved in Colorado. Centered in Central and South America, they are characterized by urban centers, religious and other public architecture, an emphasis on art during the Classic, and a waning of religious influence and an increase in militarism during the Post-Classic.

The Willey and Phillips system was largely responsible for a reawakening of the cultural evolution approach to archaeological research. The modern archaeologist, searching for processes of culture change, has roots in the work of Willey and Phillips.

The Pecos Classification

On more restricted regional levels, other archaeologists have contributed to our current classificatory systems in use in Colorado.

Concerning Southwestern United States cultures, 1927 was a watershed year. Alfred Kidder, having excavated for years at New Mexico's Pecos Pueblo, hosted a conference for the leading regional archaeologists with the intent of formulating a classification system that would standardize terminology for the types of sites being investigated at the time. He hoped that this exercise would enhance communication between professionals. The Pecos Conference exists to this day as an annual meeting where new data and ideas can be exchanged.

What emerged from the 1927 gathering was the first cultural system developed on the basis of intensive excavation. It has come to be known as the Pecos Classification. Beginning with Basketmaker I, II, and III (based on early observations that the cultures appeared to be aceramic), it progressed through Pueblo I, II, III, IV, and V (Pueblo V is modern). The Pecos Classification was designed with the idea that as new finds warranted, modifications in the system would be made. Though some alterations were attempted, the original Pecos framework essentially became rigid. Its applicability to areas peripheral to the Anasazi (Four Corners area) was limited. Eventually, this led to the abandonment of the terms among those working with the Mogollon and Hohokam to the south and west. With the addition of complex phase systems developed by some archaeologists, the Pecos Classification is still in use in Four Corners Anasazi research.

The Midwestern Taxonomic Method

During the 1930s archaeologists working in the eastern part of the continent were developing local cultural sequences but had no framework to tie them together into a cohesive synthesis. In 1932 and 1935, a number of leading authorities—including James Griffin, Fay-Cooper Cole, William McKern, and others from Michigan, Illinois and Wisconsin—convened conferences to put their data into some order. The result has been termed the Midwestern Taxonomic Method or the McKern Classification, an archaeological adaptation of a geological taxonomic system.

One of the real problems in the Mississippi drainage and the area to the east was the lack of known multi-component sites (which have since been added to the data base). Most of the knowledge came from collections with very limited contextual information. As a result, the McKern system was less concerned with chronology and geographic distribution, than with artifact typology.

The Midwestern Taxonomic Method is divided into several levels, beginning with the smallest unit, a *component*. The component can be an entire site that exhibits a singular lifeway or a single occupation level within a site that had been periodically visited by other groups. Sites or artifact assemblages that exhibit very similar traits are grouped into a *focus*. A number of foci can in turn be lumped together on the basis of similarity into the next level, an *aspect*. Aspects are grouped by traits into *phases*, which can then be combined into *patterns*. By this time, the number of divergent qualities present within a level is considerable, though at least some significant attributes are still held in common. The highest level in the system is the *base*, in which, for example, one might distinguish between horticulturalists and hunter-gatherers.

Strong, Mulloy, Frison, and Wood

The Midwestern Taxonomic Method filtered across the plains and into Colorado via the work of people like W. D. Strong of Nebraska. He employed a methodology termed the Direct Historical Approach. By starting with ethnohistoric information and known Pawnee village sites, he worked back into time, connecting historic Indians to their prehistoric ancestors. Strong utilized the Midwestern Taxonomic Method to organize the data and augmented the system with dates.

Those parts of the plains with little cultural influence from the major eastern riverine groups were in something of a terminological vacuum for many years. William T. Mulloy worked in Montana and Wyoming during the 1940s and began to sort out cultural periods for the area, using especially the data derived from the deeply stratified Pictograph Cave.

His stages were the Early Prehistoric, the Altithermal Hiatus, Middle Prehistoric (Early and Late divisions), and Late Prehistoric. Of these terms, the one that has survived in some reports is Late Prehistoric, denoting all post-Archaic peoples prior to historic contact.

Another Wyoming archaeologist, George Frison, has reworked Mulloy's system into a form that is widely used today in the literature. He employs the more standard Paleo-Indian term for Mulloy's Early Prehistoric. Mulloy thought that during the hotter and drier Altithermal the plains

Basic Culture	Phase	Aspect	Focus	Component
	Upper Mississippi	Nebraska	Omaha	Rock Bluffs, Gates Saunders, Walker Gilmore II
			St. Helena	Butte, St. Helena, etc.
Mississippi	Central Plains	Upper Republican	Lost Creek	Lost Creek, Prairie Dog Creek, etc.
			Sweetwater	Sweetwater, Munson Creek, etc.
			Medicine Creek	Medicine Creek
			North Platte	Signal Butte III
		Lower Loup (Protohistoric Pawnee?)	Beaver Creek	Burkett, Schuyler, etc.
		Lower Platte (Historic Pawnee?)	Columbus	Horse Creek, Fullerton, Linwood, etc.
			Republican	Hill, etc.
	Woodland	Iowa "Algonkian"	Sterns Creek	Walker Gilmore I
Great Plains	Early Hunting	Signal Butte II (?)	Signal Butte	Signal Butte II
		Signal Butte I	Signal Butte	Signal Butte I
		Folsom	Northern Colorado	Lindenmeier (Colo.)

Figure T-3   Strong's Plains Classification with the Midwestern Taxonomic Method. (Strong 1935.)

were generally devoid of people. Subsequent research has identified sites from this period, which Frison has termed the Early Plains Archaic. Frison puts the Middle and Late Plains Archaic where Mulloy had the Early and Late Middle Prehistoric. The Late Prehistoric is retained for the terminal occupation of the Northern Plains prior to historic contact. Frison admits that chronological problems exist for the Archaic regardless of whose terminology is used, due to cultural variability across the plains at any given time. Although his scheme is used for convenience, it is open to future modification.

John J. Wood, in his dissertation dealing with the prehistory of northeastern Colorado, utilized a revised system for the sites he was investigating. Divided into Preceramic and Ceramic Periods, it has fallen into disuse due to subsequent knowledge accumulated through better dating of additional stratified sites.

Summary

The preceding superficial overview of the terminological influences on Colorado archaeology should impress upon the reader that the current frameworks for classifying past cultures here were not built by any single individual or at any one time. These systems have developed from a wide variety of sources and have undergone criticisms, rejections, revisions, and acceptance (not necessarily in that order).

If one reads even a few archaeological reports dealing with Colorado, it is soon obvious that taxonomic standardization is yet to be accomplished by

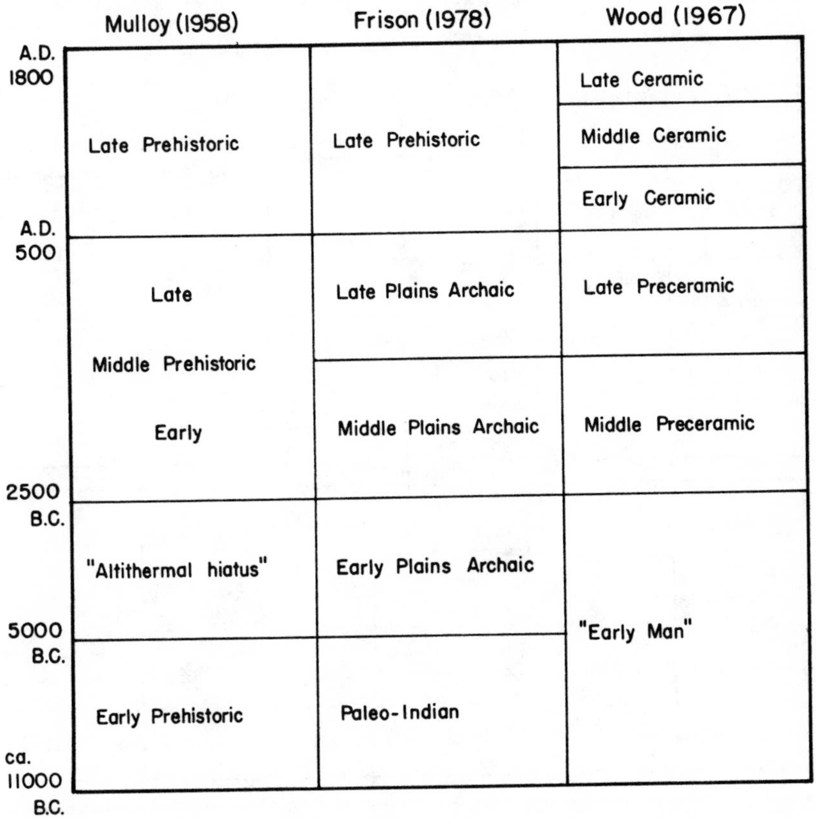

	Mulloy (1958)	Frison (1978)	Wood (1967)
A.D. 1800	Late Prehistoric	Late Prehistoric	Late Ceramic
			Middle Ceramic
			Early Ceramic
A.D. 500	Late	Late Plains Archaic	Late Preceramic
	Middle Prehistoric		
	Early	Middle Plains Archaic	Middle Preceramic
2500 B.C.	"Altithermal hiatus"	Early Plains Archaic	
5000 B.C.			"Early Man"
	Early Prehistoric	Paleo-Indian	
ca. 11000 B.C.			

Figure T-4   Other terminology schemes for the Northern and Central Plains.

STAGE	TRADITION	PERIOD	COMPLEX	PHASE	COMPONENT
Northeast Colorado					
FORMATIVE	Central Plains			Upper Republican	
	Woodland	Plains Woodland			
ARCHAIC	Archaic	Late Archaic			
		Middle Archaic	McKean		
		Early Archaic	Magic Mt. / Mt. Albion		
LITHIC	Paleo-Indian	Plano	Cody / Agate Basin / Hell Gap		
		Folsom	Folsom		
		Clovis (Llano)	Clovis		
Southeast Colorado					
FORMATIVE			Upper Purgatoire (Complex)	Late Sopris (Phase) / Early Sopris (Phase) / Initial Sopris (Phase)	
			Panhandle (Aspect)	Apishapa (Focus) / Optima (Focus) / Antelope Ck.(Focus)	
	Woodland	Plains Woodland			
ARCHAIC	Archaic	Late Archaic			
		Middle Archaic			
		Early Archaic			
LITHIC	Paleo-Indian	Plano			
		Folsom			
		Clovis (Llano)			
Northwest Colorado					
FORMATIVE	Fremont		Uinta / San Rafael	Cub Ck.	
ARCHAIC	Desert Culture		Uncompahgre		
		Middle Archaic	McKean		
LITHIC	Paleo-Indian	Plano			
		Folsom			
		Clovis (Llano)			
Southwest Colorado					
FORMATIVE	Anasazi	Pueblo III / Pueblo II / Pueblo I / Basketmaker III / Basketmaker II		various regional systems	
ARCHAIC	Desert Culture	Late Archaic (lg. projectile pt.)	Uncompahgre	Ironstone / Dry Creek / Horsefly / Roubideau / Shavano / Monitor Mesa	
		Middle Archaic			
LITHIC	Paleo-Indian	Plano			
		Folsom			
		Clovis			

Figure T-5   Colorado archaeological classifications as used in this text.

fieldworkers in the state. Often, what an archaeologist uses in categorizing finds is a blend of many systems. In addition, errors in applying various terms (some of which have become entrenched in the literature) has led to confusion.

This book is not presented as the last word on the subject of regional taxonomy. Continued theory-building, combined with rigorous fieldwork and analysis, will certainly result in many significant changes in the way we view Colorado and its prehistory.

For the moment at least the scheme in Figure T-5 will serve to define the basic taxonomic levels and the incorporated cultural terminology that are used in this book. Whether others choose to utilize it in its entirety, modify it to some degree, or reject it altogether, will depend on their background, educational influences and biases, and specific research orientations.

References

On the Willey and Phillips Historical-Developmental scheme:
    Willey and Phillips 1958; Willey and Sabloff 1974.

On Kidder's Pecos Classification:
    Kidder 1927; Willey and Sabloff 1974.

On McKern's Midwestern Taxonomic Method:
    McKern 1939; Willey and Sabloff 1974.

On Strong's Direct Historical Approach:
    Strong 1935; Willey and Sabloff 1974.

On Mulloy's terminology for the Northern Plains:
    Mulloy 1958.

On Frison's terminology for the Northern Plains:
    Frison 1978.

On Wood's terminology for northeastern Colorado:
    Wood 1967.

Radiocarbon Dates

COLORADO PALEO-INDIAN RADIOCARBON DATES

Date B.P.	Lab No.	Cultural Affiliation	Site
7,160 ± 135	SI-4849	Cody	Wetzel
7,995 ± 80	SI-4898	Cody	Nelson
8,460 ± 140	I-5449	Cody	Caribou Lake
7,870 ± 240	SI-45	Cody	Lamb Spring
8,870 ± 350	M-1463	Cody	Lamb Spring
8,910 ± 90	SI-4848	Cody	Frasca
9,070 ± 90	SI-3726	Kersey/Cody	Jurgens
9,000 ± 130	SMU-32	Agate Basin	Frazier
9,550 ± 130	SMU-31	Agate Basin	Frazier
9,700 ± 250	GX-0530	Unknown Plano	Gordon Creek
10,020 ± 320	SI-1989	Hell Gap	Jones-Miller
10,150 ± 500	A-744	Firstview/Cody	Olsen-Chubbuck
8,480 ± 85	SI-3540	Folsom	Linger
9,885 ± 140	SI-3537	Folsom	Linger
10,780 ± 375	I-141	Folsom	Lindenmeier
11,200 ± 400	GX-1282	Folsom	Lindenmeier
11,200 ± 500	I-622	Clovis	Dent
11,710 ± 150	SI-2897	Underlies Clovis	Dutton
13,600 ± 485	SI-5186	Pre-Clovis	Dutton
11,735 ± 95	SI-4850	Pre-Clovis	Lamb Spring
13,140 ± 1000	M-1464	Pre-Clovis	Lamb Spring
16,630 ± 320	SI-5185	Pre-Clovis	Selby

SELECTED COLORADO ARCHAIC RADIOCARBON DATES

Date B.P.	Lab No.	Cultural Affiliation	Site
2,060 ± 60	Beta 1970	Late Archaic	5 OR 243
2,170 ± 65	Dic-1258	Late Archaic	McEndree Ranch
2,350 ± 55	Dic-1254	Late Archaic	McEndree Ranch
2,770 ± 60	Beta-3840	Late Archaic	Kewclaw
2,900 ± 60	Beta-3339	Late Archaic	Kewclaw
3,215 ± 90	I-8281	Late Archaic	Blue Lake Valley
3,180 ± 80	UGa-456	Middle Archaic	Dipper Gap
3,520 ± 85	UGa-455	Middle Archaic	Dipper Gap
3,480 ± 65	UGa-737	Middle Archaic	Draper Cave
3,520 ± 70	UGa-736	Middle Archaic	Draper Cave
2,050 ± 65	Dic-1661	Late Archaic	Sisyphus
2,100 ± 55	Dic-1798	Late Archaic	Sisyphus
2,410 ± 70	Dic-1660	Late Archaic	Sisyphus (house)
3,240 ± 75	Dic-1698	Middle Archaic	Sisyphus
4,400 ± 95	Dic-1773	Middle Archaic	Sisyphus
4,398 ± 90	Tx-3157	Middle Archaic	5 GN 204/205
4,697 ± 80	Tx-3151	Middle Archaic	5 GN 204/205
4,840 ± 250	M-1009	Early Archaic	LoDaisKa
4,900 ± 250	W8/70-71	Early Archaic	Magic Mountain
3,460 ± 75	UGa-1069	Middle Archaic	Cherry Gulch
5,730 ± 130		Early Archaic	Cherry Gulch
2,420 ± 220	I-4582	Middle ? Archaic	Albion Boardinghouse
5,730 ± 145	I-5020	Middle ? Archaic	Albion Boardinghouse
5,220 ± 190	I-9434	Early Archaic	Hungry Whistler
5,800 ± 125	I-3267	Early Archaic	Hungry Whistler
5,861 ± 170	Tx-3155	Early Archaic	5 GN 191
5,984 ± 120	Tx-3152	Early Archaic	5 GN 191
5,880 ± 120	I-6544	Early ? Archaic	4th of July Valley
6,045 ± 120	I-6545	Early ? Archaic	4th of July Valley
2,440 ± 120	RL-1222	Late Archaic	DeBeque
3,340 ± 130	RL-1215	Middle Archaic	DeBeque
4,890 ± 160	RL-1214	Early Archaic	DeBeque
5,130 ± 170	RL-170	Early Archaic	DeBeque
5,070 ± 160	RL-1219	Early Archaic	DeBeque
6,150 ± 190	RL-1221	Early Archaic	DeBeque

Date B.P.	Lab No.	Cultural Affiliation	Site
4,620 ± 95	I-8562	Early Archaic	Ptarmigan
4,745 ± 95	I-8280	Early Archaic	Ptarmigan
6,205 ± 170	I-10,976	Early Archaic	Ptarmigan
6,450 ± 110	I-7458	Early Archaic	Ptarmigan
7,170 ± 200	Beta 2976	Early Archaic	Granby
4,400 ± 70	Beta 3569	Middle ? Archaic	Hill-Horn
7,960 ± 140	Beta 3192	Early Archaic	Hill-Horn

SELECTED EASTERN COLORADO POST-ARCHAIC
RADIOCARBON DATES

Date A.D.	Date B.P.	Lab No.	Cultural Affiliation	Site
1380	570 ± 50	UGa-4240	Panhandle	Upper Plum Canyon
1320	630 ± 50	Dic-1435	Panhandle	5 LA 1725 (Carrizo Rch)
1175	775 ± 85	GX-0719	Panhandle	Steamboat Island Fort
1140	810 ± 85	GX-0515	Panhandle	Medina Shelter
1135	815 ± 125	GX-0514	Panhandle	Pyeatt Shelter
1100	850 ± 50	DIC-1234	Panhandle	5 LA 1722 (Carrizo Rch)
1020	935 ± 225	DIC-1434	Panhandle	5 LA 1721 (Carrizo Rch)
1255	695 ± 110	GX-0566	U. Republican	Biggs
1215	735 ± 105	GX-0567	U. Republican	Biggs
1140	810 ± 125	GX-0317	U. Republican	Peavy Shelter
805	1145 ± 155	GX-0318	U. Republican	Peavy Shelter
1090 ± 41*			Sopris	5 LA 1416
1085 ± 31*			Sopris	5 LA 1211
1075 ± 15*			Sopris	5 LA 1211
1070	880 ± 180	UGa-1051	Woodland	Spring Gulch
1015	935 ± 140	UGa-1050	Woodland	Spring Gulch
875	1075 ± 135	UGa-664	Woodland	Spring Gulch
635	1315 ± 135	UGa-670	Woodland	Spring Gulch
245	1705 ± 70	UGa-673	Woodland	Spring Gulch
980	970 ± 150	M-1003	Woodland	LoDaisKa
800	1150 ± 150	M-1008	Woodland	LoDaisKa
690	1250 ± 150	M-1002	Woodland	LoDaisKa
980	970 ± 100	M-1542	Woodland	Murray Game Drive
940	1010 ± 60	DIC-758	Woodland	5 LA 1110 (Carrizo Rch)
900	1050 ± 80	UTx-16506	Woodland	Upper Plum Canyon

Date A.D.	Date B.P.	Lab No.	Cultural Affiliation	Site
900	1050 ± 250	W-616	Woodland	Van Bibber Creek
690	1260 ± 95	I-3265	Woodland	Scratching Deer
660	1290 ± 55	DIC-325	Woodland	5 LA 1053 (Carrizo Rch)
660	1290 ± 100	GX-0526	Woodland	Willowbrook
645	1305 ± 100	I-885	Woodland	Hazeltine Heights Burial
550	1400 ± 90	GX-0565	Woodland	Biggs
270	1680 ± 95	GX-0718	Woodland	Metate Cave
170	$1780 \; {}^{+\,130}_{-\,150}$	I-188	Woodland	Kerbs-Klein Burial

* Archaeomagnetic.

SELECTED FREMONT RADIOCARBON DATES

Date A. D.	Date B. P.	Lab No.	Site
1280	670 ± 270	UGa-3378	5 RB 804
600	1350 ± 60	UGa-3379	5 RB 804
1210	740 ± 85	UGa-2423	Dripping Brow
830	1120 ± 50	W-4250	Dripping Brow
480	1470 ± 70	UGa-3387	Dripping Brow
	820 ± 70	Beta-3576	5 GF 134
	950 ± 80	Beta-3574	5 GF 134
	1250 ± 90	Beta-3575	5 GF 134
	1320 ± 70	Beta-3572	5 GF 134
1000	950 ± 70	UGa-3389	5 RB 748
	1010 ± 55	DIC-1662	Sisyphus
	1210 ± 50	DIC-1663	Sisyphus
800	1150 ± 50	W-4246	Brady
650	1300 ± 50	W-4249	Brady

Colorado Archaeological Agencies and Institutions

The following is a list of the principal agencies and institutions in Colorado that deal with archaeology. A far more detailed compilation of archaeologically-related personnel and agencies, the *Directory of Cultural Resource Personnel, Organizations and Agencies for Colorado*, is available for a nominal fee at the Colorado Preservation Office in the Colorado Historical Society, 1300 Broadway, Denver, CO 80203.

State Agencies

Colorado Preservation Office
1300 Broadway
Denver, CO 80203
(303) 866-3394
- State Archaeologist
- State Historic Preservation Officer
- Coordinator of Historic Preservation

Colorado Highway Department
Archaeology Laboratory
1445 13th St.
Boulder, CO 80309
(303) 449-0601
- State Highway Archaeologist
- State Highway Paleontologist

Educational Institutions

Adams State College
Dept. of Anthropology
Alamosa, CO 81101
(303) 589-7011

Arapahoe Community College
Dept. of Anthropology
5900 So. Santa Fe
Littleton, CO 80120
(303) 794-1550

Colorado College
Dept. of Anthropology
Colorado Springs, CO 80903
(303) 473-2233

Colorado Mountain College
Dept. of Social Services
Leadville, CO 80451
(303) 486-2015

Colorado State University
Dept. of Anthropology
Fort Collins, CO 80523
(303) 491-5447

Fort Lewis College
Dept. of Anthropology
Durango, CO 81301
(303) 247-7864

Mesa College
Dept. of Anthropology
Grand Junction, CO 81501
(303) 248-1020

Metropolitan State College
Dept of Anthropology
Denver, CO 80204
(303) 629-2934

Otero State Junior College
Dept. of Anthropology
La Junta, CO 81050
(303) 384-4443

Trinidad State Junior College
Dept. of Anthropology
Trinidad, CO 81082
(303) 846-5630/5508

University of Colorado, Boulder
Dept. of Anthropology
Boulder, CO 80309
(303) 492-7947

University of Colorado,
   Colorado Springs
Dept. of Anthropology
Colorado Springs, CO 80907
(303) 598-3737

University of Denver
Dept. of Anthropology
Denver, CO 80208
(303) 753-2406

University of Southern Colorado
Dept. of Anthropology
Pueblo, CO 81001
(303) 549-2259

Museums

Denver Art Museum
100 W. 14th Ave. Parkway
Denver, CO 80204
(303) 575-2256

Denver Museum of Natural History
City Park
Denver, CO 80205
(303) 575-3561

Fort Carson Museum
Office of Chief of Military History
U.S. Army
Fort Carson
Colorado Springs, CO 80901
(303) 579-2908

Four Mile Historic Park, Inc.
715 S. Forest St.
Denver, CO 80222
(303) 399-1859

Longmont Pioneer Museum
375 Kimbark
Longmont, CO 80501
(303) 776-6050

Museum of Western Colorado
4th and Ute
Grand Junction, CO 81501
(303) 242-0971

Colorado Historical Society

   Colorado Heritage Center
   1300 Broadway
   Denver, CO 80203
   (303) 866-2136

   Bloom House
   P.O. Box 472
   Trinidad, CO 81082
   (303) 846-7217

   El Pueblo Museum
   905 So. Prairie
   Pueblo, CO 81005
   (303) 561-4635

   Fort Garland
   Fort Garland, CO 81133
   (303) 379-3512

   Fort Vasquez Visitors Center
   Platteville, CO 80651
   (303) 785-2832

   Healy House
   912 Harrison Drive
   Leadville, CO 80461
   (303) 486-0487

Ute Indian Museum
P.O. Box 1736
Montrose, CO 81401
(303) 249-3098

Georgetown National
  Historic District
Georgetown, CO 80444
(303) 569-2840

University of Colorado Museum
University of Colorado
Boulder, CO 80309
(303) 492-6165

Federal Agencies

Advisory Council on Historic
  Preservation
Western Division of Project Review
44 Union Blvd., Suite 616
Lakewood, CO 80228
(303) 234-4946

Bureau of Indian Affairs
  (Dept. of the Interior)
Environmental Quality Services
P.O. Box 8327
Albuquerque, NM 87198
(505) 766-3374

Bureau of Land Management
  (Dept. of the Interior)
Colorado State Office
2000 Arapahoe St.
Denver, CO 80205
(303) 837-3393

Bureau of Reclamation
  (Dept. of the Interior)
Engineering and Research
  Center, D-150
Denver Federal Center
P.O. Box 25007
Denver CO 80225
(303) 234-4348

Department of Housing and Urban
  Development
Region 8

Community and Planning
  Development
140 So. Curtis St.
Denver, CO 80202
(303) 837-3102

National Park Service
  (Dept. of the Interior)

Rocky Mountain Regional Office
655 Parfet
P.O. Box 25287
Lakewood, CO 80225

Mesa Verde National Park
Mesa Verde, CO 81330
(303) 529-4465

Interagency Archeological Services
655 Parfet
P.O. Box 25387
Lakewood, CO 80225

Soil Conservation Service
  (U.S. Dept. of Agriculture)
P.O. Box 17107
Denver, CO 80217
(303) 837-5651

United States Forest Service
  (U.S. Dept. of Agriculture)
Region 2
11177 W. 8th Ave.
Lakewood, CO 80228
(303) 234-4946

Colorado Antiquities Violations Can Be Reported to the Following:

State of Colorado

State Archaeologist
Colorado Preservation Office
1300 Broadway
Denver, CO 80203
(303) 866-3394

State Highway Archaeologist
Highway Department
  Archaeology Laboratory

1445 13th St.
Boulder, CO 80309
(303) 449-0601

Assistant Attorney General
Dept. of Law
1525 Sherman St.
Denver, CO 80203

Counties

Any County Sheriff

Federal Agencies

Bureau of Land Management
Archaeologist
Colorado State Office
2000 Arapahoe St.
Denver, CO 80205
(303) 837-3393

Bureau of Land Management Special
Agent in Charge
Colorado State Office

2000 Arapahoe St.
Denver, CO 80205
(303) 837-3814

United States Forest Service
Regional Archaeologist
Region 2
11177 W. 8th Ave.
Lakewood, CO 80228
(303) 234-4946

United States Forest Service Special
Agent in Charge
Region 2
11177 W. 8th Ave.
Lakewood, CO 80228
(303) 234-4211

United States Fish and Wildlife
Service Special Agent in Charge
300 So. Garrison
Denver, CO 80226
(303) 234-3723

Glossary

Adobe. Clay applied to a framework, as in wattle and daub construction, or used as mortar in masonry.

Agriculture. System of crop production, characterized by intensive use of land and human labor. Often includes irrigation, terracing, and other modifications of the landscape.

Alluvium. Soils, sands, or gravels deposited by the slowing of running water, such as those released when a stream enters a lake or a rapidly-moving mountain river reaches the plains.

Altithermal. A climatic period from 7,000 to 4,500 B.P. defined by Antevs as being substantially warmer and drier than the present day.

Articulated. Two or more bones connected at the joints. In an archaeological deposit, connected skeletal elements in animals suggest a lack of butchering, while articulations in human remains usually indicate a primary burial.

Artifact. Anything made by humans.

Aspect. A grouping of foci with similar traits, as used in the Midwestern Taxonomic System by McKern.

Atlatl. Spear-throwing implement with a handle at one end and a hook at the other. The hook is placed in a socket in the base of the spear shaft, and the atlatl becomes an extension of the arm, increasing the force of the throw.

Awl. A bone or stone tool used primarily to perforate leather for sewing or in basket weaving.

Backed Knife. Stone knife with the long edge opposite the cutting edge being intentionally dulled in order to reduce injury to the user.

Basal Grinding. Dulling the lower lateral edges of a projectile point (usually of Paleo-Indian age) by abrasion in order to reduce the chance of the sinew binding being cut after the point was seated in the shaft.

Biface. Stone tool flaked on both sides (faces). The term is sometimes used to describe a tool that is otherwise unclassifiable.

Blade. Can be either the unhafted portion of a projectile point or a long narrow flake, generally with parallel sides.

Blowout. A sandy depression lacking topsoil and highly vulnerable to wind erosion.

Burial, Bundle. An interment in a bundle of human bones that had previously been defleshed through an earlier burial, scaffold exposure, or other means. (*See* Burial, Secondary).

Burial, Extended. A type of human burial in which the body is laid in a straight alignment.

Burial, Flexed. A type of human burial in which the legs are bent, often drawn up to the chest. Can also include bent arms.

Burial, Primary. A human burial in its original placement.

Burial, Secondary. Human remains that were buried, dug up, and buried again in a new location.

Caliche. Calcium carbonate residue from ground water activity that can occur as massive deposits in the soil or a filler in joints and fractures.

Chalcedony. A type of siliceous (SiO_2) stone often used as material in the production of chipped stone tools. It is colorless, translucent, and has a waxy luster.

Channel Flake. The flake removed from the base of a Clovis or Folsom point to make the flute.

Chipped Stone. Knives, scrapers, projectile points, and other artifacts produced by removing flakes.

Coiling. A common pottery building technique of the Anasazi. The potter fashions long thin rolls of clay and coils them into vessels of various heights. The interior surface is always smoothed, while the exterior is either smoothed or corrugated.

Collateral Flaking. A knapping technique in which flakes are removed from the edge of the tool to the midline of the blade, forming a dorsal ridge. The flake scars are parallel to each other and at 90° to the long axis of the tool.

Complex. A cultural unit identified by the association of several distinct tool types.

Component. Each distinct cultural unit within a site, separated from others primarily by chronology.

Contract Archaeology. A recent development in which independent archaeologists contract with government or private companies to carry out any surveys or excavations required by antiquities laws.

Core. Nodule of stone from which flakes are removed. Typically a core is reduced until most usable flakes are obtained and then it is discarded.

Corrugated. A treatment on the outside of some pottery vessels. The coils are partially impressed into each other, which strengthens the pot and creates distinctive patterns.

Deflector. Usually a vertical slab or masonry wall located between the air inlet (ventilator shaft) and central firepit in Anasazi kivas and some pithouses. It serves to keep air from blowing directly across the fire.

Deposit. A buildup of soils or other earth material by natural processes.

Diffusion. The spreading of cultural traits across geographic areas and into different societies.

Fauna. Animals

Flake. A thin piece of stone detached from a core or partially-finished artifact.

Flaking, Bifacial. The removal of flakes from both sides (faces) of a tool. (*See* Biface).

Flaking, Unifacial. The removal of flakes from only one side of a tool.

Flintknapping. (*See* Knapping).

Flora. Plants

Flute. The large flake scars found on both basal faces of Clovis and Folsom points. They are oriented along the long axis of the tool and served to better seat the point into the foreshaft.

Focus. A grouping of components with similar traits.

Foreshaft. The leading (distal) section of a two-piece spear shaft. The projectile point is hafted to the foreshaft, which is then socketed into the main shaft. It can serve as a handle when the point is used as a knife, or it could prevent the loss of a valuable shaft if an animal escapes and takes the spear with it, as the main shaft can separate from the foreshaft and be retrieved.

Ground Stone. Artifacts produced by grinding or pecking. These include manos, metates, mortars, and pestles.

Haft. The connecting of a tool and a shaft or handle.

Hammerstone. A rock used for pounding, as in direct percussion production of chipped stone tools. Generally, the hammerstone should be harder than the material it is hitting. Usually a fist-sized cobble with battered ends.

Horizon. Used to denote a level within a site, or in the Willey and Phillips system, the cultural continuity extending across a geographical expanse at any given time.

Horticulture. A system of crop production, involving less intensive land use than in agriculture. Characterized by lack of irrigation, use of beasts of burden, and less organized human labor.

In Situ. A Latin phrase meaning "in place" and referring to the original position of any object. An important aspect in determining relationships of artifacts within a site.

Incising. The act of cutting a design into a pottery surface or the cutting of petroglyphs into a rock surface.

Indiana Jones. Swashbuckling archaeologist in the movie, *Raiders of the Lost Ark*.

Isolated Find. The occurrence, usually on the surface, of a single artifact. Considered to be something less than a true site.

Jacal. (*See* Wattle and Daub).

Jasper. Opaque, fine grained siliceous (SiO_2) stone containing various amounts of iron, an impurity that creates colors of tan and red. A common material used in the production of chipped stone tools.

Kill Site. A human activity area in which the primary function was the killing of animals for food.

Knapping. The act of flaking stone artifacts.

Knife. An implement used for cutting, as opposed to scraping and other tasks. The angle of the cutting edge is usually quite low.

Lanceolate. A long, thin artifact form, with a taper at one or both ends.

Lithic. Stone. Also, the earliest stage in the Willey and Phillips system.

Lithic Scatter. A site characterized by a number of flakes and/or tools but having an ambiguous function.

Loess. Wind-blown dust. In North America it is usually associated with the late Pleistocene.

Mano. Handstone used in conjunction with a grinding stone (metate) for the purpose of processing vegetable matter.

Metate. The large milling slab (or trough) on which vegetable matter is placed and then ground up by the motion of a mano.

Midden. A trash deposit.

Oblique Flaking. A flaking pattern in which the flake scars are oriented diagonally on the faces of the blade. Often the scars are transverse, extending across the midline and removing any vestige of a dorsal ridge.

Obsidian. Commonly known as volcanic glass, it is an igneous silicate formed by rapid cooling of lava flows. It is usually translucent and ranges in color from black to reddish-brown. When available (scarce in Colorado), it was commonly used for stone tool production.

Ocher. An iron-rich clay or soil used by aboriginals for pigment.

Ossuary. A receptacle where bones have been deposited.

Paddle and Anvil. A pottery construction technique involving an anvil (stone or human hand) inside the partially-formed vessel and a paddle (often wrapped with cordage) used to hit the outside in order to even out the wall and complete construction.

Palynology. The scientific study of pollen.

Percussion, Direct. A knapping technique in which the flaking tool (hammerstone, antler baton) is struck on the core or partially-finished tool.

Percussion, Indirect. A knapping technique in which the flaking tool (hammerstone, antler baton) is struck on an intermediate tool (punch) which in turn strikes the core or partially-finished tool.

Phase. In the Willey and Phillips scheme, a phase is a distinctive cultural entity represented by specific sites or levels within sites, similar to other definitions of a focus. In the Midwestern Taxonomic System of McKern, a phase is a larger unit composed of several aspects, which can be broken down into even more foci.

Pothunter. An individual who digs sites for pottery and other artifacts for personal gain. This person cares nothing for context, does not accurately record artifact proveniences or publish results, and often shows disdain for federal regulations which prohibit such activity on public lands.

Pressure Flaking. A method of chipped stone manufacture in which the knapper puts the tip of the flaking tool (e.g. antler tine) on the edge of the nearly-finished stone tool and then "pushes" off each flake. Pressure flaking is generally the final stage in the making of a stone implement.

Primary Flake. One of the initial flakes detached from the outside of a core. A portion of the core's weathered exterior (cortex) is retained on the flake.

Projectile Point. Normally a bifacially-flaked implement with a pointed distal end designed for penetrating an animal's hide and a blunted proximal end designed for attachment to a shaft. Can be a spear point, dart point, or arrowhead.

Provenience. The exact location of an artifact or other remains associated with a site. It must be located both horizontally and vertically on maps in order to be fully documented.

Quarry. A location where aboriginal flintknappers obtained the stone material to make their tools. Much of the reduction of large nodules was often done at the quarry, in order to avoid transporting unnecessary weight back to camp (usually in the form of crude bifaces).

Quartzite. A metamorphic sandstone with a granular texture. Commonly used to make stone tools.

Rockshelter. An overhang, usually along the base of a cliff, in which occupation by humans has taken place.

Retouch. Secondary flaking of a stone tool for the purpose of resharpening it, usually by pressure flaking.

Scraper. A tool used to remove tissue from the interior surface of hides, to smooth wood, and for other tasks. The edge angle on most scrapers is high.

Scraper, End. A scraper with the primary working edge on the narrow or short side.

Scraper, Side. Scraper with the primary working edge on the wide or long side.

Sherd. A fragment of pottery.

Sinew. Animal tendons that are dried, separated into thin strips, and used in sewing leather and attaching projectile points onto shafts.

Sipapu. "Spirit hole" found in the floors of Puebloan kivas and some pithouses. Ethnographic documentation shows that the Puebloans believed their ancestors entered this world via this opening.

Site. Any human activity area of significant content and duration.

278 THE ARCHAEOLOGY OF COLORADO

Stage. The highest level in the Willey and Phillips system, incorporating diverse cultural groups located across much of the New World, yet still sharing some basic characteristics.

Stone Ring/Circle. A circular outline of rocks marking the spot where an aboriginal dwelling once stood. Some stone circles are tipi rings, but since it is not known if most of the structures were hide-covered and cone-shaped or not, the more generic term, stone circle, is preferred.

Stratified. Soils deposited in layers (strata). If undisturbed, the Law of Superposition applies, meaning that the lowest stratum is the oldest and the highest stratum is the youngest.

Utilized Flake. A flake showing evidence of use or wear on one or more edges. No flakes have been intentionally removed, but very small flakes have incidentally detached during use. This use-wear is known as "nibbling."

Vandal. Individual who deliberately destroys or damages archaeological sites.

Wattle and Daub. A technique of construction involving a framework of poles and interwoven branches which are plastered with clay.

Bibliography

Adovasio, J. M., J. D. Gunn, J. Donahue, R. Stuckenrath, J. E. Guilday and K. Volman
1980 Yes Virginia, It Really Is That Old: A Reply to Haynes and Mead. *American Antiquity* 45 (3): 588-95.

Agenbroad, Larry D.
1978 *The Hudson-Meng Site: An Alberta Bison Kill in the Nebraska High Plains.* University Press of America.

Agogino, George A.
1960 Review of Excavations in Mancos Canyon, Colorado (Reed). *Southwestern Lore* 25.
1961 A New Point Type from Hell Gap Valley, Eastern Wyoming. *American Antiquity* 26 (4): 558-60.
1963 Progress Report on the Chemical Removal of Preservative from Radiocarbon Samples. *La Conquista*, Spring.
1964 The Cody Complex. *Wyoming Archaeologist* 7: 38-42.
1968 The Experimental Removal of Preservative from Radiocarbon Samples. *Plains Anthropologist* 13: 146-47.

Agogino, George A. and J. Duguid
1963 Scottsbluff-Eden Points and the Cody Complex. *Southwestern Lore* 28: 73-75.

Agogino, George A. and G. Egan
1965 Man's Use of Bison and Cattle on the High Plains. *Great Plains Journal* 5: 34-43.

Agogino, George A. and Franklin Folsom
1975 New Light on an Old Site: Events Leading up to the Discovery of the Folsom Type Site. *Anthropological Journal of Canada* 13 (3): 2-5.

Agogino, George A. and Al Parrish
1971 The Fowler-Parrish Site: A Folsom Campsite in Eastern Colorado. *Plains Anthropologist* 16 (52): 111-14.

Agogino, George A., David K. Patterson and Deborah E. Patterson
1976 Blackwater Draw Locality No. 1, South Bank: Report for the Summer of 1974. *Plains Anthropologist* 21 (73): 213-23.

Aikens, C. Melvin
1966 Fremont-Promontory-Plains Relationships. *University of Utah Anthropological Papers* 82.

1967   Excavations at Snake Rock Village and Bear River No. 2 Site. *University of Utah Anthropological Papers* 87.

Almquist, Alan J. and John E. Cronin
1978   *Human Origins: Problems in the Interpretation of New Evidence.* AAAS Study Guides on Contemporary Problems, American Association for the Advancement of Science.

Ambler, J. Richard
1966   Caldwell Village. *University of Utah Anthropological Papers* 84.
1969   The Temporal Span of the Fremont. *Southwestern Lore* 34 (4): 107-17.

Anderson, Adrienne
1975   "Least Cost" Strategy and Limited Activity Site Location, Upper Dry Cimarron River Valley, Northeastern New Mexico. Ph.D. Dissertation, University of Colorado.

Anderson, Duane C.
1966   The Gordon Creek Burial. *Southwestern Lore* 32 (1): 1-9.

Anderson, Jane
1976   A Techno-Functional Analysis of the Flaked Lithic Materials from Three Woodland Period Sites on the High Plains, Southeastern Colorado. MS., Colorado Preservation Office.

Anonymous
1936   Jean Jeançon, Indian Expert, Passes Away. *The Denver Post*, 11 April.
1948   Dr. Renaud Retires after 32 Years at Denver. MS., on file, Denver University Laboratory of Anthropology.
1962   Andrew Ellicott Douglass, 1867-1962. *Tree-Ring Bulletin* 24 (3-4): 3-10.
1973   Etienne Renaud. *The Denver Post*, 9 February.
1978a   Obituaries: Professor Succumbs. *Lewiston* (Idaho) *Morning Tribune*, 20 April.
1978b   Obituaries: Henry T. Irwin. *The Pullman* (Washington) *Herald*, 19 April.
1979   Local Archaeologist 'Zeke' Flora dies. *Durango Herald*, 22 March.

Antevs, Ernst
1948   Climatic Changes and pre-White Man. *Bulletin of the University of Utah* 38 (20): 168-91.
1955   Geologic-Climatic Dating in the West. *American Antiquity* 20 (4, pt. 1): 317-35.

Bair, Gerald A.
1975   Archaeological Investigations in the Upper Purgatoire River Drainage, Southeastern Colorado. *Southwestern Lore* 41 (4): 39-44.

Baker, Galen R.
1964   The Archaeology of the Park Plateau in Southeastern Colorado. *Southwestern Lore* 30 (1): 1-18.
1965a   Excavating Fort Massachusetts. *The Colorado Magazine* 24 (1): 1-15.
1965b   Final Report from Trinidad State College, Las Animas County, Raton Pass Highway Salvage. MS., Colorado Preservation Office.
1977   Comanche National Grasslands, Timpas Unit: Pike and San Isabel National Forests Cultural Resource Survey. MS., Colorado Preservation Office.
n.d.   Pasture Number 12 Pipeline, 30-Foot Tank; Pasture 24, Square Overflow Pit, Pike-San Isabel National Forests, Comanche National Grasslands. MS., Colorado Preservation Office.

Barbour, E. H. and C. Bertrand Schultz
1932   The Scottsbluff Bison Quarry and its Artifacts. *Nebraska State Museum Bulletin* 34 (1).

Benedict, James B.
1974   Early Occupation of the Caribou Lake Site, Colorado Front Range. *Plains Anthropologist* 19 (63): 1-4.
1975a   The Murray Site: A Late Prehistoric Game Drive System in the Colorado Rocky Mountains. *Plains Anthropologist* 20 (69): 161-74.
1975b   Scratching Deer: A Late Prehistoric Campsite in the Green Lakes Valley, Colorado. *Plains Anthropologist* 20 (70): 267-78.
1975c   The Albion Boardinghouse Site: Archaic Occupation of a High Mountain Valley. *Southwestern Lore* 41 (3): 1-12.
1979a   Getting Away From It All: A Study of Man, Mountains and the Two-Drought Altithermal. *Southwestern Lore* 45 (3): 1-12.
1979b   Excavation at the Blue Lake Valley Site, Front Range, Colorado. *Southwestern Lore* 45 (4): 7-17.
1981a   The Fourth of July Valley: Glacial Geology and Archaeology of the Timberline Ecotone. *Center for Mountain Archaeology, Research Report No. 2.*
1981b   Prehistoric Man, Volcanism, and Climatic Change: 7500-5000 [14]C Yr. B.P. *Abstracts with Programs 1981*, Geological Society of America 13 (7): 407.
n.d.   Arapaho Pass: Glacial Geology and Archaeology at the Crest of the Colorado Front Range. *Center for Mountain Archaeology, Research Report No. 3* (in prep.).

Benedict, James B. and Byron L. Olson
1973   Origin of the McKean Complex: Evidence from Timberline. *Plains Anthropologist* 18 (62, pts. 1-2): 323-27.
1978   The Mount Albion Complex: A Study of Man and the Altithermal. *Center for Mountain Archaeology, Research Report.*

Berthrong, Donald J.
1963   *The Southern Cheyenne.* University of Oklahoma Press.

Bilgery, Conrad, S. J.
1935   Correspondence to J. D. Figgins, Director of the Colorado Museum of Natural History, 2 August. On file at the Denver Museum of Natural History and Colorado Preservation Office.
n.d.   Evidence of Pleistocene Man in the Denver Basin: Preliminary Report. MS., Colorado Preservation Office.

Birkedal, Terje G.
1976   Basketmaker III Residence Units: A Study of Prehistoric Social Organization in the Mesa Verde Archaeological District. Ph.D. Dissertation, University of Colorado.

Bolton, Herbert E.
1972   *Pageant in the Wilderness. The Story of the Expedition to the Interior Basin, 1776.* Utah State Historical Society.

Bonnichsen, R.
1978   Critical Arguments for Pleistocene Artifacts from Old Crow Basin, Yukon: A Preliminary Statement. *In*: Early Man in America: From a Circum-Pacific Perspective (A. L. Bryan, ed.). *Occasional Papers, No. 1, Department of Anthropology, University of Alberta*: 102-18.

Borland, Lois
1949   Dr. C. T. Hurst is Mourned by College, Entire Community. *Southwestern Lore* 14 (4): 70-88.

Braidwood, Robert J.
1967   *Prehistoric Men* (7th ed.). Scott Foresman.
Breternitz, David A.
1966   An Appraisal of Tree-Ring Dated Pottery in the Southwest. *Anthropological Papers of the University of Arizona* 10.
1969   Radiocarbon Dates: Eastern Colorado. *Plains Anthropologist* 14 (44): 113-24.
1970   Archaeological Investigations in Dinosaur National Monument. Colorado-Utah, 1964-1965. *University of Colorado Studies, Series in Anthropology* 17
1971   Archaeological Investigations at the Wilbur Thomas Shelter, Carr, Colorado. *Southwestern Lore* 36 (4): 53-99.
1972   A Further Note on Burial 7, Hazeltine Heights Site. *Southwestern Lore* 38 (3): 18-19.
1975   Mesa Verde Research Center, 1975. *Southwestern Lore* 41 (4): 17-21.
1979   Archaeological Research in National Park Service Areas: The University of Colorado Example. *In*: Proceedings of the First Conference on Scientific Research in the National Parks 2 (R. M. Linn, ed.). U. S. Dept. of the Interior, *National Park Service Transactions and Proceedings Series* 5.
1981   Dolores Archaeological Program Synthetic Report, 1978-80. Report submitted to the Upper Colorado Region, Bureau of Reclamation. Salt Lake.
1982   The Four Corners Anasazi Ceramic Tradition. *In*: Southwestern Ceramics: A Comparative Review (A. H. Schroeder, ed.). *The Arizona Archaeologist* 15.
Breternitz, David A. and Barbara B. Breternitz
1965   General Index, Southwestern Lore, Volumes 21-30, 1955-65. *Southwestern Lore* 31 (1): 1-18.
Breternitz, David A. and John J. Wood
1965   Comments on the Bisterfeldt Potato Cellar Site and Flexed Burials in the Western Plains. *Southwestern Lore* 31 (3): 62-66.
Breternitz, David A. and Robert H. Lister
1968   The Salvage Excavation of Site 1104, Wetherill Mesa. *In*: Emergency Archaeology in Mesa Verde National Park, Colorado, 1948-66 (R. H. Lister, ed.). *University of Colorado Studies, Series in Anthropology* 15, *Contributions to Mesa Verde Archaeology* 5.
Breternitz, David A., Alan C. Swedlund and Duane C. Anderson
1971   An Early Burial from Gordon Creek, Colorado. *American Antiquity* 36 (2): 170-82.
Breternitz, David A. and Larry V. Norby
1972   Site MV 1824-71, A Basketmaker III Pithouse and Cist on Wetherill Mesa. *In*: Archaeological Salvage Excavations, Wetherill Mesa, Mesa Verde National Park, 1971. MS., Midwest Archaeological Center, National Park Service.
Breternitz, David A. and Jack Smith
1972   Mesa Verde: The Green Table. *Photographic and Comprehensive Guide to Rocky Mountain and Mesa Verde National Parks*. World-Wide Research and Publishing Company.
Breternitz, David A., Larry V. Norby, and Paul R. Nickens
1974   Activities of the University of Colorado Mesa Verde Archaeological Research Center for 1974. *Southwestern Lore* 40 (3-4): 15-22.

Breternitz, David A., Arthur H. Rohn, and Elizabeth A. Morris
1974   Prehistoric Ceramics of the Mesa Verde Region. *Ceramic Series 5, Museum of Northern Arizona.*

Breternitz, David A. and Adrian S. White
1976   Stabilization of Lowry Ruin. *Bureau of Land Management Colorado, Cultural Resources Series* 1.
1979   Stabilization of Escalante Ruin, 5 MT 2149, and Dominguez Ruin, 5 MT 2148, Dolores, Colorado. *In*: Archaeology and Stabilization of the Dominguez Ruins, pt. III. *Bureau of Land Management Colorado, Cultural Resources Series* 7.

Breternitz, David A., Robert A. Bye, S. E. James, A. E. Kane, and R. Knudson
1980   Research Design and Operations Management, Dolores Project. *Contract Abstracts and Cultural Resource Management Archaeology* 1 (2).

Breternitz, David A. and W. A. Lucius
1981   The Current Status of Redwares in the Mesa Verde Region. *In*: Collected Papers in Honor of Erik Kellerman Reed (A. H. Schroeder, ed.). *Papers of the Archaeological Society of New Mexico* 6.

Brew, John O.
1946   The Archaeology of Alkali Ridge, Southeastern Utah. *Papers of the Peabody Museum of Archaeology and Ethnology* 21.
1963   James A. Lancaster: Citation for Distinguished Service. *American Antiquity* 29 (2): 230-32.

Brinkley-Rogers, Paul
1981   The Big Business of Artifacts Theft. *Historic Preservation* 33 (1): 16-21.

Brown, Dee
1970   *Bury My Heart at Wounded Knee: An Indian History of the American West.* Holt, Rinehart and Winston.

Brown, Joy
1975   Preliminary Report on the 1975 Excavation at Site 5 MT 3 Near Yellowjacket, Colorado. *Southwestern Lore* 41 (4): 47-50.

Bryan, A. L. (ed.)
1978   Early Man in America: From a Circum-Pacific Perspective. *Occasional Papers* 1, *Department of Anthropology, University of Alberta.*

Bryan, Alan L. and Ruth Gruhn
1964   Problems Relating to the Neothermal Climatic Sequence. *American Antiquity* 29 (3): 307-15.

Bryson, Reid, David A. Baerreis and Wayne M. Wendlund
1970   The Character of Late Glacial and Post-Glacial Climatic Changes. *In: Pleistocene and Recent Environments of the Central Great Plains* (Dort and Jones, eds.). University of Kansas, Department of Geology, Special Publications (3): 53-74.

Buckles, William G.
1968   The Archaeology of Colorado: Part III, Archaeology in Colorado: Historic Tribes. *Southwestern Lore* 34 (3): 53-67.
1971   The Uncompahgre Complex: Historic Ute Archaeology and Prehistoric Archaeology. Ph.D. Dissertation, University of Colorado.
1981   Old Dallas Historical Archaeology Program. Draft report for the Bureau of Reclamation. MS., Colorado Preservation Office.

Buckles, William G., G. H. Ewing, Nancy Buckles, G. J. Armelagos, J. J. Wood, J. D. Haug and J. H. McCullough
 1963   The Excavations of the Hazeltine Heights Site. *Southwestern Lore* 29 (1): 1-36.
Bullard, William
 1962   The Cerro Colorado Site and Pit House Architecture in the Southwestern United States Prior to A.D. 900. *Papers of the Peabody Museum of Archaeology and Ethnology* 44 (2).
Burgh, Robert F.
 1957   Earl H. Morris. *American Anthropologist* 59 (3).
Burgh, Robert F. and Charles R. Scoggin
 1948   The Archaeology of Castle Park, Dinosaur National Monument. *University of Colorado Studies, Series in Anthropology* 2.
Burton, Robert J.
 1971   The Pictographs and Petroglyphs of Dinosaur National Monument. M.A. Thesis, University of Colorado.

Caldwell, Joseph R.
 1958   Trend and Tradition in the Prehistory of the Eastern United States. *American Anthropologist* 60 (6, pt. 2).
Campbell, Robert G.
 1963   Test Excavations of Medina Rock Shelter, Chacuaco Creek Canyon. *Southwestern Lore* 29 (3): 53-60.
 1969   Prehistoric Panhandle Culture on the Chaquaqua Plateau, Southeastern Colorado. Ph.D. Dissertation, University of Colorado.
 1976   The Panhandle Aspect of the Chaquaqua Plateau. *Texas Tech University Graduate Studies* 11.
Cannon, George L.
 1889   Notes on Aboriginal Remains Near Durango, Colorado. *Proceedings, Colorado Scientific Society* 3 (pt. 2): 200-04.
Carlson, Roy L.
 1963   Basket Maker III Sites Near Durango, Colorado. *University of Colorado Studies, Series in Anthropology* 8.
Cassells, E. Steve
 1979   An Aboriginal Scarred Tree in the Gunnison National Forest, Cebolla District, CO. MS., U. S. Forest Service, on file at the Colorado Preservation Office.
Cattanach, George S., Jr.
 1980   Long House, Mesa Verde National Park, Colorado. *Publications in Archaeology 7H, Wetherill Mesa Studies*. National Park Service.
Champe, John L.
 1946   Ash Hollow Cave: A Study of Stratigraphic Sequence in the Central Great Plains. *University of Nebraska Studies*, n.s., 1.
 1949   White Cat Village. *American Antiquity* 14 (4): 285-92.
Chapman, Hugh H., Jr.
 1973   Etienne B. Renaud, Linguist and Anthropologist, Dies. MS., Phi Sigma Iota, Pennsylvania State University, on file at the Laboratory of Anthropology, Denver University.
Charters, Ann
 1973   *Kerouac: A Biography*. Warner Books.

Chase, Halden M.
1949   The Columbia University High Plains Expedition of 1949. Field Notes. On file at the Laboratory of Anthropology, Denver University.
n.d.   Snake Blakeslee 1. MS., Laboratory of Anthropology, Denver University.
Chavez, Fray Angelico (translator) and Ted J. Warner (ed.)
1976   *The Dominguez-Escalante Journal.* Brigham Young University Press.
Chronic, Halka
1979   *Roadside Geology of Colorado.* Mountain Press Publishing Company.
Chronic, John and Halka Chronic
1972   Prairie, Peak and Plateau: A Guide to the Geology of Colorado. *Colorado Geological Society Bulletin* 32.
Clark, Grahame
1977   *World Prehistory in New Perspective* (3rd ed.) Cambridge University Press.
Coggins, Clemency
1979   Update on the Cultural Property Implementation Act and More Evidence of its Importance. *Journal of Field Archaeology* 6 (1): 104.
Colton, Harold S. (ed.)
1955   Pottery Types of the Southwest. *Museum of Northern Arizona, Ceramic Series* 3B.
Conner, Carl E. and Diana L. Langdon
1983   Battlement Mesa Community Project - Cultural Resources Study. MS., Colorado Preservation Office.
Costello, David F.
1954   Vegetation Zones in Colorado. *In: Manual of the Plants of Colorado* (H.D. Harrington). Sage Books.
Cotter, John L.
1937   The Occurrence of Flints and Extinct Animals in Pluvial Deposits near Clovis, New Mexico, pt. IV, Report on the Excavations at the Gravel Pit in 1936. *Proceedings, Philadelphia Academy of Natural Sciences* 89:2-16.
1938   The Occurrence of Flints and Extinct Animals in Pluvial Deposits near Clovis, New Mexico, pt. VI, Report on the Field Season of 1937. *Proceedings, Philadelphia Academy of Natural Sciences* 90:113-17.
1978   A Report on Field Work of the Colorado Museum of Natural History at the Lindenmeier Folsom Campsite, 1935. Appendix, *In*: Lindenmeier, 1934-1974: Concluding Report on Investigations (Wilmsen and Roberts). *Smithsonian Contributions to Anthropology* 24:181-84.
Coues, Elliott (ed.)
1965   *The History of the Lewis and Clark Expedition* (3 vols). Dover Press (orig. 1893).
Creaseman, Steven D.
1981   Archaeological Investigations in the Canyon Pintado Historic District, Rio Blanco County, Colorado: Phase I. *Reports of the Laboratory of Public Archaeology* 34, Colorado State University.
1982   Rock Art of the Canyon Pintado Historic District. *Southwestern Lore* 48 (4): 1-13.
Crouse, N. M.
1956   *La Verendrye, Fur Trader and Explorer.* Cornell University Press.
Cutler, Hugh C.
1966a   Corn, Curcurbits and Cotton from Glen Canyon. *University of Utah Anthropological Papers* 80, *Glen Canyon Series* 30.

1966b   Maize of Caldwell Village. *In*: Caldwell Village. (Richard Ambler, ed.) *University of Utah Anthropological Papers* 84:114-18.
Cutler, Hugh C. and Leonard W. Blake
1970   Corn from the Median Village Site. *In*: Median Village and Fremont Culture Regional Variation. (John P. Marwitt, ed.) *University of Utah Anthropological Papers* 95.
Cutter, Donald C.
1977   Prelude to a Pageant in the Wilderness. *The Western Historical Quarterly* 8 (1): 5-14.

Dawson, Jerry and Dennis Stanford
1975   The Linger Site: A Re-investigation. *Southwestern Lore* 41 (4): 11-16.
Day, Michael
1965   *Guide to Fossil Man: A Handbook of Human Paleontology*. World Publishing Co.
Dick, Herbert W.
1953   The Status of Colorado Archaeology, with Bibliographic Guide. *Southwestern Lore* 18 (4).
1956   The Excavation of Bent's Fort, Otero County, Colorado. *The Colorado Magazine* 33 (3).
1963   Preliminary Report: Trinidad Reservoir, Las Animas County, Colorado. MS., National Park Service, Midwest Archaeological Center.
n.d.   The Archaeology of Marigold Cave, Castle Park, Dinosaur National Monument. MS., University of Colorado Museum.
Dick, Herbert W. and Bert Mountain
1960   The Claypool Site: A Cody Complex Site in Northeastern Colorado. *American Antiquity* 26 (2): 223-35.
Dean, Jeffrey S.
1975   *Tree-Ring Dates from Colorado W: Durango Area*. Laboratory of Tree-Ring Research, University of Arizona.
Dean, Jeffrey S. and William J. Robinson
1977   *Dendroclimatic Variability in the American Southwest, A.D. 680-1970*. Laboratory of Tree-Ring Research, University of Arizona.
Doll, Marice
1977   Ute 'Medicine Trees' May Exist in Jefferson County. *Denver Post*, 28 May.

Eddy, Frank W.
1961   Excavations at Los Pinos Phase Sites in the Navajo Reservoir District. *Museum of New Mexico Papers in Anthropology* 4.
1966   Prehistory in the Navajo Reservoir District, Northwestern New Mexico. *Museum of New Mexico Papers in Anthropology* 15 (pts. 1 and 2).
1972   Cultural Ecology and Prehistory of the Navajo Reservoir District. *Southwestern Lore* 38 (1 and 2): 1-73.
1977   Archaeological Investigations at Chimney Rock Mesa: 1970-72. *Memoirs of the Colorado Archaeological Society* 1.
Eighmy, Jeffrey L.
1980   Archaeomagnetism: A Handbook for the Archeologist. *Cultural Resource Management Series, Heritage Conservation and Recreation Service*, U. S. Department of the Interior.

Elisha, M. J.
1968   The Present Status of Basketmaker II and III Sites in Colorado. *Southwestern Lore* 34 (2): 33-46.
Emery, Sloan and Dennis Stanford
1982   Preliminary Report on Archaeological Investigations at the Cattle Guard Site, Alamosa County, Colorado. *Southwestern Lore* 48 (1): 10-20.
Euler, R. Thomas and Mark A. Stiger
1981   1978 Test Excavations at Five Archeological Sites in Curecanti National Recreation Area, Intermountain Colorado. MS., National Park Service, Midwest Archeological Center.

Fewkes, Jesse Walter
1909   Antiquities of the Mesa Verde National Park, Spruce Tree House. *Bureau of American Ethnology, Bulletin 41.*
1911   Antiquities of the Mesa Verde National Park, Cliff Palace. *Bureau of American Ethnology, Bulletin 51.*
1916   The Cliff Ruins in Fewkes Canyon, Mesa Verde National Park, Colorado. *Holmes Anniversary Volume, Anthropological Essays*, Smithsonian Institution: 96-117.
1919   Prehistoric Villages, Castle and Towers of Southwestern Colorado. *Bureau of American Ethnology, Bulletin 70.*
1920   Field Work on the Mesa Verde National Park, Colorado (Square Tower House and Earth Lodge A), Explorations and Field-Work in 1919. *Smithsonian Miscellaneous Collections* 72 (1): 47-64.
1921   Archaeological Field-Work on the Mesa Verde National Park. *Smithsonian Miscellaneous Collections* 72 (15): 75-79.
1923   Archaeological Field-Work on the Mesa Verde National Park, Colorado. Exploration and Field-Work of the Smithsonian Institution in 1922. *Smithsonian Miscellaneous Collections* 74 (5): 89-119.
Figgins, J. D.
1927   The Antiquity of Man in America. *Natural History* 27 (3): 229-39.
1931   An Additional Discovery of the Association of a "Folsom" Artifact and Fossil Mammal Remains. *Proceedings, Colorado Museum of Natural History* 10 (2).
1933   A Further Contribution to the Antiquity of Man in America. *Proceedings, Colorado Museum of Natural History* 12 (2): 4-10.
1934   Folsom and Yuma Artifacts. *Proceedings, Colorado Museum of Natural History* 13 (2).
1935a   New World Man. *Proceedings, Colorado Museum of Natural History* 14 (1).
1935b   Folsom and Yuma Artifacts, part II. *Proceedings, Colorado Museum of Natural History* 14 (2).
Fitting, James E. (ed.)
1973   *The Development of North American Archaeology.* Anchor Books.
Folsom, Franklin and Mary Folsom
1982   Sinodonty and Sudadonty: An Argument with Teeth in it for Man's Arrival in the New World. *Early Man* 4 (2).
Forbes, Jack D.
1960   *Apache, Navajo and Spaniard.* University of Oklahoma Press.
Frison, George C.
1971   Shoshonean Antelope Procurement in the Upper Green River Basin, Wyoming. *Plains Anthropologist* 16 (54): 258-84.

1974   *The Casper Site: A Hell Gap Bison Kill on the High Plains.* Academic Press.
1978   *Prehistoric Hunters of the High Plains.* Academic Press.
Frison, George C. and Bruce A. Bradley
1980   *Folsom Tools and Technology at the Hanson Site, Wyoming.* University of New Mexico Press.
Frison, George C. and Dennis Stanford
1982   *The Agate Basin Site: A Record of the Paleo-Indian Occupation of the Northwestern High Plains.* Academic Press.
Fulgham, Tommy and Dennis Stanford
1982   The Frasca Site: A Preliminary Report. *Southwestern Lore* 48 (1): 1-9.

Galloway, Eugene and George A. Agogino
1961   The Johnson Site: A Folsom Campsite. *Plains Anthropologist* 6 (13): 205-08.
Gebhard, Paul H.
1943   The Excavation of an Archaeological Site on the Purgatoire River, Southeastern Colorado. *Papers of the Explorers Club* 2 (2).
1949   An Archaeological Survey of the Blowouts of Yuma County, Colorado. *American Antiquity* 15 (2): 132-43.
Gifford, Barry and Lawrence Lee
1978   *Jack's Book: An Oral Biography of Jack Kerouac.* St. Martin's Press.
Gillio, David A.
1970   A Reexamination of the Gordon Creek Burial Lithic Material. *Southwestern Lore* 36 (1): 12-14.
Gillmor, Frances and Louisa Wade Wetherill
1953   *Traders to the Navajos: The Story of the Wetherills of Kayenta.* The University of New Mexico Press.
Gladwin, Winifred and H. S. Gladwin
1934   A Method for the Designation of Cultures and their Variations. *Medallion Papers* 15, Globe, Arizona.
Gooding, John D.
1980   The Durango South Project: An Archaeological Salvage of Two Late Basketmaker III Sites in the Durango District. *Anthropological Papers of the University of Arizona* 34.
1981   The Archaeology of Vail Pass Camp: A Multicomponent Base Camp Below Treelimit in the Southern Rockies. *Highway Salvage Report* 35. Colorado Department of Highways.
Gooding, John D., Allen Kihm and William L. Shields
in prep.   The Archaeology of Sisyphus Shelter. MS., Colorado Department of Highways.
Gordon, E. K., K. J. Kranzush and D. J. Knox
1979   Final Cultural Resource Inventory Report - 1978 Taiga/Coseka Drilling Program and 1978 Northwest Pipeline West Foundation Creek Gathering System, Rio Blanco and Garfield Counties, Colorado. *Cultural Resource Inventory Report Series* 79-3. Gordon and Kranzush Archaeological Consultants.
Gordon, E. K., K. J. Kranzush, D. J. Knox, V. E. Keen and C. A. Engleman
1981   A Class III Cultural Inventory of the Texas-Missouri-Evacuation Creeks Study Area, Rio Blanco County, Colorado. *Cultural Resource Inventory Report Series* 81-3. Gordon and Kranzush Archaeological Consultants.
Grady, James
1980   Environmental Factors in Archaeological Site Locations. *Bureau of Land Management Colorado, Cultural Resources Series* 9.

Graham, Russell W.
1981   Preliminary Report on Late Pleistocene Vertebrates from the Selby and Dutton Archaeological/Paleontological Sites, Yuma County, Colorado. *Contributions to Geology*, University of Wyoming 20 (1): 33-56.
Griffin, James B.
1952   *Archaeology of the Eastern United States*. University of Chicago Press.
Grinnel, George Bird
1915   *The Fighting Cheyenne*. Charles Scribner's Sons.
1923   *The Cheyenne Indians: The History and Ways of Life* (2 vols). Yale University Press.
Gunnerson, James H.
1960a   The Fremont Culture: Internal Dimensions and External Relationships. *American Antiquity* 25 (3): 373-80.
1960b   An Introduction to Plains Apache Archaeology - The Dismal River Aspect. *Bureau of American Ethnology, Bulletin* 173.
1968   Plains Apache Archaeology: A Review. *Plains Anthropologist* 13:167-89.
1969   The Fremont Culture: A Study in Culture Dynamics in the Northern Anasazi Frontier. *Papers of the Peabody Museum of Archaeology and Ethnology*, 59 (2).
Guthrie, Mark R.
1979   Mammal, Bird, Amphibian and Reptile Bone from the Torres Cave Site (5LA1310), Southeastern Colorado. *Southwestern Lore* 45 (1 and 2): 36-42.
1983   The Aurora Burial: Site 5AH244. Paper presented at the fifth annual meeting of the Colorado Council of Professional Archaeologists, Denver.

Hackett, Charles W. (ed.)
1931   *Pichardo's Treatise on the Limits of Louisiana and Texas* 1. Austin.
1934   *Pichardo's Treatise on the Limits of Louisiana and Texas* 2. Austin.
Hagar, Ivol K.
1976   5CR1 - Draper Cave Excavation and Research Report. *Southwestern Lore* 42 (3): 1-13.
Haines, Francis
1938a   Where Did The Plains Indians Get Their Horses? *American Anthropologist*, n.s. 40:112-17.
1938b   The Northward Spread of Horses Among Plains Indians. *American Anthropologist*, n.s. 40:429-36.
1976   *The Plains Indians*. Thomas Y. Crowell Co.
Halasi, Judith Ann
1979   Archaeological Excavation at the Escalante Site, Dolores, Colorado, 1975 and 1976. *In*: The Archaeology and Stabilization of the Dominguez and Escalante Ruins: 197-425. *Bureau of Land Management Colorado, Cultural Resources Series* 2.
Hathaway, J. Holly, Jeffrey L. Eighmy and Allen E. Kane
1983   Preliminary Modification of the Southwest Virtual Geomagnetic Pole Path A.D. 700 to A.D. 900: Dolores Archaeological Program Results. *Journal of Archaeological Science* 10:51-59.
Haury, Emil W.
1962   HH-39: Recollections of a Dramatic Moment in Southwestern Archaeology. *Tree-Ring Bulletin* 24 (3-4): 11-14.
Hayes, Alden C.
1964   The Archaeological Survey of Wetherill Mesa, Mesa Verde National Park - Colorado. *Archaeological Research Series* 7A. National Park Service.

Hayes, Alden C. and James A. Lancaster
1975   Badger House Community, Mesa Verde National Park. *Publications in Archaeology 7E, Wetherill Mesa Studies*, National Park Service.
Haynes, C. Vance
1974   Archaeological Geology of Some Selected Paleo-Indian Sites. *In*: History and Prehistory of the Lubbock Lake Site (C.C. Black, ed.). *The Museum Journal* 15. West Texas Museum Association.
1980   Paleoindian Charcoal From Meadowcroft Rockshelter: Is Contamination a Problem? *American Antiquity* 45 (3): 582-87.
Haynes, C. Vance and George Agogino
1960   Geological Significance of a New Radiocarbon Date from the Lindenmeier Site. *Proceedings, Denver Museum of Natural History* 9.
Heirtzler, J. R.
1968   Sea Floor Spreading. *Scientific American* 219:66-69.
Hemmings, E. T. and C. Vance Haynes
1969   The Escapule Mammoth and Associated Projectile Points, San Pedro Valley, Arizona. *Journal of the Arizona Academy of Science* 5 (3): 84-88.
Hester, James J.
1982   Review of *The Archaeology of Vail Pass Camp: A Multicomponent Base Camp Below Treelimit in the Southern Rockies* (Gooding). *Southwestern Lore* 48 (4): 32-33.
Hester, James J. and James Grady
1982   *Introduction to Archaeology*. Holt, Reinhart and Winston.
Hester, Thomas R., Robert F. Heizer and John A. Graham
1975   *Field Methods in Archaeology*. Mayfield Publishing Co.
Hewett, Edgar L.
1906   Preservation of American Antiquities: Progress During the Last Year; Needed Legislation. *American Anthropologist* 8 (1): 109-14.
1907   Preservation of American Antiquities. *American Anthropologist* 9 (1): 233-34.
1911   The School of American Archaeology in Santa Fe, N. M. *School of American Research Bulletin* 3.
Hibben, Frank
1941   Evidence of Early Occupation of Sandia Cave, New Mexico, and Other Sites in the Sandia-Manzano Region. *Smithsonian Miscellaneous Collections* 99 (23).
Hill, J. J.
1930   Spanish and American Exploration and Trade Northwest from New Mexico into the Great Basin. *Utah Historical Quarterly* 3 (1): 3-23.
Hoffman, J. J., Ann M. Johnson and William B. Butler
1982   Review of *The Archaeology of Vail Pass Camp: A Multicomponent Base Camp Below the Treelimit in the Southern Rockies* (Gooding). *Southwestern Lore* 48 (4): 32-33.
Hoig, Stan
1961   *The Sand Creek Massacre*. University of Oklahoma Press.
Holmer, Richard and Dennis G. Weder
1980   Common Post-Archaic Projectile Points of the Fremont Area. *Antiquities Section Selected Papers* 7 (16): 55-68. State of Utah.
Holmes, W. H.
1878a   Cliff House and Ruins on the Mancos River. *In*: Survey of the Territories for 1876 (F.V. Hayden, ed.). *U. S. Geological and Geographical Survey of the Territories, 10th Annual Report*.
1878b   Report on the Ancient Ruins of Southwestern Colorado, Examined

During the Summer of 1875 and 1876. *In*: Survey of the Territories for 1876
(F.V. Hayden, ed.). *U.S. Geological and Geographical Survey of the Territories, 10th
Annual Report*.
1886   Pottery of the Ancient Pueblos. *Bureau of American Ethnology, Fourth
Annual Report*: 257-360.
Horner, Susan and Charles Horner
1974   Progress Report for Sites 5JF57 and 5JF60. *Southwestern Lore* 40 (3 and
4): 43-48.
Hothem, Lar
1978   Indian Artifacting. *Fur-Fish-Game*, August: 26-40.
Hough, Walter
1931   Jesse Walter Fewkes. *American Anthropologist*, n.s. 33 (1): 92-97.
Howell, F. Clark
1968   *Early Man*. Time-Life Books.
Howells, William
1959   *Mankind in the Making*. Doubleday and Co., Inc.
Hoyt, Steven D.
1979   Archaeological Investigations of Torres Cave (5LA1310), Las Animas
County, Colorado, 1977. *Southwestern Lore* 45 (1 and 2): 1-21.
Hurlbett, Robert E.
1977   Environmental Constraint and Settlement Predictability, Northwestern
Colorado. *Bureau of Land Management Colorado, Cultural Resources Series* 3.
Hurst, C. T.
1935a   Southwestern Lore. *Southwestern Lore* 1 (1): 1-2.
1935b   Our New Society. *Southwestern Lore* 1 (1): 2-3.
1936   We Need To Discourage Exploitation. *Southwestern Lore* 2 (1): 22.
1939   An Outline for the Study of Archaeology - I. *Southwestern Lore* 5 (3):
64-66.
1940a   An Outline for the Study of Archaeology - II. *Southwestern Lore* 5 (4):
84-85.
1940b   Preliminary Work in Tabeguache Cave - 1939. *Southwestern Lore* 6 (2):
4-18.
1940c   An Outline for the Study of Archaeology - III. *Southwestern Lore* 6 (2):
37-38.
1941   A Folsom Location in the San Luis Valley, Colorado. *Southwestern Lore* 7
(2): 31-34.
1943a   A Folsom Site in a Mountain Valley of Colorado. *American Antiquity* 8
(3): 250-53.
1943b   Preliminary Work in Tabeguache Cave - II. *Southwestern Lore* 9 (1):
10-16.
1944   1943 Excavations in Cave II, Tabeguache Canyon, Montrose County,
Colorado. *Southwestern Lore* 10 (1): 2-14.
1945   Completion of Excavations of Tabeguache Cave II. *Southwestern Lore*, 11
(1): 7-12.
1946   The 1945 Tabeguache Expedition. *Southwestern Lore* 12 (1): 7-16.
1947   Excavation of Dolores Cave - 1946. *Southwestern Lore* 13 (1): 8-17.
1948   The Cottonwood Expedition, 1947 - A Cave and a Pueblo Site. *Southwestern Lore* 14 (1): 4-19.
Hurst, C. T. and Edgar Anderson
1949   A Corn Cache from Western Colorado. *American Antiquity* 14 (3):
161-67.

Huscher, Harold A.
   1939   Influence of the Drainage Pattern of the Uncompahgre Plateau on the Movements of Primitive Peoples. *Southwestern Lore* 5 (2): 22-41.
Huscher, B. H. and H. A. Huscher
   1939   Annual Report of the Colorado Museum of Natural History. *Publications of the Colorado Museum of Natural History* 19:21-22.
   1940a   Annual Report of the Colorado Museum of Natural History. *Publications of the Colorado Museum of Natural History* 20:23.
   1940b   Conventionalized Bear-Track Petroglyphs of the Uncompahgre Plateau. *Southwestern Lore* 6 (2): 25-27.
   1940c   Potsherds in a Pinon Tree. *Masterkey* 14 (4): 137-42.
   1941   Annual Report of the Colorado Museum of Natural History. *Publications of the Colorado Museum of Natural History* 21:21-23.
   1942   Athapaskan Migration via the Intermontaine Region. *American Antiquity* 8 (1): 80-88.
Huse, Hannah
   1977   Cultural Resource Inventory Report for the Proposed Windy Gap Dam, Reservoir and Pipeline Project near Granby, Grand County, Colorado. MS., Colorado Preservation Office.
Husted, Wilfred M.
   1965   Early Occupation of the Colorado Front Range. *American Antiquity* 30 (4): 494-498.
Husted, Wilfred M. and Oscar L. Mallory
   1967   The Fremont Culture: Its Derivation and Ultimate Fate. *Plains Anthropologist* 12 (36): 222-232.

Ireland, Stephen K.
   1968   Five Apishapa Focus Sites in the Arkansas Valley, Colorado. M.A. Thesis, University of Denver.
   1971   The Upper Purgatoire Complex - A Re-Appraisal. *Southwestern Lore* 37 (2): 37-51.
Irving, W. N. and C. R. Harington
   1973   Upper Pleistocene Radiocarbon-dated Artefacts from the Northern Yukon. *Science* 179 (4071): 335-40.
Irwin, Cynthia and Henry Irwin
   1957   Archaeology of the Agate Bluff Area. *Plains Anthropologist* 8:15-38.
   1959   Excavations at the LoDaisKa Site in the Denver, Colorado area. *Proceedings, Denver Museum of Natural History* 8.
   1961   Radio-carbon Dates from the LoDaisKa Site, Colorado. *American Antiquity* 27 (1).
Irwin-Williams, Cynthia and Henry Irwin
   1966   Excavations at Magic Mountain. *Proceedings, Denver Museum of Natural History* 12.
Irwin-Williams, Cynthia, Henry Irwin, George Agogino and C. Vance Haynes, Jr.
   1973   Hell Gap: Paleo-Indian Occupation on the High Plains. *Plains Anthropologist* 18 (59): 40-53.
Irwin-Williams, Cynthia
   1973   The Oshara Tradition: Origins of Anasazi Culture. *Eastern New Mexico University Contributions in Anthropology* 5 (1).

Irwin, Henry and H. M. Wormington
1970   Paleo-Indian Tool Types in the Great Plains. *American Antiquity* 35 (1): 24-34.
Ives, Ronald L.
1941   A Cultural Hiatus in the Rocky Mountain Region. *Southwestern Lore* 41 (3): 42-46.

Jackson, William H.
1875   A Notice of the Ancient Ruins in Arizona and Utah Lying about the Rio San Juan. *U.S. Geological and Geographical Survey Bulletin* 1 (3): 25-45.
1876   *Descriptive Catalogue of the Photographs of the U.S. Geological and Geographical Surveys for the Years 1869 to 1875, Inclusive.*
1878   Report on the Ancient Ruins Examined in 1875 and 1877. *U. S. Geological and Geographical Survey Bulletin* 1: 411-50.
Jeançon, Jean A.
1922   Archaeological Research in the Northwestern San Juan Basin of Colorado During the Summer of 1921. The State Historical and Natural History Society of Colorado and the University of Denver.
Jeançon, Jean A. and Frank H. H. Roberts, Jr.
1923   Further Archaeological Research in the Northeastern San Juan Basin of Colorado, During the Summer of 1922: The Pagosa-Piedra Region. *The Colorado Magazine* 1 (1): 11-28.
1924a   Excavation Work in the Pagosa-Piedra Field during the Season of 1922. *The Colorado Magazine* 1 (2): 65-70.
1924b   Excavation Work in the Pagosa-Piedra Field during the Season of 1922. *The Colorado Magazine* 1 (3): 108-118.
1924c   Excavation Work in the Pagosa-Piedra Field during the Season of 1922. *The Colorado Magazine* 1 (4): 163-73.
Jennings, Calvin H.
1974   Regional Oil Shale Study: Environmental Inventory, Analysis, and Impact Study. MS., Thorne Ecological Institute, Boulder, Colorado.
Jennings, Jesse D.
1956   The American Southwest: A Problem in Cultural Isolation. *In*: Seminars in Archaeology: 1955 (R. Wauchope, ed.). *Memoirs of the Society for American Archaeology* 11:59-127.
1957   Danger Cave. *American Antiquity* 23 (2, pt. 2), Memoir 14.
1968   *Prehistory of North America.* McGraw-Hill Book Co.
Jepsen, Glenn L.
1953   Ancient Buffalo Hunters of Northwestern Wyoming. *Southwestern Lore* 19 (2): 19-25.
Johanson, Donald and Maitland Edey
1981   *Lucy: The Beginnings of Humankind.* Simon and Schuster.
Jones, Bruce A.
1982   The Curecanti Archeological Project: 1980 Investigations in Curecanti National Recreation Area, Colorado. *Midwest Archeological Center Occasional Studies in Anthropology* 8.
Joukowsky, Martha
1980   *A Complete Mannual of Field Archaeology: Tools and Techniques of Field Work for Archaeologists.* Prentice-Hall, Inc.
Judd, Neil M.
1968   *Men Met Along the Trail.* University of Oklahoma Press.

Judge, James W.
1974   Projectile Point Form and Function in Late Paleo-Indian Period Assemblages. *In*: History and Prehistory of the Lubbock Lake Site. *The Museum Journal* 15. West Texas Museum Association.

Kainer, Ronald E.
1974   A Brief Descriptive Summary of the Spring Gulch Site, Larimer County, Colorado. *Southwestern Lore* 40 (3 and 4): 137-41.
1976   Archaeological Investigations at the Spring Gulch Site (5LR252). M.A. Thesis, Colorado State University.

Kane, Allen E.
1979   The Dolores Archaeological Program in 1978: Introduction and Implementation of the Research Design. *Cultural Resources Series* 1. Bureau of Reclamation, Upper Colorado Region, Salt Lake City.
1981   The Prehistory of the Dolores Project Area. *In*: Dolores Archaeological Program Synthetic Report 1978-80 (D. Breternitz, ed.). Report submitted to the Upper Colorado Region, U.S. Bureau of Reclamation.

Kaplan, Howard
1973   The Man Who Found Esther and Lost Her. *Empire Magazine, The Denver Post*, 4 Nov.

Kay, Marvin
1979   Review of The Mount Albion Complex: A Study of Prehistoric Man and the Altithermal (Benedict and Olson). *Plains Anthropologist* 24 (86): 341-42.

Kerouac, Jack
1957   *On The Road*. The Viking Press.

Kidder, Alfred V.
1910   Explorations in Southeastern Utah in 1908. *American Journal of Archaeology* 14:337-59.
1923   Basket Maker Caves in the Mesa Verde. *El Palacio* 15:164-5.
1924   An Introduction to the Study of Southwestern Archaeology, with a Preliminary Account of the Excavations at Pecos. *Papers of the Phillips Academy Southwestern Expedition* 1.
1927   Southwestern Archaeological Conference. *Science* 66:489-91.
1948   Sylvanus Griswold Morley, 1883-1948. *El Palacio* 55 (9): 267-74.
1957a   Earl H. Morris. *American Antiquity* 22 (4, pt. 1).
1957b   Reminiscences in Southwestern Archaeology: I. *The Kiva* 25 (4).
1958   Pecos, New Mexico: Archaeological Notes. *Papers of the Robert S. Peabody Foundation for Archaeology* 5.

Kingsbury, Lawrence A. and Michael Nowak
1980   Archaeological Investigations on Carrizo Ranches, Inc., 1974-79. *Colorado College Publications In Archaeology* 2.

Kingsbury, Lawrence A. and Lorna H. Gabel
1981   Eastern Apache Campsites in Southeastern Colorado: An Hypothesis. Paper presented at the 39th Plains Conference, Bismarck, N.D. (in press, *Plains Anthropologist* memoir).

Kluckhohn, Clyde and William H. Kelly
1945   The Concept of Culture. *In: The Science of Man in the World Crisis* (R. Linton, ed.). Columbia University Press.

Krieger, Alex D.
1946   Culture Complexes and Chronology in North Texas, with Extension of Puebloan Datings to the Mississippi Valley. *Publication 4640*. University of Texas.

1947   The Eastward Extension of Puebloan Datings toward Culture of the Mississippi Valley. *American Antiquity* 12 (3): 141-48.

Kroeber, Alfred L. and Clyde Kluckhohn
1952   Culture: A Critical Review of Concepts and Definitions. *Papers of the Peabody Museum of American Archaeology and Ethnology* 47 (1).

Lancaster, James A. and Don Watson
1942   Excavations of Mesa Verde Pit Houses. *American Antiquity* 9 (2).
1954   Excavation of Two Late Basketmaker III Pithouses. *In:* Archaeological Excavations in Mesa Verde National Park, Colorado (Lancaster, Pinkley, Van Cleave and Watson, eds.). *National Park Service Archaeological Research Series* 2.

Lancaster, James A. and Jean M. Pinkley
1954   Excavation at Site 16 of Three Pueblo II Mesa-Top Ruins. *In:* Archaeological Excavations in Mesa Verde National Park, Colorado (Lancaster, Pinkley, Van Cleave and Watson, eds.). *National Park Service Archaeological Reserarch Series* 2.

Lancaster, James A. and Philip Van Cleave
1954   Excavation of Sun Point Pueblo. *In:* Archaeological Excavations in Mesa Verde National Park, Colorado (Lancaster, Pinkley, Van Cleave and Watson, eds.). *National Park Service Archaeological Research Series* 2.

Lancaster, James A., Jean Pinkley, Philip Van Cleave and Don Watson
1954   Archaeological Excavations in Mesa Verde National Park, Colorado. *National Park Service Archaeological Research Series* 2.

LaPoint, Halcyon J., Howard M. Davidson, Steven D. Creasman and Karen Schubert
1981   Archaeological Investigations in the Canyon Pintado Historic District, Rio Blanco County, Colorado: Phase II. *Reports of the Laboratory of Public Archaeology*, Colorado State University.

Laughlin, W. S.
1967   Human Migration and Permanent Occupation in the Bering Sea Area. *In: The Bering Land Bridge* (D. Hopkins, ed.). Stanford University Press.

Lawrence, Robert and Cheryl Muceus
1981   Pool Area Prehistoric Sites. *In:* Old Dallas Historical Archaeology Program (W. Buckles, ed.), MS., Colorado Preservation Office.

Leach, Larry L.
1966a   Excavations at Willowbrook, a Stratified Site near Morrison. *Southwestern Lore* 32 (2): 25-46
1966b   The Archaeology of Boundary Village. *University of Utah Anthropological Papers* 83.
1967   Archaeological Investigations of Deluge Shelter, Dinosaur National Monument. *Publication PB 176960*, Clearinghouse for Federal Scientific and Technical Information, Department of Commerce, Springfield, Virginia.
1980   Archaeological Investigation at Deluge Shelter in Dinosaur National Monument. Ph.D. Dissertation, University of Colorado.

Linton, Adelin and Charles Wagley
1971   *Ralph Linton*. Columbia University Press.

Lintz, Christopher
1979   The Southwestern Periphery of the Plains Caddoan Area. *Nebraska History* 60 (2): 161-82.

Lischka, Joseph J.
1980   Review of *The Mount Albion Complex: A Study of Prehistoric Man and the Altithermal* (Benedict and Olson). *Southwestern Lore* 46 (4): 25-26.

Lister, Florence C. and Robert H. Lister
   1968   *Earl Morris and Southwestern Archaeology.* University of New Mexico Press.
Lister, Robert H.
   1951   Excavations at Hells Midden, Dinosaur National Monument. *University of Colorado Studies, Series in Anthropology* 3.
   1953   The Stemmed Indented Base Point, a Possible Horizon Marker. *American Antiquity* 18:264-65.
   1961   Twenty-Five Years of Archaeology in the Greater Southwest. *American Antiquity* 27 (1): 39-45.
   1964   Contributions to Mesa Verde Archaeology I, Site 499. *University of Colorado Studies, Series in Anthropology* 9.
   1965   Contributions to Mesa Verde Archaeology II, Site 875. *University of Colorado Studies, Series in Anthropology* 11.
   1966   Contributions to Mesa Verde Archaeology III, Site 866 and the Cultural Sequence at Four Villages in the Far View Group, Mesa Verde National Park, Colorado. *University of Colorado Studies, Series in Anthropology* 12.
   1967   Contributions to Mesa Verde Archaeology IV, Site 1086, an Isolated Above Ground Kiva in Mesa Verde National Park, Colorado. *University of Colorado Studies, Series in Anthropology* 13.
   1968   Contributions to Mesa Verde Archaeology V, Emergency Archaeology in Mesa Verde National Park, Colorado, 1948-1966. *University of Colorado Studies, Series in Anthropology* 15.
   1969   Environment and Man in Mesa Verde. *Naturalist* 20 (2): 1-37.
Lister, Robert H. and Florence C. Lister
   1978   *Anasazi Pottery.* University of New Mexico Press.
Lister, Robert H. and Herbert W. Dick
   1952   Archaeology of the Glade Park Area - A Progress Report: *Southwestern Lore* 17 (4): 69-92.
Longacre, William A.
   1976   Paul Sidney Martin, 1899-1974. *American Anthropologist* 78 (1): 90-92.
Ludwickson, John, Donald Blakeslee and John O'Shea
   1981   Missouri National Recreational River: Native American Cultural Resources. MS., Interagency Archeological Services, Denver.
Lyons, Ray D.
   1973   The Colorado Campaign for a State Archaeologist. *Southwestern Lore* 39 (2): 1-17.
   1979   Floral Resources of the Torres Cave (5LA1310) Vicinity. *Southwestern Lore* 45 (1 and 2): 43-47.

Madsen, Rex E. (compiler)
   1977   Prehistoric Ceramics of the Fremont. *Museum of Northern Arizona Ceramics Series* 6.
Malde, Harold E.
   1960   Geological Age of the Claypool Site, Northeastern Colorado. *American Antiquity* 26 (2): 235-43.
Martin, Paul Schultz and Peter J. Mehringer
   1965   Pleistocene Pollen Analysis and Biogeography of the Southwest. *In: The Quaternary of the United States* (Wright and Frey, eds.). Princeton University Press.

Martin, Paul Schultz and H. E. Wright, Jr.
1967   *Pleistocene Extinctions: The Search for a Cause.* Yale University Press.
Martin, Paul Sidney
1929   The 1928 Archaeological Expedition of the State Historical Society of Colorado. *Colorado Magazine* 6 (1): 1-35.
1930   Archaeological Expedition of the State Historical Society of Colorado in Cooperation with the Smithsonian Institution. *Colorado Magazine* 7 (1): 1-40.
1938   Archaeological Work in the Ackmen-Lowry Area, Southwestern Colorado, 1937. *Field Museum of Natural History, Anthropological Series* 23 (2).
1939   Modified Basketmaker Sites in the Ackmen-Lowry Area, Southwestern Colorado, 1938. *Field Museum of Natural History, Anthropological Series* 23 (3).
Martin, Paul Sidney, Lawrence Roy and G. von Bonin
1936   Lowry Ruin in Southwestern Colorado. *Field Museum of Natural History, Anthropological Series* 23 (1).
Martorano, Marilyn A.
1981   Scarred Ponderosa Pine Trees Reflecting Cultural Utilization of Bark. M.A. Thesis, Colorado State University.
Marwitt, John P.
1970   Median Village and Fremont Culture Regional Variation. *University of Utah Anthropological Papers* 95.
Mason, Ronald J.
1981   *Great Lakes Archaeology.* Academic Press.
McCabe, Helen
1973   The Settlement System of Five Prehistoric Pueblo Sites of the Upper Purgatoire Complex. *Southwestern Lore* 39 (3): 12-29.
McGimsey, Charles R., III and Hester A. Davis (eds.)
1977   The Management of Archaeological Resources: The Arlie House Report. *Special Publication of the Society for American Archaeology.*
McKern, William C.
1939   The Midwestern Taxonomic Method as an Aid to Archaeological Study. *American Antiquity* 4 (4): 301-13.
McNitt, Frank
1957   *Richard Wetherill: Anasazi.* The University of New Mexico Press.
Mead, Jim I.
1980   Is It Really That Old? A Comment About the Meadowcroft Rockshelter "Overview". *American Antiquity* 45 (3): 579-82.
Medina, Douglas M.
1974   Excavations at Ken Caryl Ranch, 1973 and 1974: Report on Bradford House III. *Southwestern Lore* 40 (3 and 4): 46-47.
1975   Preliminary Report on the Excavation of the Bradford House III Site - Ken Caryl Ranch. *Southwestern Lore* 41 (4): 51-56.
Metcalf, Michael D.
1973   Archaeology at Dipper Gap: An Archaic Campsite, Logan County, CO. M.A. Thesis, Colorado State University.
Meyer, Karl
1973   *The Plundered Past.* Atheneum Press.
Moorehead, Wayne
1979   'Zeke' Flora. *Durango Herald*, 25 March.
Morley, Sylvanus G.
1908   The Excavation of the Cannonball Ruins in Southwestern Colorado. *American Anthropologist* 10 (4): 596-610.

Morley, Sylvanus G. and A. V. Kidder
1917   The Archaeology of McElmo Canyon, Colorado. *El Palacio* 4: 41-70.
Morris, Ann Axtell
1978   *Digging in the Southwest.* Peregrine Smith, Inc.(orig. 1933).
Morris, Earl H.
1911   The Cliff Dwellers of the San Juan. *Colorado* 2 (7): 27-30.
1919   Preliminary Account of the Antiquities of the Region between the Mancos and La Plata Rivers in Southwestern Colorado. *Thirty-Third Annual Report, Bureau of American Ethnology*: 155-206.
1927   The Beginnings of Pottery Making in the San Juan Area, Unfired Prototypes and the Wares of the Earliest Ceramic Period. *Anthropological Papers* 28 (2). American Museum of Natural History.
1929   Archaeological Field Work in North America during 1928: Arizona. *American Anthropologist*, n.s. 31: 339-40.
1931   Archaeological Research in Southwestern United States: the San Juan Basin, *Carnegie Institution of Washington Yearbook* 30: 398-405.
1939   Archaeological Studies in the La Plata District. *Carnegie Institution of Washington, Publication* 519.
1944   Anasazi Sandals. *News Letters* 68/69:239-41. Clearing House for Western Museums.
1949   Basket Maker II Dwellings near Durango, Colorado. *Tree-Ring Bulletin* 15 (4): 33-34.
1952   Note on the Durango Dates. *Tree-Ring Bulletin* 18 (4): 36.
Morris, Earl H. and Robert F. Burgh
1941   Anasazi Basketry: BMIII-PIII, A Study Based on Specimens from the San Juan River. *Carnegie Institution of Washington, Publication* 535.
1954   Basketmaker II Sites near Durango, Colorado. *Carnegie Institution of Washington, Publication* 601.
Morris, Elizabeth Ann
1981   Alan Peter Olson, 1926-1978. *American Antiquity* 46 (2): 342-45.
Morss, Noel
1931   The Ancient Culture of the Fremont River in Utah: Report on the Explorations under the Claflin-Emerson Fund, 1928-29. *Papers of the Peabody Museum of American Archaeology and Ethnology* 12 (3).
1954   Clay Figurines of the American Southwest. *Papers of the Peabody Museum of American Archaeology and Ethnology* 49 (1).
1957   Figurines. *In:* Two Fremont Sites and their Position in. Southwestern Prehistory. *University of Utah Anthropological Papers* 29: 167-70.
Moss, John H., in collaboration with Kirk Bryan, G. William Holmes, Linton Satterthwaite, Jr., Henry P. Hansen, C. Bertrand Schultz ahd W. D. Frankforter.
1951   Early Man in the Eden Valley. *University of Pennsylvania, Museum Monographs* 6.
Müller-Beck, H.
1967   On Migrations of Hunters across the Bering Land Bridge in the Upper Pleistocene. *In: The Bering Land Bridge* (D. Hopkins, ed.). Stanford University Press.
Mulloy, William T.
1954   The McKean Site in Northwestern Wyoming. *Southwestern Journal of Anthropology* 10 (4): 432-60.
1958   A Preliminary Historical Outline for the Northwestern Plains. *University of Wyoming Publications in Science* 22 (1).

1959   The James Allen Site near Laramie, Wyoming. *American Antiquity* 25 (1): 112-16.

Nelson, Charles E.
1967   The Archaeology of Hall-Woodland Cave. *Southwestern Lore* 33 (1): 1-13.
1969   Salvage Archaeology on Van Bibber Creek, Site 5JF10. *Southwestern Lore* 34 (4): 85-106.
1971   The George W. Lindsay Ranch Site, 5JF11. *Southwestern Lore* 37 (1): 1-14.
1981   Cherry Gulch Site (5JF63): A Projectile Point Study. *Southwestern Lore* 47 (2): 1-27.
Nelson, Charles E. and Jesse M. Graeber
1966   Excavation of Graeber Cave, North Turkey Creek. *Southwestern Lore* 32 (2): 47-54.
Nelson, Sarah M.
1983   Franktown Cave Mapping Project, Franktown, Colorado. MS., Colorado Preservation Office.
Neuman, Robert W.
1967   Radiocarbon-Dated Archaeological Remains on the Northern and Central Great Plains. *American Antiquity* 32 (4): 471-86.
Nickens, Paul R.
1977   Colorado's Archaeological Sites need Protection. *Colorado Outdoors* 26 (4): 7-10.
1982   (with Deborah A. Hull) San Juan Resource Area. *In*: Archaeological Resources of Southwestern Colorado. *Bureau of Land Management Colorado, Cultural Resources Series* 13.
Nickens, Paul R., Signa L. Larralde and Gordon C. Tucker, Jr.
1981   A Survey of Vandalism to Archaeological Resources in Southwestern Colorado. *Bureau of Land Management Colorado, Cultural Resources Series* 11.
Nordenskiöld, Gustav Eric Adolf
1901   *The Cliff Dwellers of the Mesa Verde.* (translated by D. I. Morgan). Stechert Publishing.
Nusbaum, Jesse L.
1922   A Basket-Maker Cave in Kane County, Utah . . . with Notes on the Artifacts by A. V. Kidder and S. J. Guernsey. *Museum of the American Indian, Heye Foundation, Indian Notes and Monographs, Miscellaneous* 29.
1981   The 1926 Re-Excavation of Step House Cave. *Mesa Verde Research Series, Paper* 1.
Nykamp, Robert H.
1982   South Divide Timber Sales. MS., U.S. Forest Service, on file, Colorado Preservation Office.

O'Bryan, Deric
1950   Excavations in Mesa Verde National Park, 1947-48. *Medallion Papers* 39. Globe, Arizona.
Olson, Alan P.
1953   Excavation of the Lyons Rock Shelter. *Southwestern Lore* 19:1-3.
1976   An Archaeological Survey Assessment for Rio Blanco Oil Shale Project 1976. MS., Bureau of Land Management, on file, Colorado Preservation Office.

Olson, Alan P., Robert Rowland, and Betty J. LaFree
    1976   Archaeological Survey, Florissant National Monument, August-November, 1974. MS., National Park Service.
Olson, Alan P., Tom Bridge and Betty J. LaFree
    1976   Archaeology Excavation, Florissant National Monument, September 1975. MS., National Park Service.

Park, Edwards
    1978   The Ginsberg Caper: Hacking it as in the Stone Age. *Smithsonian* 9 (4): 85-96.
Patterson, David and George A. Agogino
    1976   The Linger Skull: A Find of Possible Folsom Age. *The Greater Llano Estacado Southwest Heritage* 6 (2).
Peckham, Stewart
    1976   Jesse Logan Nusbaum. *El Palacio* 82 (1): 42-43.
Perry, Richard J.
    1980   The Apachean Transition from the Subarctic to the Southwest. *Plains Anthropologist* 25 (90): 279-96.
Phenice, T. W.
    1972   *Hominid Fossils: An Illustrated Key*. William C. Brown Co., Publishers.
Poirier, Frank E.
    1977   *Fossil Evidence: The Human Evolutionary Journey* (2nd ed.) The C. V. Mosby Co.
Powell, Peter J.
    1969   *Sweet Medicine: The Continuing Role of the Sacred Arrows, the Sundance and the Sacred Buffalo Hat in Northern Cheyenne History*. University of Oklahoma Press.
    1980   *The Cheyenne, Ma²heo²o's People: A Critical Bibliography*. Indiana University Press.

Rancier, James, Gary Haynes and Dennis Stanford
    1982   1981 Investigations of Lamb Spring. *Southwestern Lore* 48 (2): 1-17.
Rathbun, Fred
    1979   Archaeological Geology of Torres Cave (5LA1310), Las Animas County, Colorado. *Southwestern Lore* 45 (1 and 2): 22-35.
Reed, Alan D. and Ronald E. Kainer
    1978   The Tamarron Site: A Basketmaker II Site in Southwestern Colorado. *Southwestern Lore* 44 (2): 1-47.
Reed, Alan D. and Paul R. Nickens
    1980   Archeological Investigations at the DeBeque Rockshelter: A Stratified Archaic Site in West-Central Colorado. MS., Colorado Preservation Office.
Reed, Alan D. and Douglas D. Scott
    1982   The Archaeological Resources of the Uncompahgre and Gunnison Resource Areas, West Central Colorado. *In*: Archaeological Resources in Southwestern Colorado. *Bureau of Land Management Colorado, Cultural Resources Series* 13.
Reed, Erik K..
    1958   Excavations in Mancos Canyon, Colorado. *University of Utah Anthropological Papers* 35.
Reeves, Brian
    1973   The Concept of an Altithermal Cultural Hiatus in Northern Plains Prehistory. *American Anthropologist,* 75 (5): 1221-53.

Renaud, E. B.
1931 Archaeological Survey of Eastern Colorado, First Report. *Archaeological Survey, Department of Anthropology, University of Denver.*
1932a Archaeological Survey of Eastern Colorado, Second Report. *Archaeological Survey, Department of Anthropology, University of Denver.*
1932b Yuma and Folsom Artifacts, New Material. *Proceedings,* Colorado Museum of Natural History 11 (2).
1933 Archaeological Survey of Eastern Colorado, Third Report. *Archaeological Survey, Department of Anthropology, University of Denver.*
1934a Archaeological Survey of Western Nebraska, Sixth Report. *Archaeological Survey, Department of Anthropology, University of Denver.*
1934b The First Thousand Yuma-Folsom Artifacts, First Paper. *Archaeological Series, Department of Anthropology, University of Denver.*
1935 The Archaeological Survey of Eastern Colorado, Fourth Report. *Archaeological Survey, Department of Anthropology, University of Denver.*
1936a The Archaeological Survey of the High Western Plains, Southern Wyoming and Southwest South Dakota, Seventh Report. *Archaeological Survey, Department of Anthropology, University of Denver.*
1936b The Archaeological Survey of the High Western Plains. Pictographs and Petroglyphs of the High Western Plains, Eighth Report. *Archaeological Survey, Department of Anthropology, University of Denver.*
1937 The Archaeological Survey of the High Western Plains. Northeastern New Mexico, Ninth Report. *Archaeological Survey, Department of Anthropology, University of Denver.*
1938a The Archaeological Survey of the High Western Plains. Black's Fork Culture of Southwest Wyoming, Tenth Report. *Archaeologial Survey, Department of Anthropology, University of Denver.*
1938b The Archaeological Survey Series. Petroglyphs of North Central New Mexico, Eleventh Report. *Archaeological Survey, Department of Anthropology, University of Denver.*
1940 The Archaeological Survey Series. Further Research Work in the Black's Fork Basin, Southwest Wyoming, Twelfth Report. *Archaeological Survey, Department of Anthropology, University of Denver.*
1942a Indian Stone Enclosures of Colorado and New Mexico, Second Paper. *Archaeological Series, Department of Anthropology, University of Denver.*
1942b Reconnaissance Work in the Upper Rio Grande Valley, Third Paper. *Archaeological Series, Department of Anthropology, University of Denver.*
1943 Archaeological Sites of the Cuchara Drainage, Southern Colorado, Fourth Paper. *Archaeological Series, Department of Anthropology, University of Denver.*
1945 Archaeological Survey of South Park, Colorado, Fifth Paper. *Archaeological Series, Department of Anthropology, University of Denver.*
1946 Archaeology of the Upper Rio Grande Basin in Southern Colorado and Northern New Mexico, Sixth Paper. *Archaeological Series, Department of Anthropology, University of Denver.*
1947 Archaeology of the High Western Plains - Seventeen Years of Archaeological Research. *Miscellaneous Paper, Department of Anthropology, University of Denver.*
1960 Typology of Yuma, Folsoms and other Weapon Points. *Southwestern Lore* 26 (2): 37-42.

Reyman, Jonathan E.
1979   Vandalism and Site Destruction at some National Parks and Monuments: A Call for Action. *A.S.C.A. Newsletter* 6:4-9.
Richardson, Charles
1974   Summary of Excavations at the Ken Caryl Ranch, 1973. *Southwestern Lore* 40 (3 and 4): 48-49.
Rippeteau, Bruce E.
1978   A Colorado Book of the Dead: The Prehistoric Era. *The Colorado Magazine* 55 (4).
1979   Antiquities Enforcement in Colorado. *Journal of Field Archaeology* 6 (1): 84-103.
Roberts, Frank, H. H., Jr.
1925   Report on Archaeological Reconnaissance in Southwestern Colorado in the Summer of 1923. *The Colorado Magazine* 2 (2): 1-80.
1929   Certain Early Pueblo Villages in Southwestern Colorado. *Explorations and Field-Work of the Smithsonian Institution in 1928*: 161-68.
1930   Early Pueblo Ruins in the Piedra District, Southwestern Colorado. *Bureau of American Ethnology, Bulletin* 96.
1934   True Folsom Points. *Literary Digest* 118 (4): 18.
1935a   A Folsom Camp Site and Workshop. *Explorations and Field-Work of the Smithsonian Institution in 1934*:61-64.
1935b   A Folsom Complex: Preliminary Report on the Investigations at the Lindenmeier Site in Northern Colorado. *Smithsonian Miscellaneous Collections* 94 (4).
1935c   Folsom Complex: Preliminary Report on the Investigations at the Lindenmeier Site in Northern Colorado (a summary). *Nature* 136:535-38.
1935d   A Survey of Southwestern Archaeology. *American Antiquity* 37 (1): 1-35.
1936a   Additional Information on the Folsom Complex: Report on the Second Season's Investigations at the Lindenmeier Site in Northern Colorado. *Smithsonian Miscellaneous Collections* 95 (10).
1936b   Recent Discoveries in the Material Culture of Folsom Man. *The American Naturalist* 70:337-45.
1936c   Further Investigations at a Folsom Campsite in Northern Colorado. *Explorations and Field-Work of the Smithsonian Institution in 1935*: 69-74.
1937a   New Developments in the Problem of the Folsom Complex. *Explorations and Field-Work of the Smithsonian Institution in 1936*: 69-74.
1937b   The Material Culture of Folsom Man as Revealed at the Lindenmeier Site. *Southwestern Lore* 2 (4): 67-73.
1938   The Lindenmeier Site in Northern Colorado Contributes Additional Data on the Folsom Complex. *Explorations and Field-Work of the Smithsonian Institution in 1937*: 115-18.
1940a   Excavations at the Lindenmeier Site Contributes New Information on the Folsom Complex. *Explorations and Field-Work of the Smithsonian Institution in 1939*: 87-92.
1940b   Developments in the Problem of the North American Paleo-Indian. *In*: Essays in Historical Anthropology in North America. *Smithsonian Miscellaneous Collections* 100:51-116.
1941   Latest Excavations at the Lindenmeier Site Add to Information on the Folsom Complex. *Explorations and Field-Work of the Smithsonian Institution in 1940*: 79-82.

1944   Charles R. Scoggin, 1914-1944. *American Antiquity* 10 (2): 198-201.
1946a   Prehistoric Peoples of Colorado. *The Colorado Magazine* 23 (4): 145-56.
1946b   Prehistoric Peoples of Colorado. *The Colorado Magazine* 23 (5): 215-30 (a continuation of the above).
1951   The Early Americans. *Scientific American* 184 (2): 15-19.
1961   The Agate Basin Complex. *In: Homenaje a Pablo Martinez del Rio*. Instituto Nacional de Antropologia y Historia. Mexico.

Robinson, William J. and Bruce G. Harrill
1974   *Tree Ring Dates from Colorado V: Mesa Verde Area*. Laboratory of Tree-Ring Research, University of Arizona.

Rohn, Arthur H.
1971   Mug House, Mesa Verde National Park - Colorado. *Publications in Archaeology* 72. National Park Service.

Roys, R. L. and M. W. Harrison
1948   Sylvanus Griswold Morley, 1883-1948. *American Antiquity* 14 (2): 215-21.

Rudy, Jack R.
1953   Archaeological Survey of Western Utah. *University of Utah Anthropological Papers* 22.

Runcorn, S. K. (ed.)
1962   *Continental Drift*. International Geophysical Series 3. Academic Press.

Schaafsma, Polly
1971   The Rock Art of Utah: A Study from the Donald Scott Collection. *Papers of the Peabody Museum of Archaeology and Ethnology* 65.

Schiffer, Michael B. and George J. Gumerman (eds.)
1977   *Conservation Archaeology: A Guide for Cultural Resource Management*. Academic Press.

Schoenwetter, James and Frank Eddy
1964   Alluvial and Palynological Reconstruction of Environments, Navajo Reservoir District. *Museum of New Mexico Papers in Anthropology* 13.

Schroeder, Albert H.
1965   A Brief History of Southern Utah. *Southwestern Lore* 30 (4): 53-78.

Schroedl, Alan R.
1977   The Paleo-Indian Period on the Colorado Plateau. *Southwestern Lore* 43 (3): 1-9.

Schubert, Karen C., Christopher S. Arthur, Bruce R. Miller, and Calvin H. Jennings.
1981   Archaeological Investigations along the Breckenridge to Malta Transmission Line, Lake Park and Summit Counties, Colorado. *Reports of the Laboratory of Public Archaeology* 54. Colorado State University.

Scoggin, Charles R.
1939   Folsom and Nepesta Points. *American Antiquity* 5 (4): 290-98.
1941   Preliminary Report of the Archaeological Field Work of the University of Colorado Museum in Yampa Canyon, 1939-40. MS., University of Colorado Museum.
1942   Report of Reconnaissance in Dinosaur National Monument, Season 1941. MS., University of Colorado Museum.

Scott, Douglas D.
1972   The Nordenskiöld Campsite: A Test in Historic Archaeology. *The Kiva* 37 (3): 128-40.

1977   Two Vandalized Pueblo III Burials: Some Key Factors Affecting Vandalism of Sites. *Southwestern Lore* 43 (3): 10-14.
1979   A New Note on Colorado Plains Woodland Mortuary Practices. *Southwestern Lore* 45 (3): 13-24.
1980   Pothunting in Southwestern Colorado. *Colorado Council of Professional Archaeologists Newsletter* 2 (1):3.

Scott, Douglas D. and Terje G. Birkedal
1972   The Archaeology and Physical Anthropology of the Gahagan-Lipe Site with Comments on Colorado Woodland Mortuary Practices. *Southwestern Lore* 38 (3): 1-18.

Scott, Linda J.
1982   Pollen and Fiber Analysis of the McEndree Ranch Site, 5 BA 30, Southwestern Colorado. *Southwestern Lore* 48 (2): 18-24.

Sellards, E. H.
1952   *Early Man in America.* University of Texas Press.

Sharrock, Floyd W.
1966   Prehistoric Occupation Patterns in Southwest Wyoming and Cultural Relationships with the Great Basin and Plains Culture Areas. *University of Utah Anthropological Papers,* 77.

Sheets, Payson D.
1969   The Archaeology of Ely Caves, Dinosaur National Monument. Clearinghouse for Federal Scientific and Technical Information, Department of Commerce, Springfield, Virginia.
1973   The Pillage of Prehistory. *American Antiquity* 38 (3): 317-20.

Shields, William Lane
1980   Preliminary Investigations at the McEndree Ranch Site, 5 BA 30. *Southwestern Lore* 46 (3): 1-17.

Simonich, Edward
1980   Arnie Withers, oral history. Tape recordings on file, Pueblo Public Library.

Smith, Jack E.
1981   The Nusbaum Years. *Mesa Verde Occasional Papers* 1 (1 and 2).

Smith, Watson
1962   Robert Frederick Burgh, 1907-1962. *American Antiquity* 28 (1): 83-86.

Spikard, Lynda
1972   Progress Report of a Dent Site Investigation. MS., Colorado Preservation Office.

Stanford, Dennis
1974   Preliminary Report of the Excavation of the Jones-Miller Hell Gap Site, Yuma County, Colorado. *Southwestern Lore* 40 (3 and 4): 29-36.
1975   The 1975 Excavations at the Jones-Miller Site, Yuma County, Colorado. *Southwestern Lore* 41 (4): 34-38.
1979a   The Selby and Dutton Sites: Evidence for a Possible Pre-Clovis Occupation of the High Plains. *In: Pre-Llano Cultures of the Americas: Paradoxes and Possibilities* (Humphrey and Stanford, eds.). The Anthropological Society of Washington: 101-23.
1979b   Bison Kill by Ice Age Hunters. *National Geographic* 155 (1): 114-21.
1981   Book Review of *The Hudson-Meng Site: An Alberta Bison Kill in the Nebraska High Plains* (Agenbroad). *Plains Anthropologist* 26 (94): 339-41.
1982   A Critical Review of Archaeological Evidence Relating to the Antiquity of the Human Occupation of the New World. *In*: Plains Indian Studies: A

Collection of Essays in Honor of John C. Ewers and Waldo Wedel (Ubelaker and Viola, eds.). *Smithsonian Contributions to Anthropology* 30.
1983   Pre-Clovis Occupation South of the Ice Sheets. *In: Early Man in the New World* (R. Shutler, ed.): 65-72. Sage Publications.
Stanford, Dennis, Robson Bonnichson and Richard E. Morland
1981   The Ginsberg Experiment: Modern and Prehistoric Evidence of a Bone Flaking Technology. *Science* 212: 438-40.
Stanford, Dennis, Waldo R. Wedel and Glenn R. Scott
1981   Archaeological Investigations of the Lamb Spring Site. *Southwestern Lore* 47 (1): 14-27.
Stanford, Dennis and John Albanese
1975   Preliminary Results of the Smithsonian Institution Excavation at the Claypool Site, Washington County, Colorado. *Southwestern Lore* 41 (4).
Steen, Charlie R.
1955   *Prehistoric Man in the Arkansas-White-Red River Basins.* National Park Service.
Stephenson, Robert L.
1967   Frank H. H. Roberts, Jr., 1897-1966. *American Antiquity* 32 (1): 84-94.
Stevens, Dominique E. and George A. Agogino
1975   Sandia Cave: A Study in Controversy. *Contributions in Anthropology* 7 (1). Eastern New Mexico University, Paleo-Indian Institute.
Steward, Julian H.
1933   Archaeological Problems of the Northern Periphery of the Southwest. *Museum of Northern Arizona Bulletin 5.*
1936   Pueblo Material Culture in Western Utah. *University of New Mexico Bulletin* 287, *Anthropological Science* 1 (3).
Stewart, Omer C.
1941   The Southern Ute Peyote Cult. *American Anthropologist* n.s., 43:303-08.
1942   Cultural Element Distributions XVIII: Ute-Southern Paiute. *University of California Anthropological Records* 6 (4): 231-355.
1947a   Objectives and Methods for an Archaeological Survey. *Southwestern Lore* 12 (4).
1947b   Archaeology, Ethnology and History in Colorado. *Southwestern Lore* 13 (2): 24-28.
1948   Ute Peyotism: A Study of a Cultural Complex. *University of Colorado Studies, Series in Anthropology* 1.
1949   The Colorado Archaeological Society: Monument to Dr. C. T. Hurst. *Southwestern Lore* 15 (4): 79-87.
1963   Review of *The World of the Past* (Hewkes). *Southwestern Lore* 29 (3): 67-68.
1966   Ute Indians: Before and After White Contact. *Bureau of Anthropological Research, Institute of Behavioral Science.* Publication 5L, University of Colorado.
1971   Ethnohistorical Bibliography of the Ute Indians of Colorado. *University of Colorado Studies, Series in Anthropology* 18.
1977   Review of *American Indians in Colorado* (Hughes). *Southwestern Lore* 43 (3): 30.
1979   Review of *America B.C., Ancient Settlers in the New World* (Fell). *Southwestern Lore* 45 (1 and 2): 54-55.
1982   *Indians of the Great Basin: A Critical Bibliography.* Indiana University Press.

Stoltman, James B.
   1966   New Radiocarbon Dates for Southeastern Fiber-Tempered Pottery.
   American Antiquity 31 (6): 872-74.
Strong, W. Duncan
   1935   An Introduction to Nebraska Archaeology. *Smithsonian Miscellaneous
   Collections* 93 (10).
   1940   From History to Prehistory in the Northern Great Plains. *Smithsonian
   Miscellaneous Collections* 100:353-94.
Struever, Stuart (ed.)
   1971   *Prehistoric Agriculture.* The Natural History Press.
Struever, Stuart and Felicia A. Holton
   1979   *Koster: Americans in Search of their Past.* Doubleday and Co.
Stuart, David E. and Rory P. Gauthier
   1981   *Prehistoric New Mexico: Background for Survey.* State Historic Preservation
   Bureau, Santa Fe.
Sudler, Barbara
   1983   H. M. Wormington: An Exceptional Archaeologist. *Colorado Heritage
   News*, 1 April.
Suess, H. E.
   1965   Secular Variations of the Cosmic-Ray Produced Carbon-14 in the At-
   mosphere. *Journal of Geophysical Research* 70.

Tarling, Don and Maureen Tarling
   1971   *Continental Drift: A Study of the Earth's Moving Surface.* Anchor Books.
Taylor, Walter
   1948   *A Study of Archaeology.* Memoir Series of the American Anthropological
   Association 69.
Thomas, A. B.
   1935   *After Coronado.* University of Oklahoma Press.
Thompson, Ian M.
   1982   Looters and Losers in the San Juan Country. *Early Man* 4 (2).
Thompson, J. Eric S.
   1949   Sylvanus Griswold Morley, 1883-1948. *American Anthropologist 51 (2):
   293-297.*
Toll, Henry Wolcott, III
   1971   Dolores River Archaeology: Canyon Adaptations as seen through Survey. *Bureau of Land Management Colorado, Cultural Resources Series* 4.
Trautman, M. A. and E. H. Willis
   1966   Radiocarbon Measurements V, Isotopes, Inc. *Radiocarbon* 8:161-203.
Turner, Christy G., II
   1981   Dental Evidence for the Peopling of the Americas. Paper presented at
   the 46th Annual Meeting of the Society for American Archaeology.
   1983   Dental Evidence for the Peopling of the Americas. *In: Early Man in the
   New World* (R. Shutler, ed.): 147-57. Sage Publications.
Tyler, S. Lyman
   1951   Before Escalante: An Early History of the Yuta Indians and the Area
   North of New Mexico. Ph.D Dissertation, University of Utah.
Tyrell, J. B.
   1916   David Thompson's Narrative of his Explorations in Western America,
   1784-1812. *The Publications of the Champlain Society* 12.

Vitelli, Karen D.
  1982   The ABC's of the Antiquities Market. *Early Man* 4 (1): 29-32.

Walter, Paul A.
  1947   Edgar Lee Hewett, Americanist, 1865-1946. *American Anthropologist* 49
  (1): 260-69.
Watson, Virginia
  1950   The Optima Focus of the Panhandle Aspect: Description and Analysis.
  Bulletin of the Texas Archaeological and Paleontological Society 21: 7-68.
Wauchope, Robert
  1965   Alfred Vincent Kidder, 1885-1963. *American Antiquity* 31 (2, pt. 1):
  149-71.
Webb, Walter Prescott
  1931   *The Great Plains.* Grosset and Dunlap.
Wettlaufer, Boyd
  1955   The Mortlach Site in the Besant Valley of Central Saskatchewan. *Saskatchewan Museum of Natural History, Anthropological Series* 1.
Wedel, Waldo R.
  1954   Earthenware and Steatite Vessels from Northwestern Wyoming. *American Antiquity* 19 (4): 403-09.
  1961   *Prehistoric Man on the Great Plains.* University of Oklahoma Press.
  1964   Primitive Man in the Boulder Area. *In*: Natural History of the Boulder
  Area. *University of Colorado Museum, Leaflet* 13.
Weir, Glendon H.
  1977   Pollen Evidence for Environmental Change at Hovenweep National
  Monument A.D. 900-A.D. 1300. *In*: Hovenweep 1976 (J. Winter, ed.) *San
  Jose State University Archaeology Report* 3:246-78.
Wendorf, Fred and James J. Hester
  1962   Early Man's Utilization of the Great Plains Environment. *American
  Antiquity* 28 (2): 159-71.
Wenger, Gilbert R.
  1955   A Brief Summary of the Archaeology of Southern Blue Mountain and
  Douglas Creek in Northwestern Colorado. *In*: A Reappraisal of the Fremont
  Culture (Wormington). *Proceedings, Denver Museum of Natural History* 1:140-42.
  1956   An Archaeological Survey of Southern Blue Mountain and Douglas
  Creek in Northwestern Colorado. M.A. Thesis, University of Denver.
  1980   *The Mesa Verde Story.* Mesa Verde Museum Association.
  1981   *Archeological Techniques Used at Mesa Verde.* Mesa Verde Museum Association.
Wheat, Joe Ben
  1955   MT-1, A Basketmaker III Site Near Yellow Jacket, Colorado (A Progress Report). *Southwestern Lore* 21 (2).
  1967   A Paleo-Indian Bison Kill. *Scientific American* 216 (1): 44-52.
  1972   The Olsen-Chubbuck Site: A Paleo-Indian Bison Kill. *Society for American Archaeology Memoir* 26.
  1979   The Jurgens Site. *Plains Anthropologist* 24 (82, pt. 2), Memoir 15.
Wheeler, Charles W. and Gary Martin
  1982   The Granby Site: Early-Middle Archaic Wattle and Daub Structures.
  Southwestern Lore 48 (3): 16-25.
Wheeler, Richard P.
  1952   A Note on the "McKean Lanceolate Point." *Plains Anthropological Conference Newsletter* 4 (4): 39-44.

1954   Two New Projectile Point Types: Duncan and Hanna Points. *Plains Anthropologist* 1:7-14.
White, Thain
1952   *Scarred Trees in Western Montana.* Flathead Lake Lookout Museum, Lakeside, Montana.
Willey, Gordon R. and Philip Phillips
1958   *Method and Theory in American Archaeology.* University of Chicago Press.
Willey, Gordon R. and Jeremy A. Sabloff
1974   *A History of American Archaeology.* W. H. Freeman and Co.
Williams, Lance R.
1977   Vandalism to Cultural Resources of the Rocky Mountain West. M. A. Thesis, Recreational Resources Department, Colorado State University.
Wilmsen, Edwin N.
1974   *Lindenmeier: A Pleistocene Hunting Society.* Harper and Row.
Wilmsen, Edwin N. and Frank H. H. Roberts, Jr.
1978   Lindenmeier, 1934-1974: Concluding Report on Investigations. *Smithsonian Contributions to Anthropology* 24.
Wissler, Clark
1914   The Influence of the Horse in the Development of Plains Culture. *American Anthropologist*, n.s., 16 (1): 1-25.
Withers, Arnold M.
1954   Reports of Archaeological Fieldwork in Colorado, Wyoming, New Mexico, Arizona, and Utah in 1952 and 1953 - University of Denver Archaeological Fieldwork. *Southwestern Lore* 19 (4): 1-3.
1964a   Northwestern Pueblo County and Adjacent Parts of El Paso and Fremont Counties to be Appropriated for Fort Carson. MS., Colorado Preservation Office.
1964b   Ruedi Reservoir: Frying Pan-Arkansas Project of the Bureau of Reclamation. MS., Colorado Preservation Office.
1965   Sugarloaf, Twin Lakes and Pueblo Reservoirs: Frying Pan-Arkansas Project. MS., Colorado Preservation Office.
1972   Arapaho County Archaeological Survey of Chatfield Reservoir. MS., Colorado Preservation Office.
1981   The View From My Front Porch. *Archaeological Society of New Mexico Anthropological Papers* 6.
1982   The View From My Front Porch. *The Midden*, Pueblo Archaeological and Historical Society 2 (9).
Withers, Arnold M. and Frank H. H. Roberts, Jr.
1948   Blue River-South Platte Project: Preliminary Study of the Archaeological Resources. MS., Colorado Preservation Office.
Withers, Arnold M. and Thomas Huffman
1966   Pueblo Reservoir: Frying Pan-Arkansas Project of the Bureau of Reclamation. MS., Colorado Preservation Office.
Witkind, Max
1971   An Archaeological Interpretation of the Roberts Buffalo Jump Site, Larimer County, Colorado. M.S. Thesis, Department of Anthropology, Colorado State University.
Wood, Caryl
1974   Excavations in Trinchera Cave: A Preliminary Report. *Southwestern Lore* 49 (3 and 4): 53-56.
Wood, Caryl E. and Gerald A. Bair
1980   Trinidad Lake Cultural Resources Study, Part II: The Prehistoric Occu-

pation of the Upper Purgatoire River Valley, Southeastern Colorado. MS.,
Interagency Archaeological Services, on file, Colorado Preservation Office.
Wood, John J.
1967   Archaeological Investigations in Northeastern Colorado. Ph.D Dissertation, University of Colorado.
Wood, Raymond
1971   Pottery Sites near Limon, Colorado. *Southwestern Lore* 37 (3): 53-85.
Wood-Simpson, Caryl
1976   Trinchera Cave: A Rock Shelter in Southeastern Colorado. M. A.
Thesis, University of Wyoming.
Woodbury, Richard B.
1973   *Alfred V. Kidder.* Columbia University Press.
Wormington, H. M.
1946   Jesse Dade Figgins, 1867-1944. *American Anthropologist* 48 (1): 57-77.
1947   Prehistoric Indians of the Southwest. *Denver Museum of Natural History
Popular Series* 7.
1948   A Proposed Revision of Yuma Point Terminology. *Proceedings, Colorado
Museum of Natural History* 18 (2).
1955   A Reappraisal of the Fremont Culture, with a Summary of the Archaeology of the Northern Periphery. *Denver Museum of Natural History Popular Series* 1.
1957   Ancient Man in North America. *Denver Museum of Natural History
Popular Series* 4.
1962   A Survey of Early American Prehistory. *American Scientist* 50 (1): 230-
42.
1979   William Thomas Mulloy, 1917-1978. *American Antiquity* 44 (3).
in prep.   *Ancient Hunters and Gatherers of the Americas: The Archaeological Record
Before 6,000 B.C.* Academic Press.
Wormington, H. M. and Robert H. Lister
1956   Archaeological Investigations on the Uncompahgre Plateau. *Denver
Museum of Natural History Popular Series* 2.
Wyckoff, Don G.
1977   Secondary Forest Succession Following Abandonment of Mesa Verde.
The Kiva 42 (3 and 4): 215-31.

Index

THE AUTHOR

Educated at Chadron State College and the University of Arizona, E. Steve Cassells has his own contract firm, Plano Archaeological Consultants, and was elected president of the Colorado Council of Professional Archaeologists for 1984-85. He currently resides in Longmont, Colorado.